ENDURING AND EMERGING ISSUES
IN SOUTH ASIAN SECURITY

ENDURING AND EMERGING ISSUES IN SOUTH ASIAN SECURITY

Edited by
ŠUMIT GANGULY
DINSHAW MISTRY

BROOKINGS INSTITUTION PRESS
Washington, D.C.

Copyright © 2022
THE BROOKINGS INSTITUTION
1775 Massachusetts Avenue, N.W.
Washington, D.C. 20036
www.brookings.edu

All rights reserved. No part of this publication may be reproduced or transmitted in any form or by any means without permission in writing from the Brookings Institution Press.

The Brookings Institution is a private nonprofit organization devoted to research, education, and publication on important issues of domestic and foreign policy. Its principal purpose is to bring the highest quality independent research and analysis to bear on current and emerging policy problems. Interpretations or conclusions in Brookings publications should be understood to be solely those of the authors.

Library of Congress Control Number: 2021950362

ISBN 9780815738848 (pbk)
ISBN 9780815738855 (ebook)

9 8 7 6 5 4 3 2 1

Typeset in Adobe Caslon Pro

Composition by Elliott Beard

Contents

Preface	vii
ONE U.S. Foreign Policy and Security and Governance in South Asia DINSHAW MISTRY	1
TWO Pakistan, India, and U.S. Strategic Interests DINSHAW MISTRY	25
THREE Security Issues in Sino-Indian Relations ŠUMIT GANGULY	49
FOUR Governance Challenges: Legitimacy and Citizenship in China and India EDWARD KOLODZIEJ	66

FIVE
Cooperation and Defection Cycles 86
in India-Pakistan Relations
KANTI BAJPAI

SIX
Nuclear Stability in South Asia 109
DINSHAW MISTRY

SEVEN
Building Up the Indian Air Force 133
AMIT GUPTA

EIGHT
Pakistan's Political Culture 148
and Its Implications for Democracy
MARVIN G. WEINBAUM

NINE
Baloch Nationalism and the Garrison State in Pakistan 172
KAVITA R. KHORY

TEN
Internal Security Threats in Nepal, Bangladesh, 190
Maldives, and Other Cases:
Learning from Comparative Responses
CHETAN KUMAR

Contributors 213
Index 217

Preface

The security landscape in South Asia is diverse. Major enduring issues include India-Pakistan relations, India-China relations, conventional forces, and nuclear weapons. Some underexplored security and governance issues include authoritarian hardening in China and democratic backsliding trends in India; Pakistan's political culture and its implications for democracy; insurgency in its Baluchistan province; and internal security challenges in other states, such as Nepal, Bangladesh, and Maldives. This book examines these issues.

The volume does not cover all major topics in South Asian security. Many chapters focus on traditional political and military issues in India and Pakistan, and, while China is discussed in some chapters, its role in South Asia has acquired prominence in the 2020s and requires more detailed examination. Also, the volume does not have much coverage of nontraditional security issues, human security, and emerging technologies or the cyber domain. The book nevertheless examines important issues confronting governments and societies in the region, issues that are also significant for U.S. foreign policy in and beyond South Asia. It accordingly begins by discussing American foreign policy interests in the region, which range from strategic issues to democracy and development.

This book is a tribute to longtime Brookings Institution scholar Stephen Philip Cohen and a recognition of his contributions to scholarship and policymaking on South Asia. Cohen was professor of history and political science at the University of Illinois, Urbana-Champaign (1965–1998);

and Brookings senior fellow (1998–2017) and senior fellow emeritus (from 2017 until his passing in 2019). He was the first American scholar to work in the field of South Asian security studies. He largely defined the field and was himself its most experienced and insightful scholar-practitioner.

In 2016, Brookings published *The South Asia Papers*, a compilation of Cohen's prior writings on the region's military history, state-building efforts, armed ethnic groups, military forces, nuclear arsenals, interstate relations, and American engagement with the region. The chapters in this volume expand upon these topics. Two contributors to the book, Marvin Weinbaum and Edward Kolodziej, were Cohen's closest departmental colleagues at the University of Illinois. Cohen was dissertation adviser in the 1980s–1990s for the six other contributors. (Cohen chaired four other dissertations whose authors were approached but could not write for this book; they contributed to an earlier edited volume, *Security and South Asia: Ideas, Institutions and Initiatives*). Šumit Ganguly initiated the idea for this book project and provided its subvention. Dinshaw Mistry worked with the authors to develop the contents and provided editorial inputs on the chapters.

The editors acknowledge helpful comments from the reviewers of this manuscript. We also thank Bill Finan and the team at the Brookings Institution Press for their assistance with the publication of this book.

ONE

U.S. Foreign Policy and Security and Governance in South Asia

DINSHAW MISTRY

American foreign policy in South Asia has focused on security, economic, and governance issues. The United States has undertaken military, diplomatic, and economic initiatives toward its objectives in these areas. This chapter briefly reviews these American interests and investments in South Asia. It looks at trends in U.S. strategic interests, development aid, and democracy objectives in the region. It thereby provides the context for examining the security and governance issues that are covered in this book.

Security Issues

U.S. security interests in South Asia, which are significantly influenced by regional and world events, have varied across the decades. They include much-examined topics such as nuclear proliferation and terrorism, less prominent issues such as South Asia's role in Indian Ocean security and United Nations (UN) peacekeeping, and emerging areas such as China's involvement in the region.

In the 1990s, nuclear proliferation was arguably the foremost U.S. security concern in the subcontinent, though embedded within broader regional objectives. Just after India's May 1998 nuclear tests, administration officials noted that, in prior years, they had worked "to broaden and deepen our ties with India and the rest of South Asia, and to pursue our non-proliferation objectives vigorously within the context of our overall relationship," but, after the nuclear tests, they "need[ed] to put much of the cooperative side of our agenda on hold and deal with the consequences of India's actions."[1] The Clinton administration engaged in diplomatic talks with, and substantially reduced economic aid to, India and Pakistan in an unsuccessful effort to get them to sign the Comprehensive Nuclear Test Ban Treaty and undertake other nuclear restraints. Subsequently, in 1999 and 2001–2002, the Clinton and Bush administrations, respectively, were successful in crisis management, helping prevent India-Pakistan military tensions from expanding into larger conventional battles, which American officials feared could have led to the use of nuclear weapons.

After September 11, 2001, the issues of terrorism and violent extremism, the war in Afghanistan, and the "Af-Pak" (Afghanistan-Pakistan) policy were the most pressing U.S. concerns in the region. From 2001 to 2020, U.S. military expenditures in Afghanistan were an estimated $800–$900 billion; U.S. troop fatalities were near 2,400; and U.S. aid to Afghanistan was about $140 billion, one-fourth ($35 billion) for development and three-fifths ($86 billion) in security aid to fund the Afghan security forces; annual disbursements were typically $4 billion in security aid and $1 billion in economic aid.[2] In the same period, the United States provided $14 billion in coalition support funds, $11 billion in economic aid, and $8 billion in security aid to Pakistan, toward "our primary goal of helping Pakistan reach its objective of becoming a moderate, prosperous state, and preventing terrorism—directly through security programs and also through democracy, development and outreach programs that combat extremism and instability."[3] Stability in Pakistan became a major U.S. interest, especially since state failure in Pakistan would increase risks of the transfer of Pakistan's nuclear assets.

The Bush administration simultaneously advanced relations with India, influenced by the same factors that had guided prior American engagement with New Delhi—India's democratic credentials and its potential role in advancing U.S. strategic objectives.[4] The week before September 11, 2001, in his first public remarks as ambassador to India, Robert Blackwill noted that "President Bush has a global approach to U.S.-India relations, consistent with the rise of India as a world power"; that there was much appeal in a "democratic India, a billion-strong, heterogeneous, multilingual, secular . . . [country that could be] a bridgehead of effervescent liberty on the Asian continent"; and that the United States would partner with India to promote its democratic values and advance its strategic interests.[5] To further a partnership with India, the administration made a huge diplomatic investment in a civilian nuclear agreement. This agreement exempted India from long-standing U.S. nonproliferation policy against civilian nuclear transfers to countries without full-scope safeguards. India thereby became the sixth country in the world—alongside the five nuclear weapons states defined in the nuclear Nonproliferation Treaty (NPT)—that could keep nuclear weapons and still engage in civilian nuclear transactions. The Bush administration also convened meetings of the international Nuclear Suppliers Group (NSG) to gain its acceptance of this approach.

During the first term of the Obama administration, the United States announced its support for India's entry into the NSG and permanent membership in the UN Security Council. Still, India slid down Washington's global priority list, and there were some disappointments in U.S.-India relations.[6] In particular, India's nuclear liability legislation dissuaded American firms from reactor sales, possibly worth $50 billion, and India rejected American fighter aircraft for a potential $15 billion arms deal. U.S.-India strategic ties regained momentum during the Obama administration's second term. Thereafter, the Trump administration gave India an important place in its Asia policy, noting that India had a "leadership role in Indian Ocean security and throughout the broader region," and that this helps in a situation where "a geopolitical competition between free and repressive visions of world order is taking place in the Indo-Pacific region."[7] The Biden foreign policy team, during the 2020 election campaign, affirmed that it "will place a high priority on continuing to strengthen the U.S.-India relationship"; it added that "as the world's oldest and largest democracies, the United States and India are bound together by our shared democratic values."[8] The administration's March 2021 national security guidance document mentioned that it "will deepen our partnership with India."[9]

Beyond these high-profile issues, U.S. policymakers acknowledged South Asia's role in other areas such as UN peacekeeping. For example, a 1995 congressional testimony noted that "We would not have imagined even five years ago that shared approaches to conflict resolution would have put South Asian and U.S. peacekeepers side-by-side."[10] Over the years, South Asian countries made strong contributions on this issue. In 2010, the top three peacekeeping contributors were Pakistan (10,000), Bangladesh (10,000), and India (9,000), with Nepal ranked sixth (5,000); these four states contributed one-third of the 100,000 peacekeepers worldwide. In 2020, four of the top six peacekeeping contributors were Bangladesh (6,500), Nepal (5,600), India (5,500), and Pakistan (4,500), accounting for one-fourth of the 82,000 peacekeepers worldwide.

U.S. policymakers also recognized that South Asian states could help in maritime security because of their location along sea lanes linking East Asia with the Middle East and Europe. Washington sought to "strengthen the capacity of emerging partners in South Asia, including the Maldives, Bangladesh, and Sri Lanka," and to "establish a new initiative with South Asian partners modeled on the Maritime Security Initiative in Southeast Asia to improve maritime domain awareness, interoperability, and data sharing with the United States."[11] The U.S. Navy undertook significant exchanges with India and smaller-scale initiatives with Pakistan, Bangladesh, and Sri Lanka. It made port calls to these states; participated in exercises with their navies to build cooperation on humanitarian assistance, disaster relief, and maritime security; and sought to bolster their patrol, interdiction, and search and rescue abilities. In addition, India and Pakistan contributed one or two frigates each to the international antipiracy coalition in the late 2000s and early 2010s.

Security, Economics, and China in South Asia

Since the late 2010s, Washington gave more attention to an issue combining economic and security dimensions—China's role in South Asia, especially via its Belt and Road Initiative (BRI) infrastructure investments.[12] A 2019 administration testimony highlighted concerns on the issue, stating that "We cannot allow China . . . to subvert our partners through unsustainable infrastructure projects that push economies into unsustainable debt, or by contributing to an erosion of transparency and democratic norms."[13]

Three background points on this issue should be noted. First, Washington was concerned about Chinese investments and influence across Asia and globally, rather than just in South Asia. Accordingly, the U.S. approach toward China's investments in South Asia drew upon its general foreign policy response on the issue. Washington recognized that it could not counter Chinese financing dollar for dollar. Instead, it sought to create greater awareness about the costs and debt burdens of borrowing from China; it developed the Blue Dot Network with Japan and Australia to certify the quality of infrastructure projects; and it highlighted that Western donors offered better and more transparent aid compared to China, especially since Western development aid was mostly through grants rather than loans. It then suggested three alternatives to Chinese financing. One was traditional U.S. bilateral aid, which was mostly not for infrastructure, though additional Millennium Challenge Corporation (MCC) possibilities covered some infrastructure projects in Nepal and Sri Lanka.[14] A second alternative was a refurbished U.S. development finance corporation, created in 2018–2019, with an overall lending capacity of $60 billion. Still, this institution and its predecessor did not finance many projects in South Asia beyond India—it had only a few projects in Pakistan, Afghanistan, and Sri Lanka.[15] A third was U.S. allies and partners (Japan, Australia, India, European countries, and multilateral banks) and the private sector.[16] In practice, in the late 2010s and early 2020s, infrastructure investment through these avenues was much less than that disbursed by China for most South Asian states.

A second general point is that the connections between economic interdependence, debt, and political or security influence are not straightforward. For example, the magnitude of donor or lender influence does not correlate well with the size of donor or lender investments in particular countries or with the causal mechanisms enabling influence (debt traps, elite capture, socialization, or other avenues).[17] Further, the notion of Chinese-induced debt traps is contested because countries borrow from multiple lenders—China, Western donors, multilateral banks, and private bond holders—and their debt and debt sustainability problems arise from the collective lending by all these sources rather than from China alone.[18]

A third issue is that China's political, economic, and security ties vary widely across states within a region. For example, states in Southeast Asia differ considerably in their political leaning toward or distance from China, and China's economic ties are much greater than its security links with the region.[19] Similar trends are seen in the Middle East.[20] And, as noted above, the connection between most of these economic or security links and Chinese "influence" is ambiguous.

The above points provide the background for analyzing China's economic ties and investments in South Asian countries. On debt issues, analyses for the late 2010s indicated that overall debt distress and vulnerability to Chinese debt was relatively higher for Pakistan and Maldives, moderate for Sri Lanka, and lesser for Bangladesh and Nepal.[21] Other data for this period are indicated below, showing cumulative infrastructure investment where the data are unclear; cumulative arms imports; and single-year goods trade (2018 data). They suggest that China's economic and security links were substantial with Pakistan, but relatively moderate or lesser with Bangladesh, Sri Lanka, and Nepal. India also made some infrastructure investments in these states as part of its regional connectivity strategy, and a handful of these were cofinanced by Japan.[22] And India had more security interaction than China with Nepal, Sri Lanka, and Maldives, often involving joint military exercises and the training of military officers.

For Bangladesh, about half of its $40 billion exports were to European countries and one-sixth to the United States; one-third of its $55 billion imports were from China and one-sixth from India. Further, while China was a large investor, India, Japan, and Russia also had substantial infrastructure investments in Bangladesh. China committed $26 billion, though by 2020 its actual investment was about $10 billion, for projects such as the Padma River road and rail bridge, an industrial park, and a deep-sea port.[23] Japan's estimated $5–7 billion investment (some of it part of its regular development aid) included a deep-sea port near Chittagong to be completed in the early 2020s, a new terminal at Dhaka airport, modernizing the Dhaka metro rail system, and a power project.[24] Russia is building two nuclear plants, costing $12 billion, scheduled to start in 2024–2025. India, in 2017, committed to investments worth about $9 billion, including $2 billion for the power sector and $4.5 billion for seventeen infrastructure projects (covering the upgrade of three ports, an airport, new power transmission lines, and railway lines and equipment); it is unclear how much of this materialized by the early 2020s. Also, about three-fourths of Bangladesh's arms procurements were from China, mostly naval craft such as two submarines and four frigates, and one-sixth were from Russia, mostly armored personnel carriers and Mi-17 transport helicopters.

Sri Lanka's $11 billion exports were mainly to the United States (one-fourth); three European countries—Germany, the United Kingdom, and Italy (collectively about one-fifth); and India (one-tenth). Its $17 billion imports were mostly from India (one-fifth), China (one-fifth), and East Asian states Singapore, Japan, and Malaysia (collectively about one-fifth). China was Sri Lanka's main infrastructure investor, with investments worth $5.4 billion for fifteen projects in the pre-BRI period (2006–2012), and $6.8 billion for thirteen projects in the BRI period (2013–2019).[25] The latter included less controversial items such as the southern and central road expressways, as well as the controversial Hambantota Port (which was leased to China when Sri Lanka could not repay the debt), and the nearby, largely unused, Mattala Rajapaksa International Airport. India committed lines of credit worth $1.3 billion for Sri Lanka's railway sector. Other major development aid donors (though it is unclear how much of their aid covered infrastructure investment) included Japan and the World Bank. And Sri Lanka's main arms suppliers were China, the United States, and India—it received a 3,000-ton U.S. Coast Guard cutter in 2019, a 2,300-ton Chinese frigate in 2019, and bought two 2,300-ton Indian patrol vessels in 2017–2018. Further, about 500 foreign vessels made port calls to Sri Lanka in the 2010s, with half of these from India (110), Japan (80), and China (40).[26]

For Nepal, three-fifth of its $10 billion imports are from India, and three-fifths of its $800 million exports are to India. India has traditionally been Nepal's dominant infrastructure investor, though in the late 2010s Chinese investments were larger than India's, involving an airport, a hydropower plant, and other projects.

In Maldives, China's investments of about $1.7 billion (including airport modernization and a highway and bridge) gave rise to debt burdens.[27] India, after a new Maldivian government assumed office in late 2018, extended about $1.4 billion to Maldives, including $200 million for budgetary support, a $400 million currency swap, and $800 million for infrastructure projects such as a bridge between Maldivian islands. The timeline for disbursing these funds is unclear. Chinese security interaction with Maldives was limited to occasional "goodwill visits" by naval vessels; Maldives has more substantial security exchanges with the United States and India. U.S.-Maldives military exercises in the 2010s simulated events ranging from terrorist control over an island to emergency medical assistance; the United States and Maldives also signed a framework agreement for defense cooperation in 2020.

Democracy and Development

The issues of democracy, human rights, and development have been long-standing U.S. foreign policy objectives in South Asia (notwithstanding critiques that Washington supported military regimes and downplayed human rights in certain cases). They are routinely highlighted in U.S. policy statements. For example, in a 1995 testimony, administration officials noted that "supporting and strengthening democracy remains a fundamental [U.S.] aim in South Asia"; that, beyond India, "over 200 million

South Asians live in countries with revitalized or newly installed and still fragile democratic institutions. [W]e are working to reinforce those institutions"; that "sustainable development is a critical need for South Asia"; that the United States sought to "encourag[e] free market economies and U.S. trade and investment"; and that "advancing universally recognized human rights in South Asia is a key U.S. interest."[28]

These same issues were prominent in subsequent years, with nuances to reflect democratic advances or backsliding in particular countries. For example, a 2004 testimony noted that "a return to full democracy in Pakistan is central to long-term stability."[29] It observed that, in Bangladesh, "political rivalries" and "corruption" could "threaten democratic stability and impede economic growth," which could "increase . . . the attractiveness of radical alternatives." In Sri Lanka, the United States aimed for "providing both an incentive to peace and a boost to reconstruction and reconciliation in war-torn areas." It also noted that "a fragile democracy is at stake in Nepal, where a Maoist insurgency has unraveled the weak political and economic threads that held it together." And it mentioned that, in Maldives, the United States was "encouraged by the proposed sweeping constitutional changes designed to strengthen democratic institutions and human rights and head off radicalism."

Subsequently, in 2011, administration testimony noted that in Sri Lanka, "the Government's worrisome record on human rights, weakening of democratic institutions and practices, and the way in which it conducted the final months of its conflict against the Tamil Tigers hamper our ability to fully engage."[30] It added that "Nepal continues its dramatic transformation from a caste-bound constitutional monarchy, wracked by a bloody Maoist insurgency . . . to a federal republic that represents and includes all minorities and ethnicities." It also noted that "we seek to reinforce the peaceful democratic transition that occurred in the Maldives in 2008."

In 2016, administration officials noted that, in Bangladesh, "many of the gains that Bangladesh has made in human development and economic growth risk being undermined by the escalating extremist violence."[31] On Sri Lanka, they stated that "our bilateral relationship has been transformed over the past year, thanks to a unity government [that is] committed to reforms that can benefit all Sri Lankans." On Maldives, they mentioned that "we remain greatly concerned about the narrowing of legitimate political space: too many opposition politicians still remain behind bars. . . . We are also concerned about the fertile ground for recruitment that violent extremists find in Maldives."

A 2019 congressional testimony stated that South Asia "includes several of the world's largest democracies, [and] offers growing opportunities for trade and investment benefitting U.S. firms."[32] Still, in a separate testimony that year, administration officials (Robert Destro, assistant secretary for human rights, and Alice Wells, acting assistant secretary for South Asia) expressed concerns that "as a whole, South Asia has experienced backsliding on democracy and human rights in recent months and years."[33]

These officials observed that, while "India's 2019 elections were the largest single democratic exercise in human history . . . , we are compelled to underscore human rights issues of increasing concern precisely because, if left unchecked, they could undermine India's democratic success."[34] These concerns were the "detention of local political leaders and activists" in Kashmir and the religious criteria in India's citizenship amendment act,[35] as well as "violence and discrimination against minorities in India, including cow vigilante attacks against members of the Dalit and Muslim communities."[36]

On Pakistan, the administration noted serious concerns about "restrictions on civil society, overly strict regulations on international NGOs, severe harassment of journalists, blasphemy laws . . . and overt discrimination against members of minority groups."[37] It also noted "restrictions on the Ahmadiyya Muslim community," and arbitrary arrests and enforced disappearances of "Pashtun rights activists, as well as Sindhi and Baloch nationalists."[38]

On Sri Lanka, the administration highlighted concerns about the stalling of "constitutional reform," "a truth and reconciliation commission," and a "credible judicial mechanism to address accountability for atrocities [at the end of the civil war]."[39] It also noted concerns "about violence against members of religious minorities, such as members of the Christian and Muslim communities, particularly in the aftermath of the April 21 [terrorist] attacks."

On Bangladesh, it stated that "the most recent elections in Bangladesh were neither free nor fair and were marred by irregularities," and that "we retain acute concerns about security forces suppressing, intimidating and detaining civil society, members of the media, and political opposition."[40]

On other cases, the administration noted that "Nepal is making progress in its democratic journey," and that "we are working with the government to advance its transition to federalism."[41] It added that, in Maldives, "the 2018 election of President Solih ushered in a new chapter in Maldivian history and placed the country on a clear upward trajectory on democratic governance and human rights metrics."[42]

In a 2021 hearing, administration officials reiterated their concerns with democratic backsliding in South Asia, noting that "constraints to freedom of expression, association, and religion" were undermining democracy in the region.[43]

A modest amount of foreign aid has been applied in pursuit of American political and economic development objectives for South Asia. In the mid and late 2010s, annual U.S. economic aid averaged about $400 million collectively for Bangladesh ($190 million, focused on economic development and health); India ($90 million, mostly for health programs); Nepal ($90 million, two-thirds for economic development and one-third for health programs); Sri Lanka ($40 million, mostly for economic development); and Maldives ($3 million).[44] It was a higher $600–700 million for Pakistan—two-thirds economic and one-third security aid—which declined to no security aid and about $100 million economic aid in fiscal year 2018.[45] Overall, the United States accounted for one-sixth of the $3.4 billion annual international grant aid to Bangladesh ($1.2 billion), India ($1.1 billion), Nepal ($800–900 million), and Sri Lanka ($250 million).[46] It contributed one-third to one-fourth of the more than $2 billion annual international economic aid to Pakistan before its aid cuts in the late 2010s, resulting in annual international aid to Pakistan then dropping to about $1.5 billion.[47] Also, while South Asia received only about 5 percent of U.S. foreign aid in the late 1990s (95 percent went to other regions of the world), its share increased to 16 percent in fiscal year 2007 and 15 percent in fiscal year 2017, largely because of aid to Afghanistan and Pakistan; these percentages declined after U.S. aid cuts to Pakistan and aid reductions to Afghanistan starting in fiscal year 2018.

The substantial international economic aid to South Asia reflects the significant development challenges in the region. The per capita GDP for the region's almost 1.8 billion population (2019 data), measured by purchasing power, was only near $6,500—varying across Sri Lanka ($13,500), India ($7,000), Pakistan ($5,000), Bangladesh ($5,000), Nepal ($3,500), and Afghanistan ($2,000). In comparison, per capita GDP for Southeast Asia's 650 million persons (excluding high-income Singapore and Brunei) was $12,000, while China's was almost $17,000. And Human Development Index scores were 0.63 for South Asia—varying across Afghanistan (0.50), Pakistan (0.56), Nepal (0.60), Bangladesh (0.61), India (0.64), and Sri Lanka (0.78)—compared to 0.67 for Southeast Asia and 0.76 for China.

Another indicator for development is the Fragile States Index (on a scale of 1–120, where 120 is the highest fragility), which shows that fragility levels ranged from moderate to high for South Asian states. The relevant scores for 2019 varied across India (74), Sri Lanka (84), Nepal (85), Bangladesh (87), Pakistan (94), and Afghanistan (105). In comparison, fragility scores for China and many Southeast Asian states were 70–75.

On issues of democracy, scores in South Asia are slightly greater than in Southeast Asia, where the averages are depressed by some authoritarian states. Thus, for 2020, the Freedom House political freedom score on a 1–100 scale ranged from moderate levels in India (67, declining from 71 in 2019, and 76 in 2018), Sri Lanka (56), and Nepal (56) to lower scores in Bangladesh (39), Pakistan (37), and Afghanistan (27). Scores in Southeast Asia were 48–59 for the top four and 13–30 for the lowest five countries, while China's score was 10. On the Democracy Index (on a 1–10 scale), scores in 2019 varied across India (6.90, down from 7.23 in 2018), Sri Lanka (6.27), Bangladesh (5.88), Nepal (5.25), Pakistan (4.25), and Afghanistan (2.97).[48] In Southeast Asia, the top five country scores were 6.0–7.1, while the lowest four were 2.1–3.5, and China was 2.26.

As alluded to above, the United States also has an economic interest in South Asia, especially in India. It has urged South Asian states to open their economies to greater U.S. investment and exports, and called upon India to reduce the trade deficit (U.S.-India goods and services trade was $146 billion (2019), when U.S. exports to India were $59 billion and imports were $87 billion, resulting in a trade deficit of $28 billion). U.S.-India relations have also included discussions and initiatives in science and technology, health, energy, people-to-people relations, immigration, and climate change. These issues are not discussed in this volume.

To summarize, U.S. foreign policy toward South Asia is impacted by regional security issues—ranging from China-India and Pakistan-India relations to nuclear stability—and also has development and governance objectives. Some of these issues are examined in this book.

A Tour of the Book
Pakistan, India, and U.S. Strategic Interests

The next chapter, chapter 2, examines the fit between the expectations and reality in U.S. strategic relations with India and Pakistan. The substantial U.S. diplomatic effort to build relations with India correlated with moderate alignment between New Delhi's policies and U.S. strategic objectives. New Delhi's policies converged with U.S. interests, albeit to a lesser magnitude than U.S. expectations, in the cases of balancing China, bilateral defense collaboration, Indian Ocean security, and oil sanctions against Iran. However, contrary to U.S. preferences, New Delhi persisted in arms deals with Russia.

The huge U.S. economic aid package to Pakistan likely had some positive impact on development but did not bring commensurate strategic rewards, instead correlating with significant divergence between Pakistan's foreign policies and U.S. security interests for much of the 2000s–2010s.[49] Thus, in Afghanistan, Pakistan's support for the Taliban strongly diverged from the U.S. strategy of fighting that group, but when the U.S. strategy changed to talking with the Taliban, Pakistan's approach converged with that of the United States. On China, there has been manageable divergence between Pakistan's policies and U.S. interests, but this could worsen. And on securing Pakistan's nuclear assets from theft and transfer, Pakistan took positive steps that converged with U.S. objectives, albeit with limitations.

Sino-Indian Security Relations

Chapter 3 examines security issues in Sino-Indian relations.[50] It notes that, from the standpoint of New Delhi, China constitutes the principal long-term security threat to India. The threat stems from China's unresolved border dispute with India, military capabilities, behavior in India's South Asian neighborhood, hostility toward India in various international forums, and the negative outlook on India's ties with the United States. Looking ahead, the chapter argues that as long as Sino-American relations remain troubled, the United States could court India as a viable strategic partner in Asia, and India's policymakers could follow a hedging strategy with the United States versus China. On the other hand, if China keeps increasing its economic, military, and diplomatic capabilities versus India, then India would end up in a situation of permanent strategic inferiority versus China in the broader Asian region, with its reach mostly confined to South Asia. Here, on some basic indicators, China widened the gap with India—between 2010 and 2019, India's GDP increased by 70 percent from $1.7 trillion to $2.9 trillion, while China's rose by 135 percent from $6.0 trillion to $14.3 trillion. China's GDP was 3.6 times as large as India's in 2010 and 5.0 times as large by 2019; to revert to the 2010 figure of 3.6, India's annual economic growth would have to be 3 percent greater than China's for a decade, which is unlikely in the 2020s.

Political Hardening in India and China

Chapter 4 looks at governance issues in China and India. In authoritarian China (political freedom score of 10), there has been political hardening under the leadership of Xi Jinping. As for democratic India, its political freedom score regressed to 67 (2020) from 76 (2018), leading to concerns that India was moving from "liberal" toward "ill" and "illiberal" democracy.[51] These developments have significant implications for U.S. foreign policy and global governance. The Biden administration's national security adviser noted (a year before he assumed this role) that political hardening in China can exert a pull toward autocracy and authoritarianism in other countries, and China's support for autocrats and democratic backsliders would challenge American values.[52] This administration's first national security document repeatedly stated that "democracy is essential to meeting the challenges of our time," and mentioned a policy objective of "standing up for our values abroad, including by uniting the world's democracies to combat threats to free societies."[53] Others note that India's democratic backsliding could make it difficult for the United States to credibly position India as an alternative to Beijing's authoritarian model.[54] Further, one aspect of U.S. policy in Asia emphasizes cooperation among democracies, including the Quadrilateral Security Dialogue (Quad), comprising Australia, India, Japan, and the United States. Despite India's democratic backsliding in 2019–2020, the Quad countries advanced their arrangement in 2021 through a national leaders' meeting, though further such backsliding could make it harder to position the Quad as a concert of genuinely liberal democracies.

Cycles of Cooperation and Defection in India-Pakistan Relations

Chapter 5 examines India-Pakistan diplomatic talks (cooperation) and their breakdown (defection). Between 1996 and 2016, New Delhi and Islamabad were involved in three cycles of cooperation and defection, influenced by systemic and domestic factors. The main systemic forces inducing negotiations were the desire for military stability and the quest to demonstrate international responsibility after their nuclear tests, as well as U.S. diplomatic cajoling. Domestic factors, such as an economic growth agenda and the worry over chronic terrorism, also underlined the need for cooperation. Other domestic factors, primarily divisions within ruling groups in both countries, meant that national leaders could not count on their counterparts to deliver on key objectives, and negotiations repeatedly ran aground. For India, the crucial objective was Pakistan reining in cross-border terrorism; for Pakistan, it was India seriously engaging on a Kashmir settlement. The chapter concludes with the observation that, despite its periodic interventions, the United States had neither the capacity nor willingness to bridge the India-Pakistan commitment gap. The chapter does not cover events in the early 2020s. In 2021, Pakistan and India took limited steps toward a dialogue and revived a ceasefire agreement to halt cross-border firing.

Nuclear Stability in South Asia

Chapter 6 examines two key nuclear challenges in South Asia. The first is the prospect of an India-Pakistan military crisis escalating to the use of nuclear weapons. India-Pakistan crises in the late 2010s were less severe than those in 1999–2002; thus, there was a lesser probability of nuclear use in these latter crises. Still, during these episodes, both sides ratcheted up their planned and actual military action; such action could undermine crisis stability in the future. The second issue concerns arms buildups. Here, India and Pakistan enlarged their nuclear arsenals at modest rates in the 2000s and 2010s. This did not, and future similar rates of growth would not necessarily, undermine basic deterrence stability. Over the long term, however, arms buildups could have negative consequences that could worsen crisis stability and complicate the challenge of nuclear security. Finally, the India-China dyad raises fewer nuclear stability concerns than the India-Pakistan dyad.

Indian Air Force Modernization

The Indian Air Force (IAF) has twenty-nine combat aircraft squadrons (each typically having sixteen aircraft, plus trainers and reserves), comprising thirteen Sukhoi-30, three MiG-29, six Jaguar, three Mirage-2000, two Rafale, and two Indian Light Combat Aircraft / Tejas Mark 1 squadrons. Not counted in these numbers are the last three MiG-21 squadrons to be retired around 2022–2023. Beyond these, the IAF plans to acquire four squadrons with eighty-three Tejas Mark 1As between 2024 and 2028. It would still fall short of its aspiration for forty combat squadrons, and this problem would be compounded by the early 2030s, when the MiG-29s, Mirage-2000s, and Jaguars—which all began midlife upgrades in the late

2010s—would approach retirement. To make up for its fighter deficit, the IAF plans to procure some combination of 114 medium multirole combat fighters (six squadrons), 125 or more fifth-generation Advanced Medium Combat Aircraft made in India (seven squadrons), and 100–125 Tejas Mark 2s (five or six squadrons). Any competition for the medium multirole aircraft could involve several contenders—a 2018 request for information on this issue generated responses from the Eurofighter Typhoon, French Rafale, Swedish Gripen, Russian MiG-35 and Sukhoi-35, and American F-18 and F-16/F-21.

Chapter 7 examines the above issues in IAF modernization. It covers Indian Air Force capabilities and limitations for conventional operations versus Pakistan and China, the pathologies in India's weapons acquisition policies, and their implications for the aircraft India would select to modernize its fleet. The chapter also discusses how the United States could assist India's air force, such as by transferring the C-17 transport aircraft production line to India, helping with the redesign of the Tejas Mark 2, and building up India's drone fleet.

Pakistan's Political Culture and Implications for Democracy

Political development is sometimes conceptualized as the development of institutions and of political culture, and political culture is one of five components determining a state's democracy score in some indexes. Chapter 8 notes that a study of Pakistan's political culture is essential for a full appreciation of the country's long and difficult struggle with governance, above all in its experiences with democracy. Certain deep-seated values in Pakistan can promote national unity and comity but also contribute to civic intolerance and violence. In the popular culture, attitudes of distrust, detachment, distortion, and denial serve as negative influences on democracy. Beyond its popular culture, Pakistan's political makeup contains distinctive political subcultures for its urban educated middle class, its bureaucracy, and the military. These can drive Pakistan's political reform agenda but also pose obstacles to change. Despite the many elements of Pakistan's political culture militating against the creation of a well-governed polity, the country's founding ideas, liberal aspirations, and resilience stand as redeeming political and social features.

*Pakistan's Internal Security Challenges and
the Insurgency in Balochistan*

From 2000 to 2020, about 65,000 persons were killed in militancy and political violence in Pakistan—over 20,000 civilians, 7,000–8,000 security forces, and 33,000 militants.[55] The civilian fatalities were mostly in Khyber province, including the former Federally Administered Tribal Areas (FATA) (47 percent), followed by Sindh (24 percent), Balochistan (21 percent), and Punjab (8 percent), while security force fatalities were largely in Khyber province (64 percent), followed by Balochistan (21 percent) and Sindh (9 percent). Much of the violence in Khyber/FATA and Punjab involved groups fighting the Pakistani state under the umbrella of the Pakistani Taliban, who also undertook attacks in other provinces. Violence in Sindh centered around sectarian conflict in Karachi, and violence in Balochistan was mostly linked to Baloch insurgents. Still, 87 percent of the 65,000 fatalities occurred in 2007–2015, and terrorist incidents in Pakistan declined considerably by the late 2010s. In the two years 2019–2020, about 310 civilians and 315 security force personnel were killed in militant violence—a large number of civilian fatalities were in Balochistan (170) and Khyber province (90), and security force fatalities were also mostly in Balochistan (150) and Khyber province (130).

The above information provides the context for chapter 9, which examines the insurgency in Pakistan's Balochistan province. The chapter first traces the emergence of Baloch nationalism in relation to the broader nation- and state-building endeavors in Pakistan, endeavors that have disregarded local identities and suppressed competing claims for political legitimacy and power. Second, it examines the sources of conflict and the motivations of Baloch leaders, who have sometimes cooperated with, and on other occasions resorted to armed resistance against, the central government. It also explores the "resource curse": Balochis have long complained that the province, though resource-rich, exercises little control over the earnings from its resources. Third, the chapter analyzes the state's responses, from cooptation to coercion to counterinsurgency measures. It concludes by looking at the implications of the conflict for Pakistan's security and foreign policy.

Internal Security Threats in Other States:
Learning from Comparative Responses

Internal security threats have resulted in thousands of fatalities in South Asia. An estimated 160,000 persons have been killed in the war in Afghanistan since 2001—45,000 civilians, 60,000 Afghan security forces, 3,500 U.S. and coalition forces, and tens of thousands of insurgents.[56] Elsewhere in South Asia, for 2000–2020, fatalities from terrorism, political violence, and civil war were high in Pakistan (65,000); India (45,000—14,000 civilians, 7,000 security forces, and 23,000 insurgents); and Sri Lanka (41,000—12,000 civilians, 5,500 security forces, and 22,000 insurgents); and somewhat fewer in Nepal (14,000—1,200 civilians, 2,400 security forces, and 10,300 insurgents) and Bangladesh (2,300—780 civilians, 80 security forces, and 1,400 extremists).[57] In most cases, the 2000s and early 2010s were much more violent than the late 2010s and early 2020s (the exception was Afghanistan, where civilian and security force fatalities greatly increased since the mid-2010s).

In India, the 45,000 fatalities were largely in Kashmir (21,000, three-fourths of these in 2000–2005) and northeast India (11,000, four-fifths in 2000–2009), or due to Maoist violence (10,000, half in 2005–2011) or Islamist/other terrorism (1,300, two-thirds in 2005–2008). In Sri Lanka, the fatalities occurred during that country's civil war, mostly in 2000–2001 and 2006–2009, and Sri Lanka then faced virtually no domestic terrorism until the April 2019 Islamist terrorist attack, which killed 260 civilians.[58] In Nepal, the violence was largely linked to the Maoist insurgency in 2000–2006. In Bangladesh, the fatalities were equally distributed among left-wing extremism (mostly in 2004–2009) and Islamist terrorism (which heightened in 2002–2005 and 2013–2017), though terrorist-related fatalities were in the single digits in 2019–2020.[59]

The above data provide the context for chapter 10, which examines two types of internal security threats in South Asia's less-examined states—insurgencies around identity and marginalization, contrasting Nepal and a nearby Southeast Asian state (Myanmar), and preventing and countering violent extremism, illustrated in Maldives and Bangladesh.

Nepal witnessed a successful nationally led peace process, with the 2006 peace agreement culminating in a new constitution ten years later, and with the main insurgent group integrated into the political system and the army. Myanmar, in contrast, has seen a stalled peace process. Such cases suggest that South Asian states and their neighbors have not applied lessons from other peacemaking and peacebuilding cases. Additionally, many subnational conflicts in South Asia originate from accumulated grievances over perceptions of marginalization, prolonged local violence and internal displacement over land and natural resources, and environmental damage. Addressing these conflict drivers can help both peace and development.

On the issue of radicalization and violent extremism, Bangladesh and Maldives were, despite some tactical successes in the late 2010s, still searching for a long-term strategy to keep aggrieved individuals from joining extremist groups. Such a strategy could involve engaging three constituencies that have been successful in pulling alienated individuals away from extremism: youth (especially on social media), women (especially within their families and communities), and faith-based leaders.

Summing Up

The security and governance landscape in South Asia involves some complex interstate and intrastate issues, and these have significant implications for the region as well as for U.S. foreign policy in the region. In most countries, internal security threats from terrorist and militant groups appeared less severe in the late 2010s and early 2020s, compared to the 2000s and early 2010s, and such trends can help stability and development. Still, democracy in the region saw progress but also some backsliding. And U.S. security objectives in the region encountered both setbacks and advances. For example, despite a heavy economic and military investment, the United States did not accomplish its major objective of defeating the Taliban in Afghanistan. Moreover, the considerable U.S. aid package to Pakistan did not bridge U.S.-Pakistan disagreement and divergence on China and Afghanistan. On the other hand, U.S. efforts to build a partnership with India brought about moderate alignment between India's policies and U.S. strategic interests.

Overall, America's South Asia policy in the 2000s and early 2010s was significantly focused on Afghanistan, Pakistan, and India-Pakistan issues. These issues continued to be important in the mid-2010s and 2020s, though Washington also focused on other issues such as maritime security (involving several of South Asia's less-examined states) and India's role in Asia and in balancing China. The following chapters examine these issues.

NOTES

1. Karl Inderfurth, Assistant Secretary of State for South Asia, Testimony before the Senate Committee on Foreign Relations, Subcommittee on Near Eastern and South Asian Affairs, May 13, 1998.

2. Congressional Research Service, *Afghanistan: Background and Policy Brief*, June 25, 2020. The $4 billion yearly U.S. security aid funded three-fourths of the Afghan security force budget, with the balance of this budget coming from U.S. allies ($1 billion) and the Afghan government ($500 million). U.S. economic aid to Afghanistan averaged $1 billion annually in the early and mid-2010s, but was about $500 million by the late 2010s. In 2021, after the Taliban took power in Afghanistan, the United States anticipated spending $6 billion for humanitarian and refugee assistance.

3. Christina B. Rocca, Assistant Secretary for South Asian Affairs, Statement before the House Committee on International Relations, June 22, 2004.

4. As a historical example, the Reagan administration pursued its limited opening to India because its status as "the world's largest democracy" appealed to "pro-democracy ideologues," and for realpolitik considerations. Stephen P. Cohen, *The South Asia Papers* (Brookings, 2016), p. 21.

5. Robert Blackwill, "The Future of US-India Relations," Remarks to the Indo-American Chamber of Commerce and Indo-American Society, Mumbai, September 6, 2001.

6. Nicholas Burns, "Passage to India: What Washington Can Do to Revive Relations with New Delhi," *Foreign Affairs* 93, no. 5 (September/October 2014).

7. The White House, *A New National Security Strategy for a New Era*, December 18, 2017.

8. See "Joe Biden's Agenda for the Indian American Community," https://joebiden.com/indian-americans/.

9. The White House, "Interim National Security Guidance," March 3, 2021, www.whitehouse.gov/briefing-room/statements-releases/2021/03/03/interim-national-security-strategic-guidance/.

10. Statement by Robin Raphel, Assistant Secretary of State for South Asian Affairs, before the Senate Committee on Foreign Relations, Subcommittee on Near Eastern and South Asian Affairs, March 7, 1995.

11. See a document titled, "US Strategic Framework for the IndoPacific," released by Robert C. O'Brien, Assistant to the President for National Security Affairs, January 5, 2021.

12. Jennifer Hillman and David Sacks, *China's Belt and Road: Implications for the United States* (New York: Council on Foreign Relations, 2021).

13. Statement by Alice G. Wells, Senior Bureau Official for South and Central Asian Affairs, before the House Committee on Foreign Affairs, Subcommittee for Asia, the Pacific, and Nonproliferation, "U.S. Interests in South Asia and the FY 2020 Budget," June 13, 2019.

14. The United States and Nepal signed a $500 million five-year Millennium Challenge Corporation (MCC) compact in 2017, for power and road/highway

projects. At the time of this writing in 2021, Nepal had not formally approved the arrangement. For Sri Lanka, the MCC approved a five-year, $480 million package in 2019 but discontinued it in December 2020. Sri Lanka stalled on accepting the package in 2019–2020 and stated in early 2021 that it would not sign the compact (these projects focused on transportation in the capital and between the capital and other regions; and private and public sector land management, related to land use for agriculture, services, and industrial investors).

15. From 2007 to mid-2021, it supported projects worth $2.5 billion in India (including $1.2 billion since 2019); $636 million in Pakistan (but none since 2019); $175 million in Afghanistan (but only $0.5 million since 2019); $60 million in Sri Lanka (including $40 million since 2019); $2 million in Nepal; and $1 million in Bangladesh. This information is compiled from the website of the U.S. International Development Finance Corporation, www.dfc.gov/our-impact/all-active-projects.

16. In 2021, the United States announced an initiative whereby the G7 countries, like-minded partners, and the private sector would mobilize hundreds of billions of dollars for infrastructure projects in developing countries, with a focus on climate change, health, digital technology, and gender equity. The amount of this financing that would be directed to South Asia remains unclear.

17. See, for example, Theodor Tudoroiu, ed., *China's International Socialization of Political Elites in the Belt and Road Initiative* (London: Routledge, 2021); Jordan Calinoff and David Gordon, "Port Investments in the Belt and Road Initiative: Is Beijing Grabbing Strategic Assets?" *Survival* 62, no. 4 (July 2020), pp. 59–80; Michael Mazarr, *Understanding Influence in the Strategic Competition with China* (Santa Monica, CA: Rand Corporation, 2021).

18. Countries rationally allocate Chinese investment for infrastructure, while relying on Western donors for the social sector and private bondholders for general short-term budget finance. This occurs because the U.S. International Development Finance Corporation offers small amounts of investment compared to China's infrastructure lending, and multilateral development banks prefer to finance social services, administration, and democracy-promotion rather than hard infrastructure. See David Dollar, "Seven Years into China's Belt and Road," *Order from Chaos* (blog), October 1, 2020, www.brookings.edu/blog/order-from-chaos/2020/10/01/seven-years-into-chinas-belt-and-road/.

19. David Shambaugh, "U.S.-China Rivalry in Southeast Asia: Power Shift or Competitive Coexistence," *International Security* 42, no. 4 (Spring 2018). China's ties with Southeast Asia are primarily economic and diplomatic, rather than security-oriented. In contrast, the United States has a broader outreach with the region, comprising traditional and public diplomacy, civilian and military assistance and security cooperation, economic and commercial relations, and coordinated and complementary engagement from its allies. Also, countries in Southeast Asia vary in their closeness to China. They include "capitulationists," which are almost totally aligned with China; "chafers," which are significantly dependent on China but only because they have few alternatives, and wish they

were not; "aligned accommodationists," which have good ties with both the United States and China; "balanced hedgers," which have defense ties with the United States and commercial and diplomatic ties with China; and "outliers," which do not seek especially close relations with either the United States or China.

20. Camille Lons, Jonathan Fulton, Degang Sun, and Naser Al-Tamimi, "China's Great Game in the Middle East," Policy Brief (London: European Council on Foreign Relations, October 21, 2019). In the Middle East, China's relationships are largely political and economic, motivated by energy imports from and infrastructure construction in the region, with only a small security component; the United States is the major security provider. China has different types of partnerships with regional countries—comprehensive strategic partnerships with Egypt, Saudi Arabia, and Iran; an innovation partnership with Israel; a strategic cooperative relationship with Turkey; and strategic partnerships with some midsize and small Gulf countries.

21. John Hurley, Scott Morris, and Gailyn Portelance, "Examining the Debt Implications of the Belt and Road Initiative from a Policy Perspective," Center for Global Development Policy Paper 121, March 2018.

22. Riya Sinha and Niara Sareen, *India's Limited Trade Connectivity with South Asia* (New Delhi: Brookings Institution India Centre, 2020); Constantino Xavier and Riya Sinha, *When Land Comes in the Way: India's Connectivity Infrastructure in Nepal* (New Delhi: Brookings Institution India Centre, 2020).

23. David Brewster, "Bangladesh's Road to the BRI," *The Interpreter*, May 30, 2019, www.lowyinstitute.org/the-interpreter/bangladesh-road-bri.

24. Jagaran Chakma, "Bangladesh: A Fertile Plain for Japanese Investment," *Daily Star*, March 8, 2020.

25. See a study on this issue, Ganeshan Wignaraja and others, *Chinese Investment and the BRI in Sri Lanka* (London: Chatham House Asia Pacific Program, 2020).

26. See an interview with Sri Lanka's foreign secretary, "As Far as Strategic Security Considerations Go, Sri Lanka Has an India First Approach," *Times of India*, August 14, 2020.

27. See Simon Mundy and Kathrin Hille, "The Maldives Counts the Costs of Its Debts to China," *Financial Times*, February 10, 2019; and Sanjeev Miglani and Mohamed Junayd, "After a Building Spree, Just How Much Does the Maldives Owe China," Reuters, November 23, 2018.

28. Raphel, Statement before the Senate Committee on Foreign Relations, Subcommittee on Near Eastern and South Asian Affairs, March 7, 1995.

29. Rocca, Statement before the House Committee on International Relations, June 22, 2004.

30. Testimony of Robert O. Blake Jr., Assistant Secretary, Bureau of South and Central Asian Affairs, House Committee on Foreign Affairs, Subcommittee on the Middle East and South Asia, April 5, 2011.

31. Testimony of Nisha Desai Biswal, Assistant Secretary, Bureau of South

and Central Asian Affairs, House Committee on Foreign Affairs, Subcommittee on Asia and the Pacific, May 11, 2016.

32. Statement by Wells before the House Committee on Foreign Affairs, Subcommittee for Asia, the Pacific, and Nonproliferation, "U.S. Interests in South Asia and the FY 2020 Budget," June 13, 2019.

33. Testimony of Robert Destro, Assistant Secretary of State, Bureau of Democracy, Human Rights and Labor, House Committee on Foreign Affairs, Subcommittee for Asia, the Pacific, and Nonproliferation, October 22, 2019. The parallel testimony was the Statement of Alice G. Wells, Acting Assistant Secretary, Bureau for South and Central Asian Affairs, before the House Committee on Foreign Affairs, Subcommittee for Asia and the Pacific, October 22, 2019.

34. Testimony of Destro, House Committee on Foreign Affairs, Subcommittee for Asia, the Pacific, and Nonproliferation, October 22, 2019.

35. Ibid.

36. Statement of Wells, October 22, 2019.

37. Testimony of Destro, October 22, 2019.

38. Ibid.

39. Ibid.

40. Ibid.

41. Statement of Wells, October 22, 2019.

42. Ibid.

43. Testimony of Dean Thompson, Acting Assistant Secretary, Bureau of South and Central Asian Affairs, U.S. Department of State, before the House Committee on Foreign Affairs, Subcommittee on Asia, the Pacific, Central Asia, and Nonproliferation, June 9, 2021.

44. Data are the annual average for fiscal years 2014–2019. These data exclude some additional aid outside State Department and USAID budget lines for this region. They also exclude about $200 million annually for Rohingya refugees in Bangladesh and Myanmar since late 2017, and Millennium Challenge Corporation (MCC) possibilities for Sri Lanka and Nepal that were discussed earlier in this chapter.

45. Cumulative U.S. economic aid to Pakistan from 2001 to 2019 was $11 billion—comprising $8.7 billion for economic support funds and development, and the remainder for disaster relief, food aid, migration and refugee assistance, and health.

46. Data are for net grant aid (they exclude loan aid—for example, each year in 2017 and 2018, Bangladesh received about $1.3 billion loan aid from Organization for Economic Cooperation and Development (OECD) lenders, mostly from Japan, while India received $3 billion, largely from Japan, Germany, and the European Union [EU]). Beyond the United States, the principal annual aid donors to South Asia were Japan ($200 million); European countries and the EU ($1.5 billion); and the World Bank, Asian Development Bank, and others (over $1 billion). The $3.4 billion annual figure includes Bhutan ($74 million)

and Maldives ($28 million); it counts American aid as $520 million (one-sixth of the $3.4 billion figure), which is higher than the $400 million in U.S. State Department budget figures. These data are the annual average for 2014–2017, though averages for 2014–2019 were similar. OECD, *Geographical Distribution of Financial Flows to Developing Countries 2019. Disbursements, Commitments, Country Indicators* (Paris: OECD Publishing, 2019).

47. Cumulative international economic aid to Pakistan since 2001 (OECD data up to 2019) was about $44 billion, with the main donors being the World Bank and the United States ($10–$11 billion each), the United Kingdom ($5.7 billion), Japan ($3.4 billion), EU ($2 billion), Germany ($1.5 billion), Canada ($700 million), and Australia ($700 million).

48. In the Democracy Index (from the Economist Intelligence Unit), scores are as follows: full democracy = 8–10; flawed/deficient democracy = 6–8; hybrid regime = 4–6; and authoritarian regime = below 4.

49. On development aid challenges, see Samia Altaf, *So Much Aid, So Little Development: Stories from Pakistan* (Johns Hopkins University Press, 2011).

50. For more on Sino-India relations, see Kanti Bajpai, Selina Ho, and Manjari Chatterjee Miller, *The Routledge Handbook of China–India Relations* (New York: Routledge, 2020).

51. See Rob Jenkins, "India's Democracy: Ill but Not Illiberal," *Washington Post*, March 31, 2017; and Ramachandra Guha, "The Gutting of Indian Democracy by Modi-Shah," NDTV, July 14, 2020, www.ndtv.com/opinion/.

52. Kurt Campbell and Jake Sullivan, "Competition without Catastrophe," *Foreign Affairs* 98 (September/October 2019).

53. The White House, "Interim National Security Guidance," March 3, 2021, www.whitehouse.gov/briefing-room/statements-releases/2021/03/03/interim-national-security-strategic-guidance/.

54. Alyssa Ayres, "Democratic Values No Longer Define US-India Relations," *Foreign Affairs*, March 11, 2020, www.foreignaffairs.com/articles/india/2020-03-11/democratic-values-no-longer-define-us-indian-relations.

55. Data from South Asia Terrorist Portal, www.satp.org; other databases give slightly different figures.

56. For an estimate of 157,000 war-related fatalities in Afghanistan until late 2019, see Neta Crawford and Catherine Lutz, "Human Cost of Post-9/11 Wars," November 13, 2019, Costs of War project, Watson Institute, Brown University, https://watson.brown.edu/costsofwar/costs/human/civilians/afghan.

57. Data from South Asia Terrorist Portal, www.satp.org; other databases give different figures.

58. The data for Sri Lanka include 10,000 civilian deaths in 2009, though other sources, including a UN expert panel, suggest 10,000–40,000 civilian fatalities during military operations ending the civil war that year.

59. Different constellations of factors were influential during different historical stages of Islamist terrorism in Bangladesh. These were the wider processes of Islamization: political conflict between the country's two main political parties

and authoritarian governance; weaknesses in Bangladesh's security and justice system; and international events such as the Soviet-Afghanistan war, influences from the Gulf, and the increased interest of al Qaeda and the Islamic State in South Asia. Jasmin Lorch, "Terrorism in Bangladesh: Understanding a Complex Phenomenon," *Asian Survey* 60, no. 4 (July/August 2020), pp. 778–802.

TWO

Pakistan, India, and U.S. Strategic Interests

DINSHAW MISTRY

Since the early 2000s, American policymakers have focused on two sets of strategic issues in the relationship with India.[1] First, they looked toward India to help maintain a balance of power against China, which, by the late 2010s, was officially regarded as America's main "strategic competitor" that "seeks to displace the United States" in Asia.[2] Second, they assumed that India could assist with other American regional and international security objectives. As for Pakistan, the main U.S. strategic interests concerned its role in the war in Afghanistan, its ties with China, and the security of its nuclear arsenal. This chapter assesses how well India's and Pakistan's policies on these issues aligned with U.S. interests.[3]

In most cases, India's policies converged with U.S. objectives, but often only gradually, and with limitations. Thus, in balancing China, India increased its military capabilities and forged stronger relations with some of China's neighbors, though it did not pursue "hard balancing" against China. On bilateral defense collaboration, India obtained a substantial amount of arms from the United States, signed defense interoperability agreements, and participated in one significant joint naval exercise, but the scale of other U.S.-India military exercises were small. Similarly, in the area of Indian Ocean security, India undertook some useful, albeit small-scale, patrolling and disaster relief operations. On Iran, India complied with U.S. sanctions by cutting back its oil imports. However, U.S. sanctions did not dissuade India from arms deals with Russia.

Pakistan had a mixed record in its convergence with U.S. objectives across the three principal areas. On Afghanistan, for much of the 2000s and 2010s, Pakistan permitted safe havens to the Taliban, which undermined the American war effort. In 2019–2020, when the U.S. strategy changed to talking with the Taliban, Pakistan supported these talks, which led to a U.S.-Taliban deal. On China, Pakistan substantially increased its military and economic ties with Beijing; these did not directly and immediately, but could over the long term, offer challenges for U.S. regional interests. And on nuclear issues, Pakistan strengthened its relevant practices; its policies therefore converged with U.S. interests, albeit with limitations.

India

Balancing China

U.S. policy discourse about India's role in balancing China does not define what such balancing entails, though it generally emphasizes military strength. A key Trump administration Asia policy document noted that "a strong India, in cooperation with like-minded countries, would act as a counterbalance to China," and that the U.S. objective should be to "accelerate India's rise and capacity to serve as a net provider of security and Major Defense Partner."[4] Scholars and analysts note that balancing involves some aggregate power capabilities, as well as internal and external components. India has balanced China in all these ways, albeit with limitations.

In terms of aggregate economic and military indicators, India adds perhaps 20 percent to the weight of America's three Asian allies in closing the gap with China. Illustrating this, as per 2019 data, the combined GDP of Australia ($1.4 trillion), Japan ($5.1 trillion), and South Korea ($1.6 trillion) was $8.1 billion, or 57 percent of China's GDP ($14.3 trillion). Adding India ($2.9 trillion), the combined GDP of the three allies and India was $11.0 trillion, or 77 percent of China's GDP. India makes a similar contribution when looking at military expenditures. As per the Stockholm International Peace Research Institute (SIPRI) data (2019), the combined military spending of Australia ($26 billion), Japan ($47 billion), and South Korea ($44 billion) was $117 billion, or 45 percent that of China's $261 billion (this is higher than China's defense budget of $190 billion). Adding India ($71 billion), the combined military expenditure of these four countries is $188 billion, or 72 percent that of China. And on the Lowy Institute 100-point scale of power, which includes economic and military capabilities and regional networks and influence, Japan (41), South Korea (32), and Australia (31) were collectively 137 percent the score of China (76); adding India (40), the combined score of these four countries was 190 percent that of China. It should still be noted that aggregate indicators have shortcomings. For example, India's defense forces focus not just on China but also Pakistan, and most of South Korea's defense focus is on North Korea rather than China. More generally, indicators such as GDP and military expenditure do not correlate well with military prowess and the historical rise and fall of states in international politics.[5]

Internal balancing involves building up national military capabilities against a rival, and India has internally balanced China in three ways. First, India somewhat increased its land and air forces in sectors along the Chinese border. For example, it fielded three Su-30 fighter squadrons in Assam, and a Rafale squadron in West Bengal near the Bhutan border; these deployments enable its air force to reach much of Tibet, especially with midair refueling. Also, India's U.S.-acquired C-130 and C-17 transport aircraft and Chinook heavy-lift helicopters allow it to rapidly deploy troops and armaments to the Chinese border. Still, India has been slow to build up its land forces on this front. It upgraded roads and infrastructure along the Chinese border, enabling it to deploy tanks and infantry combat vehicles to the region. But its plans for a mountain strike corps with two divisions were truncated in 2016–2018 to just one division having six brigades (three infantry, one engineer, one air defense, and one artillery brigade).

Second, India maintained a modestly sized naval fleet, replacing retiring vessels with new ones. It had one aircraft carrier (with a second expected to start sea trials in 2022); ten destroyers (with four more planned for the early to mid-2020s, to replace four nearing retirement by then); thirteen frigates (with eleven more planned for the early and mid-2020s, which would offset at least four near retirement); four large and sixteen small corvettes; and ten corvette-type patrol vessels.[6] It also acquired six French Scorpène submarines from 2017 to the early 2020s, and leased a Russian nuclear-powered attack submarine, although these would be insufficient to replace an obsolete fleet of eight Russian and four German submarines (India's plans to obtain six additional conventional attack submarines and build six nuclear-powered attack submarines would not materialize until the 2030s). For comparison, India's destroyer and frigate strength was not that large—it was comparable to South Korea's, half that of Japan's (50), and much less than China's (80–90). This naval force enables India to impose limited pressure on Chinese assets in, and trade transiting through, the Indian Ocean and the Malacca Straits; and to better protect Indian (as well as American and other) shipping against Chinese pressure in these regions. It would not give India the capability to conduct major sustained operations in the East and South China Seas. Even in the Indian Ocean, some analysts note that China has a sufficient number of naval forces and logistics support from Chinese overseas facilities to threaten India's maritime operations.[7]

Third, India built intermediate-range missiles to give it a minimal nuclear deterrent versus China. Still, in the early 2020s, it fielded only about twenty such missiles, comprising the Agni-3 (which had to be deployed in somewhat vulnerable locations in northeast India to reach China's heartland) and Agni-4. It would have a better deterrent after it inducted the more capable Agni-5, which could reach China's major cities from more secure launch sites in south India, and built comparable submarine-launched missiles.

Overall, the above internal balancing mechanisms give India defensive capabilities to offset Chinese political and military pressure, which Beijing could apply to dissuade India from supporting the United States, its allies, and Southeast Asian states in any crisis between them and China. They also enable India to strike Chinese military assets at limited distances across the border.[8] Nevertheless, China's larger economy and military forces give it advantages in any war of attrition versus India.

External balancing involves military alignments with other states to balance a rival. Here, India increased its defense and security interactions with Southeast Asian states and with U.S. allies in Asia, as well as with the United States, but it did not pursue stronger balancing involving defense pacts or military alliances.

First, India strengthened security and defense ties with the United States, as noted below. Second, India advanced bilateral defense interactions with some countries in China's vicinity, especially Singapore, Vietnam, and U.S. allies Japan and Australia.

Singapore and India have held an annual defense ministers' dialogue since 2016; they signed a logistics agreement to access each other's military bases and offer reciprocal logistics support for naval vessels; Singapore used Indian military bases for exercises and training of its mechanized forces, artillery, and F-16 fighter jets; and the two countries conducted maritime exercises that also included Thailand. Vietnam and India have held annual security dialogues since the early 2000s, when India supplied spare parts and servicing for some of Vietnam's Russian-acquired weapons systems. Subsequently, India helped train Vietnamese pilots and sailors for Vietnam's Su-30 aircraft and Kilo-class submarines. Also, Indian Navy vessels made regular port calls in Vietnam, and India sold ten high-speed patrol vessels to Vietnam with deliveries starting in 2021.

Japan and India developed a strategic partnership that had a small defense component. They held annual 2 + 2 meetings of their foreign and defense ministers in 2019, following a decade of such meetings between their foreign and defense secretaries. They conducted bilateral naval exercises with one to two ships, which complement Japan's participation in the larger Malabar exercises; engaged in small air force exercises involving two transport aircraft on each side, simulating disaster relief in 2018 and tactical interoperability in 2019; held low-level army drills since 2018, involving about twenty-five soldiers and sharing experience in counterterrorism and counterinsurgency; and signed a logistics support agreement in 2020. India and Australia entered into a comprehensive strategic partnership and signed a logistics support agreement in 2020.

In addition, India participated in trilateral national leader summits with the United States and Japan in 2018 and 2019 (on the sidelines of the G20 meetings), following a decade of such meetings among their foreign ministers or senior bureaucrats. These meetings were useful for discussing issues such as disaster relief, maritime security, and 5G cellular technologies. Also, India has held trilaterals with Australia and Japan since 2015, at the level of foreign secretaries.

Moreover, the Quadrilateral Security Dialogue (Quad), which facilitates strategic consultations between Australia, India, Japan, and the United States, was upgraded to the level of a foreign ministers' dialogue in 2019. These states' shared concerns about issues such as the coronavirus pandemic and Chinese assertiveness resulted in intensified Quad activities in 2020; the 2020 Quad foreign ministers' meeting was significant because it was a stand-alone event, while previous meetings had taken place on the sidelines of other summits.[9] The Quad was elevated to a national leaders' meeting in 2021. Here the group committed to a "shared vision for a free and open Indo-Pacific" that is "anchored by democratic values," and it established working groups on vaccines, standards for emerging technologies, and climate-related actions.[10] Quad members also reached out to other states for issue-specific initiatives. These ranged from COVID-related discussions with New Zealand, South Korea, Vietnam, Brazil, and Israel to a naval exercise with France.[11] In the end, the Quad facilitated dialogue on contemporary policy issues, though the substantive outcomes of its initiatives are unclear.

Third, as part of its "Look East" and then "Act East" approach, India increased its diplomatic profile in Southeast Asia.[12] It has participated in an annual summit with the Association of Southeast Asian Nations (ASEAN) since 2002, the East Asia Summit since it began in 2005, and the ASEAN Regional Forum. On a related note, India's diplomatic statements expressed support for a rules-based regional order, based on respect for sovereignty, territorial integrity, and international law, which reflected the line taken by the United States and by Southeast Asian countries. Still, India is not a major strategic or economic player in Southeast Asia; only 2 to 3 percent of Southeast Asia's trade is with India, and India has stayed out of the Regional Comprehensive Economic Partnership trade pact involving Southeast Asian and East Asian countries.

In sum, India's internal and external balancing initiatives dovetailed with the U.S. interest that India help balance China. Yet the scale of India's balancing endeavors was insufficient to facilitate large-scale military pressure against China's heartland. India did not have the economic capability nor the political inclination to pursue "hard balancing" against China.[13] Its China strategy has been described as one of competitive engagement, and a mix of cooperation, competition, and hedging against conflict.[14] And on diplomatic issues, New Delhi walked a fine line to not offend Beijing—it toned down its criticism of the Belt and Road Initiative, and refrained from commenting on the Uighur issue, Hong Kong, the South China Sea, and China's mishandling of the COVID-19 outbreak.[15] Moreover, in the 2010s, China was one of India's large trade partners—China, including Hong Kong, accounted for one-sixth of India's imports and one-tenth of its exports, though New Delhi moved to reduce imports from China in 2020.[16]

U.S.-India Defense Relations

Four issues are prominent in U.S.-India defense relations. Among these, India's arms purchases from the United States have been substantial; India also entered into agreements enhancing military exchanges and undertook military exercises with the United States; but U.S.-India defense coproduction ventures faltered.

First, India's arms imports from the United States were a cumulative $15 billion from the mid-2000s to the late 2010s, which compares well with the $20–30 billion in U.S. arms sales to each of its three Asian allies and four largest arms buyers in the Middle East. The majority involved air assets with heavy-lift or long-range patrol capability. These included twelve Lockheed Martin C-130J Hercules transport aircraft for $2 billion; twelve Boeing P-8 Poseidon maritime patrol aircraft for $3 billion; ten Boeing C-17 Globemaster transport aircraft for $4 billion; twenty-two Boeing Apache attack helicopters valued at $1.4 billion; fifteen Boeing Chinook heavy-lift helicopters for $1 billion; 145 howitzers for $885 million; and 120 GE aircraft engines valued at $900 million for India's Light Combat Aircraft. India deployed many of these in its 2020 military standoff with China.[17]

It should also be noted that the above contracts often took years to negotiate, and some arms deals faltered. Thus, in 2011, India opted for French Rafale jets instead of the F-16 and F-18; it eventually bought thirty-six Rafales for $8 billion, and these began entering service in 2020–2021. Also, India's plans for 180 Honeywell engines to upgrade its Jaguar aircraft were frozen in 2019 because of the high $2 billion price.

Beyond the above items, in 2020, India finalized or planned additional arms deals worth around $5 billion. These included twenty-four Sikorsky MH-60 naval helicopters for $2.6 billion; six more Apache helicopters for $930 million; and six more P-8s for $1.8 billion, having enhanced communications-protected equipment, which became possible after India signed a communications agreement with the United States in 2018. And in 2021, India was considering a $3 billion deal for thirty armed Predator drones as well as a $700 million deal for one hundred engines for future Light Combat Aircraft.

Second, India signed defense interoperability or coordination-enabling agreements similar to those that the United States has with several allies and partners. The first, in 2016, took several years to negotiate, while the others took relatively less time but still faced bureaucratic and information awareness hurdles before Indian policymakers came aboard.[18] These agreements were as follows: a logistics arrangement enabling access to each other's military facilities for fuel and supplies (2016); a communications agreement allowing the United States to transfer secure data and communication equipment to India (2018); the industrial security annex allowing for classified military information sharing between the U.S. and Indian defense industries (2019); and an agreement for sharing geospatial data (2020). Further, in 2016, the United States designated India as a "major defense partner," allowing license-free transfers of some dual-use technology. And, in 2018, India became a U.S. strategic trade authorization partner, which again facilitated some high-technology transfers.

Third, the U.S. and Indian militaries engaged in one significant annual exercise, the Malabar naval exercise. This typically involved three to five vessels from each country, and, in some years, an aircraft carrier. Japan has participated in the exercise since 2014, and Australia joined it in 2020. Still, additional U.S.-India military exercises only involved several tens to a few hundred personnel, and were much smaller than typical U.S. exercises with its NATO and Asian allies. The U.S. and Indian Armies undertook small-scale exercises. Also, the two countries held a tri-service amphibious exercise, beginning in late 2019, and planned annually thereafter, focusing on humanitarian assistance and disaster relief. Despite these exercises, India was reluctant to join the United States in some types of military operations, such as patrols in the South China Sea.[19]

Fourth, U.S. efforts to partner with India in defense coproduction faltered. In 2012, under a Defense Technology and Trade Initiative, Washington was considering providing technology for, and building in India, the Sikorsky Seahawk naval helicopter, the Javelin anti-tank missile, a 127 millimeter (mm) naval gun, and a delivery system for scatterable mines. In 2016, the United States floated plans to coproduce the Raven mini-unmanned aerial vehicle, a surveillance module for the C-130J Hercules aircraft, mobile hybrid-electric power sources, and uniforms integrated with chemical and biological protection measures. None of these materialized. However, Indian companies have made low-end components for the U.S. defense industry.[20]

Overall, while U.S.-India defense collaboration was substantial, the output was less than the effort toward building the relationship. Analyzing the record until 2018, a defense department official noted: "The overall output resulting from numerous dialogues, military exercises, and engagements and the tangible impact on Indian and U.S. security objectives are less than one would expect given the level of input and the number of years spent working toward these goals."[21] In 2019–2021, this output slightly increased after the realization of additional U.S.-India defense interoperability agreements and arms sales, but the depth of U.S. defense and intelligence ties with India was still less than that of U.S. ties with its closest allies. Analysts note that in contrast to mature defense partnerships that involve a common view of the threat environment and joint responses with shared missions or a division of labor among partners, U.S.-India defense relations are less developed and mostly involve lower-level platform- and exercise-specific initiatives.[22]

Indian Ocean Security

U.S. officials have frequently noted that they desire India to "be a partner and net provider of security in the Indian Ocean."[23] India's policies converged moderately with these U.S. interests in three ways. First, and most generally, the Indian Navy and Coast Guard were capable of providing some security for (but not routine monitoring of) international shipping lanes off India's coasts. Second, since the mid-2000s, India increased its security interactions with nearby Indian Ocean states, enabling it to play a greater security role in the region. In particular, it developed a maritime initiative with Seychelles, Maldives, Mauritius, and Sri Lanka, which included setting up radar stations in some of these states, securing berthing rights for its vessels, and holding joint naval exercises. Most of these involve the Indian Navy's smaller corvettes and patrol vessels rather than its more capable frigates and destroyers.

Third, the Indian Navy undertook some significant patrol and disaster relief operations. In 2004–2005, it quickly deployed a dozen vessels and over a thousand personnel toward tsunami relief operations in Sri Lanka, Maldives, and Indonesia. In the late 2000s and early 2010s, it sent one to two ships to assist international antipiracy efforts in the Gulf of Aden. Since 2017, Indian Navy vessels went on patrol pre-equipped and prepared for antipiracy and humanitarian assistance operations. These helped in 2019, when three such vessels quickly delivered relief supplies and rescue assistance during Intense Tropical Cyclone Idai in Mozambique, and in 2020, when an Indian naval vessel carried relief supplies during Cyclone Diane in Madagascar.

Russia

New Delhi maintained strong relations with Moscow even as it enhanced ties with Washington. New Delhi and Moscow held annual summits throughout the 2000s and 2010s. To be sure, there were some irritants in the India-Russia relationship. For example, Moscow was critical of the

U.S. "Indo-Pacific" strategy and the Quad, both of which New Delhi favored. Also, contrary to Indian preferences, Moscow did not strongly support India during its 2020 standoff with China, instead preferring to mediate evenly between these two countries. Still, key areas of Russia-India strategic cooperation included nuclear reactor deals and arms sales. Two Russian-built 1,000-megawatt (MW) reactors were connected to India's electricity grid in the mid-2010s, and two more were scheduled for completion in 2023–2024. And Russian arms deals with India were often finalized during their bilateral summits.

From the 2000s to mid-2010s, Russian arms sales to India were worth $20–25 billion. These included air assets such as 270 Su-30 fighter jets ($12 billion); forty-five naval MiG-29K fighters ($2 billion); the modernization of sixty Indian Air Force MiG-29s ($900 million); 150 Mi-17 transport helicopters ($3 billion); and fourteen naval Ka-31 helicopters (around $300 million). They also included naval vessels and army hardware, such as an Akula nuclear-powered submarine on lease ($1 billion); the Gorshkov aircraft carrier ($2.3 billion); six Talwar-class frigates ($2 billion); and over 1,000 T90 tanks ($2.5 billion).

Subsequently, in the late 2010s and 2020, India finalized or planned additional Russian arms imports worth over $12 billion, though not all may eventually materialize. These included 200 Ka-226 light utility helicopters for $3 billion (60 built in Russia, and 140 to be assembled in India beginning around 2025); ten additional naval Ka-31 helicopters for $500 million; four upgraded Talwar-class frigates for $2 billion (two built in Russia, to be delivered around 2022, and two built in India thereafter); five S-400 air defense missile systems for $5.4 billion (to be delivered in the early 2020s); and a 2020–2021 proposal for twelve Su-30s and twenty-one MiG-29s valued at $2 billion.

Washington did not object to most of the above Russian arms sales. However, it began expressing concerns in the late 2010s in the context of the Countering America's Adversaries Through Sanctions Act (CAATSA) sanctions and future defense interoperability issues. U.S. officials noted that India's S-400 purchases "effectively could limit India's ability to increase our own interoperability."[24] The S-400 could preclude future Indian acquisition of F-35 aircraft. And, more generally, U.S. officials noted that "at a certain point, India will have to make sort of a strategic commitment to technologies and platforms," meaning it would be better if it selected a primary defense partner for a range of technologies and platforms rather than buying weapons from multiple vendors that include Russia, "and we think we have the best technologies and platforms."[25]

Iran

New Delhi maintained high-level diplomatic exchanges with Tehran throughout the 2000s and 2010s. However, it complied with U.S. oil sanctions against Iran, and Washington accepted New Delhi's case for a sanctions waiver on the Chabahar Port.

On the diplomatic front, the foreign ministers, other cabinet ministers, and senior officials from India and Iran routinely met in bilateral or multilateral settings. The two countries held annual Joint Commission meetings, often chaired by their foreign ministers. Prime Minister Narendra Modi visited Tehran in 2016 for India-Iran-Afghanistan trilateral meetings (this was the first official visit by an Indian prime minister to Iran since 2001, though Prime Minister Manmohan Singh had participated in the 2012 Summit of the Non-Aligned Movement in Tehran). President Hassan Rouhani subsequently visited India in 2018.

India nevertheless cut its oil imports from Tehran to comply with U.S. sanctions. Thus, with the tightening of sanctions in 2010–2011, India reduced its Iranian oil purchases by half (from 21.8 million tons in 2009–2010 to 11 million tons in 2013–2014). When sanctions were lifted in 2016, India's oil purchases from Iran neared presanctions levels—Iran accounted for about 10–12 percent of India's oil imports, compared to 20 percent each for Iraq and Saudi Arabia. In 2019, India entirely halted Iranian oil imports after the Trump administration reintroduced sanctions.

The administration gave India a sanctions waiver on the Chabahar Port project, on the grounds that it helped reconstruction in Afghanistan. New Delhi sought to develop Chabahar Port and build rail links to complement the road from Chabahar to the Afghan border, in its quest for connectivity to Afghanistan and Central Asia while bypassing Pakistan. In 2017, India started using the road route from Chabahar for some exports into Afghanistan. In 2018, under a lease from Iran, Indian firms took over terminal and cargo handling operations at a part of Chabahar Port. However, U.S. sanctions dissuaded companies from contract work in Chabahar, and Iran canceled India's rail link plan in 2020.[26] Thus, Iran represents a case where India accommodated a U.S. security objective by complying with oil sanctions, and the United States somewhat accommodated India's regional interests on the Chabahar Port—though logistical obstacles, partly related to U.S. sanctions, still disrupted this project.

Afghanistan

India made small positive contributions to the U.S. objective of state-building in Afghanistan, but Pakistan's reaction, along with other factors, set back the U.S. counterinsurgency campaign in Afghanistan.

India disbursed about $1.0–1.2 billion in economic aid to Afghanistan, typically in annual installments of $50–100 million.[27] India's aid was a small fraction of the approximately $72 billion in international economic aid to Afghanistan (as per Organisation for Economic Co-operation and Development [OECD] data for 2001–2019)—with the largest donors being the United States at $30 billion, Japan and Germany each near $6 billion, the United Kingdom and the European Union (EU) each near $5.5 billion, the World Bank at $3 billion, Canada at $2.5 billion, Australia and Sweden each near $1.5 billion, and Norway and Denmark each around $1 billion.

Indian assistance to Afghanistan covered humanitarian aid such as food supplies ($250–300 million in wheat from 2002 to 2018); education and human capacity-building, including scholarships for Afghan nationals to study in India (valued at $60–80 million from 2012 to 2021); and community development projects worth over $100 million. It also involved infrastructure projects, principally the Afghan Parliament building (completed in 2015, costing about $150 million); the Salma Hydroelectric Dam (completed in 2016, costing $300 million); a 200 kilometer (km) road from the Kandahar-Herat Highway to the Iranian border, which goes onto Chabahar Port (completed in 2009, costing $130 million); and electric transmission lines and substations ($30–40 million).

Washington recognized that India's involvement in Afghanistan would heighten Pakistan's security concerns, and New Delhi refrained from much of a security role in Afghanistan.[28] Indian paramilitary forces provided security for its consulates and certain economic projects in Afghanistan, but India's weapons transfers to Afghanistan were insignificant (the main heavy arms were four Soviet-era attack helicopters and three light utility helicopters in the early 2010s, replaced by four additional attack helicopters in the late 2010s). Still, in 2011, India entered into a strategic partnership with Afghanistan, where the two sides agreed to "close political cooperation"; to "establish a Strategic Dialogue to provide a framework for cooperation in the area of national security"; and where "India agrees to assist, as mutually determined, in the training, equipping and capacity building programmes for Afghan National Security Forces."[29]

Pakistan's security establishment reacted to India's role in Afghanistan by supporting the Taliban (despite incurring a costly blowback from this approach, as noted below), and the Taliban insurgency disrupted the U.S. war effort in Afghanistan.[30] Ultimately, would Pakistan's level of support for the Taliban have lessened with corresponding reductions in India's economic, diplomatic, and strategic involvement in Afghanistan? Arguably, since Pakistan had supported the Taliban well before 2001, it may have continued such a pro-Taliban policy even if India's post-2001 involvement in Afghanistan was minimal.[31] Could the United States have facilitated a Pakistan-India understanding, or a broader framework for international actors in Afghanistan, so that Pakistan did not have a zero-sum response to India by supporting the Taliban? There are no definitive answers to this counterfactual, though it holds important lessons on how U.S. strategic objectives can be thwarted by India-Pakistan rivalry.

Pakistan
The War in Afghanistan

In the war in Afghanistan, key U.S. objectives involving Pakistan were availing of supply routes into Afghanistan, and getting Pakistan to act against Taliban and al Qaeda militants on its territory. To secure Pakistan's cooperation, the United States provided $14 billion in Coalition Support Funds, which reimbursed Pakistan for its military and logistics efforts in border areas; $8 billion in military aid and heavy arms; and $11 billion in economic aid.

Ultimately, Pakistan acted against al Qaeda and Pakistani militants, but not against the Afghan Taliban. It arrested a number of high- and mid-ranking al Qaeda members. However, Osama bin Laden hid in a safehouse in Pakistan from 2005 until he was killed in a U.S. military raid in 2011. Moreover, some al Qaeda leaders hid in Pakistani cities. Bin Laden's deputy, Ayman al Zawahari, operated from Pakistan and announced the formation of al-Qaeda in the Indian subcontinent in 2014. Pakistan's military also moved against domestic militants who controlled border areas with Afghanistan, thereby displacing the Afghan Taliban from these areas.

Islamabad took no direct military action against the Afghan Taliban and the Taliban-affiliated Haqqani network. It assumed that the Taliban insurgency would prevent the consolidation of an Afghan government friendly toward India, or would at least give Pakistan a stake in preventing a future Indian role in Afghanistan. This Pakistani justification of its actions in Afghanistan as defensive and motivated by a fear of India can be contested with the argument that India did not have the presence, influence, or ethnic and other links in Afghanistan that Pakistan has consistently enjoyed and used. More important, Islamabad's policies had a major blowback—the Taliban insurgency led to instability in Afghanistan that spilled over into Pakistan, contributing to the rise of the Pakistani Taliban, whose attacks substantially undermined Pakistan's security and development. Despite these heavy costs, Islamabad permitted the Afghan Taliban and Haqqani network sanctuary in Pakistani territory, and the Afghan Taliban leadership hid in Quetta and other Pakistani cities such as Peshawar and Karachi. Pakistani safe havens were one of the main factors enabling the Taliban insurgency to disrupt the U.S. war effort (another major factor was corruption and governance limitations associated with the Afghan government and its warlord allies, which fomented grievances that contributed to the insurgency).[32]

After refraining from direct public criticism of Pakistan in the 2000s, the United States gradually raised this issue in the 2010s. In 2011, after the Haqqani network attacked the U.S. embassy in Kabul, Admiral Michael Mullen, chairman of the Joint Chiefs of Staff, publicly accused the group of acting as "a veritable arm" of Pakistan's security intelligence agency. The Trump administration's South Asia strategy stated that "We can no longer be silent about Pakistan's safe havens for terrorist organizations, the Taliban, and other groups."[33] For principally this reason, it drastically cut aid to Pakistan, from $600 to $700 million annually in prior years to just $100 million in economic aid and no security assistance in Fiscal Year 2018.

U.S.-Pakistan divergence on Afghanistan lessened in 2019–2020, when U.S. strategy shifted from fighting the Taliban to talking with it to facilitate a troop withdrawal (critiques of this strategy shift, questioning the Taliban's intentions and its compatibility with modernization, gender rights, and political development, are not covered in this chapter).[34] While its role should not be overstated, Pakistan helped these talks, which led to the February 2020 U.S.-Taliban agreement.[35] In December 2018, President Donald Trump sent a letter to Prime Minister Imran Khan, requesting Pakistan's assistance in talks with the Taliban. Pakistan released a senior Taliban official who became the Taliban's chief negotiator and deputy prime minister, and it prodded the Taliban to take negotiations seriously when they appeared to falter. During U.S.-Taliban talks in Doha, Qatar, as well as intra-Afghan talks subsequently, Taliban delegations traveled to Pakistan for consultations with the Taliban leadership and field commanders. Also, the Taliban negotiating leadership visited Pakistan and met its foreign minister and intelligence chief in October 2019, and again in August and December 2020 during intra-Afghan talks. Most generally, Islamabad assumed that any power or power-sharing arrangement involving the Taliban could result in a Pakistan-friendly government in Kabul, or could at least preclude an India-leaning government.

China

Pakistan's policies toward China in the 2010s represent a case of manageable divergence with U.S. preferences. Pakistan considerably strengthened its security and economic ties with China, which, as noted previously, had emerged as America's principal "strategic competitor." While these did not immediately and directly undermine U.S. interests, they held the possibility of doing so over the long term.

On security and military ties, Pakistan obtained the majority of its new heavy arms from China, especially naval frigates, submarines, and fighter aircraft. The Pakistan Navy acquired four Chinese frigates, one built in Pakistan, in 2008–2013; ordered four additional Chinese frigates to be delivered in the early 2020s; and ordered eight Chinese submarines to be delivered in the mid and late 2020s. Pakistan's Air Force obtained 100 JF-17 fighters in the 2010s, coproduced with China and manufactured in Pakistan, and planned to acquire fifty additional improved versions by 2024.[36] Pakistan also acquired four Chinese early-warning aircraft. Pakistan nevertheless received arms from other suppliers. It procured eighteen F-16 fighter aircraft with its own funding, and received, via the U.S. security aid package, eight P-3 Orion maritime patrol aircraft, six C-130 Hercules heavy transport aircraft, a naval frigate, fourteen F-16s, twenty-six Bell utility helicopters, twenty Cobra attack helicopters, and fifteen Viper attack helicopters—some of these helicopters and fighter aircraft were used in counterinsurgency operations.[37] It also bought three early-warning aircraft from Sweden, and sought Turkish attack-helicopters, which were blocked by U.S. sanctions.

On economics, China accounted for one-fourth of Pakistan's $61 billion imports, though only 7 percent of its $27 billion exports (data for

2018). More significantly, Chinese infrastructure investment in Pakistan greatly increased through the China-Pakistan Economic Corridor (CPEC). CPEC, formalized in 2015, comprised mostly energy and transportation projects—the latter facilitated connectivity across Pakistan while also linking China's western regions to the Indian Ocean port of Gwadar.[38] By 2020, CPEC projects worth $12 billion were complete ($8 billion in the energy sector and $4 billion on highways), and $18 billion were in progress (including $9 billion for energy projects and an estimated $7 billion for the Karachi-Lahore rail line).[39]

Washington initially understood that CPEC could assist Pakistan's economic development, and also acknowledged that the United States was not able to provide tens of billions of dollars in development financing.[40] It nevertheless had two concerns. First, it was hesitant to support International Monetary Fund (IMF) loans to ease Pakistan's debt burden because some of this debt was incurred due to Chinese and CPEC projects. In November 2019, the acting assistant secretary for South Asia noted that Pakistan had "an estimated $15 billion in debt to the Chinese government and another $6.7 billion in Chinese commercial debt."[41] Pakistan responded that its total public debt was $74 billion, of which $18 billion was owed to China; and earlier, in 2018, Pakistan's Central Bank said that its $95 billion external debt included $23 billion to China. It is not clear how many CPEC-era and pre-CPEC projects are counted in the above figures.

Second, China's military could use CPEC projects such as Gwadar or other sites as a logistics hub or a naval or air base. These concerns did not materialize in the 2010s because, while a Chinese firm took over port operations at Gwadar in the mid-2010s, there was limited commercial activity and no Chinese naval visits at this port.[42] Instead, the better-developed ports at Karachi and Qasim handled most of Pakistan's maritime trade, and Chinese naval vessels made occasional port visits to Karachi. In the future, U.S. interests would be undermined if China uses Gwadar or other sites in Pakistan for military power projection against the United States or its partners; or if Pakistan uses Chinese-built infrastructure and weapons in military operations against U.S. partners. In the 2020 India-China standoff, press reports mentioned that India had detected Chinese J-10 fighter jets and Il-78 refueling aircraft at Skardu Air Base in Pakistan-held Kashmir, which is just 100 km from India's Leh airfield. Although Skardu Air Base is not a CPEC project, this example illustrates how China could use infrastructure in Pakistan for military power projection against U.S. partners.

Nuclear Security

The United States has long been concerned about the security of Pakistan's nuclear assets and the possibility of their theft or transfer to other states or nonstate actors. This concern became prominent after revelations in 2004 that a leading Pakistani nuclear scientist, A. Q. Khan, had transferred centrifuges and related technology to North Korea, Libya, and Iran in the previous decade. Pakistan eventually strengthened control over its nuclear assets.[43] Most of its actions followed standard international practices, and were assisted by the International Atomic Energy Agency (IAEA) and the U.S. Department of Energy, which allocated about $100 million toward these efforts in the 2000s.[44]

Thus, Pakistan increased physical security over its nuclear installations and infrastructure. It also better monitored its nuclear workforce through personnel reliability programs. Further, it adopted stronger nuclear security training and developed a nuclear security culture. And it took steps to prevent the unauthorized use of nuclear weapons in the event they are stolen. It kept nuclear weapon systems de-mated in peacetime, so that warheads are separated from delivery systems and from fissile cores,[45] and adopted two-person and three-person requirements to initiate a nuclear detonation.[46]

Despite these steps, factors stemming from Pakistan's internal and external security environment contributed to concerns about its nuclear security. In the late 2000s, militants attacked military facilities that could be associated with Pakistan's nuclear program; although these attacks were not directed at nuclear assets, they illustrated weaknesses in Pakistan's physical security measures. In addition, Pakistan faced an "insider" threat to its nuclear assets, in the sense that some Pakistani military personnel sympathized with jihadist-oriented groups. Moreover, Pakistan had plans to disperse its weapons to remote areas during crises with India, where they were more vulnerable to militant attacks.

A second U.S. nuclear-related concern involving Pakistan is the breaking of the taboo against the nonuse of nuclear weapons during any India-Pakistan skirmishes. Pakistan's induction of tactical nuclear weapons (which it began testing in 2011), and its first-use doctrine, increases the likelihood of such nuclear use.

Overall, Pakistan's improved nuclear security practices, despite their limitations, represent convergence with U.S. interests. Pakistan's tactical nuclear weapons and first-use policies represent divergence from U.S. interests, though such divergence was arguably manageable as long as India and Pakistan were not involved in serious military crises.

Conclusions

This chapter has assessed India and Pakistan's alignment with U.S. strategic interests, regionally and globally. India was not a major player in many important U.S. foreign policy initiatives of the early twenty-first century, such as those in the Middle East, Europe, and Northeast Asia. On broader international security issues, India made useful contributions to UN peacekeeping and also adopted strong nonproliferation export controls. It joined the Missile Technology Control Regime (2016), the Wassenaar Arrangement on conventional arms exports (2017), and the Australia Group on chemical and biological controls (2018). And India, as well as Pakistan, actively participated in the nuclear security summits of 2010–2016. On the issues discussed in this chapter—issues that mattered to the United States in Asia and in some other areas, and where India and Pakistan were relevant—India's policies mostly aligned with U.S. strategic interests while Pakistan had a mixed record. The reasons for these outcomes include each state's strategic interests, its capabilities on the issue, and cost-benefit or incentive-disincentive considerations. Three points should be noted.

First, convergence between Pakistan's policies and U.S. interests varied across the three main cases of concern to the United States. There was strong divergence in the war in Afghanistan, but this changed in 2019–2020, when Pakistan assisted in U.S.-Taliban talks. There was manageable divergence in the case of China, though this could worsen under certain circumstances. And there was convergence with limitations on nuclear security. A fourth significant U.S. interest was Pakistan's cracking down on anti-India terrorist groups. The United States assessed that "Pakistan took modest steps . . . to counter terror financing and to restrain some India-focused militant groups," but "Islamabad has yet to take decisive actions against" these groups; "Pakistan's progress on the most difficult aspects of its 2015 National Action Plan to counter terrorism remains unfulfilled—specifically its pledge to dismantle all terrorist organizations without delay and discrimination."[47] As a result of its policies in this area, Pakistan avoided being placed on the blacklist of the international Financial Action Task Force (FATF), but was in the FATF gray list of "jurisdictions with strategic deficiencies" in 2008, 2012–2015, and again in 2018–2021.

Second, many cases where Pakistani policies diverged from U.S. interests were influenced by a fundamental strategic consideration—Pakistan's security threat perceptions about India. The reasons behind this perception are complex. They include the historical legacy of Kashmir; Pakistan's economic and conventional military imbalance versus India; Pakistan's suspicions about growing U.S. ties with India; and the Pakistani military's reluctance to accept Indian regional hegemony. These factors, along with the military's dominance in security policymaking, led Pakistan to confront India—by backing the Taliban and anti-India militants; growing its nuclear program, especially tactical nuclear weapons; and strengthening ties with China—and these policies, to varying degrees, diverged from U.S. strategic interests. This observation has an important implication: as long as Pakistan perceives a strong security threat from India, such strategic considerations could lead it to pursue policies that diverge from U.S. interests on relevant issues.

Third, India had a much better record in its alignment with U.S. strategic interests. In several cases, its policies converged with U.S. objectives, but, because of its limited capabilities or bureaucratic obstacles, to a lesser magnitude and at a slower pace than U.S. expectations.[48] These include the cases of balancing China, India-U.S. defense collaboration, Indian Ocean security, and Iran. It is worth noting that New Delhi would have preferred to not disrupt ties with, and instead continue oil purchases from, Iran. Yet the costs of doing so (incurring U.S. secondary sanctions and rupturing ties with the United States) were significant, and it is likely that this reasoning influenced New Delhi to cut oil imports from Tehran. In the case of arms procurements from Russia, however, strategic and cost-benefit considerations led to India's policies diverging, albeit to a manageable extent, from U.S. interests. Here, the strategic benefits (of securing important arms deliveries) appeared to outweigh the costs (of incurring U.S. secondary sanctions), especially if the costs were reduced through diplomatic engagement with, in the hope for a sanctions waiver from, the United States. Further, despite India's interest in the U.S.-backed Quad process to balance China, it was active in diplomatic arrangements with Russia and China that did not have U.S. involvement. These included the

Shanghai Cooperation Organization (covering Russia, the former Soviet Central Asian republics, and China) and the Brazil, Russia, India, China, South Africa (BRICS) group.

In summary, as is intuitive, in cases where India's and Pakistan's strategic interests are the same as those of the United States—and there were many more such cases for India than for Pakistan—their policies converge with U.S. objectives. Still, the magnitude and pace of such convergence may be much less than U.S. expectations. In cases where India's or Pakistan's strategic interests differ from those of the United States, there is divergence between their relevant policies and U.S. interests. In such cases, however, cost-benefit considerations and American incentive-disincentive offers could bring about some degree of convergence. Such dynamics are more likely to apply in cases where the state has lower stakes (India on issues related to Iran) rather than higher stakes (Pakistan on issues related to Afghanistan). Finally, some cases are complex, as in Afghanistan. Here, India's economic contributions helped U.S. objectives of state-building in that country, but these positive effects were offset by Pakistan's actions, which, along with other factors, undermined the U.S. war effort—illustrating the manner in which the India-Pakistan rivalry can complicate U.S. strategic objectives in South Asia.

NOTES

1. Robert Blackwill and Ashley J. Tellis, "The India Dividend: New Delhi Remains Washington's Best Hope in Asia," *Foreign Affairs* 98, no. 5 (September/October 2019), pp. 173–83.

2. The White House, *National Security Strategy of the United States of America* (December 2017); and Department of Defense, "Summary of the 2018 National Defense Strategy of the United States of America: Sharpening the American Military's Competitive Edge," January 2018.

3. The analysis builds upon the author's earlier writings: Dinshaw Mistry, *Aligning Unevenly: India and the United States*, Policy Studies 74 (Honolulu: East-West Center, April 2016); and Dinshaw Mistry, "Divergence and Convergence in U.S.-Pakistan Security Relations," *Asian Security* 16, no. 2 (2020; published online September 2019).

4. See a document titled "U.S. Strategic Framework for the IndoPacific," released by Robert C. O'Brien, Assistant to the President for National Security Affairs, January 5, 2021.

5. Michael Beckley, "Stop Obsessing about China: Why Beijing Will Not Imperil U.S. Hegemony," *Foreign Affairs*, September 21, 2018.

6. Of the ten destroyers, three Indian-built Kolkata-class Project 15A were

inducted in 2014–2017; three Indian-built Delhi-class in 1997–2001; and four Russian-built Rajput-class in 1980–1988. Three of the four Project 15B (improved Kolkata-class) destroyers had been built by 2020 and would be inducted after sea trials in the early 2020s. Of the thirteen frigates, three Indian-built Shivalik-class Project 17 stealth frigates were inducted in 2010–2012; six Russian-supplied Talwar-class frigates in 2003–2013; three Indian-built Brahmaputra-class in 2000–2005; and one Indian-built Godavri-class in 1988 (others of this class had retired). Further, seven Nilgiri-class Project 17A improved stealth frigates could be inducted in the early and mid 2020s—the keels for four were laid down in 2017–2020, and the first began sea trials in 2019. Four Russian-supplied Grigorovich (improved Talwar-class) frigates are also planned for the mid-2020s.

Some major Indian naval vessels used General Electric (GE) LM 2500 gas turbines, assembled under license by Hindustan Aeronautics Limited (HAL) in Bangalore. India's second aircraft carrier was powered by four such turbines; the three Project 17 and seven Project 17A frigates each had two such turbines.

7. Daniel Kliman, Iskander Rehman, Kristine Lee, and Joshua Fitt, *Imbalance of Power: India's Military Choices in an Era of Strategic Competition with China* (Washington, D.C.: Center for New American Security, October 2019). For another perspective, see Oriana Skylar Mastro and Arzan Tarapore, "Asymmetric But Uneven: The China-India Conventional Military Balance," in *Routledge Handbook of China-India Relations*, edited by Kanti Bajpai, Selina Ho, and Manjari Chatterjee Miller (New York: Routledge, 2020), pp. 240–51.

8. Yogesh Joshi and Anit Mukherjee, "From Denial to Punishment: The Security Dilemma and Changes in India's Military," *Asian Security* 15, no. 1 (2019), pp. 25–43.

9. Tanvi Madan, "What You Need to Know about the Quad, in Charts," *Order from Chaos* (blog), Brookings, October 5, 2020.

10. The White House, "Quad Leaders' Joint Statement," March 3, 2021, www.whitehouse.gov/briefing-room/statements-releases/2021/03/12/quad-leaders-joint-statement-the-spirit-of-the-quad/.

11. Dhruva Jaishankar and Tanvi Madan, "How the Quad Can Match the Hype. It's the Best Hope for Balancing China in the Indo-Pacific," *Foreign Affairs*, April 15, 2021.

12. Dhruva Jaishankar, *Acting East: India in the Indo-Pacific* (Brookings Institution India Center, 2019).

13. Hard balancing involves internal military buildups as well as external military alliances against a rival. Some argue that India's limited security interactions with the United States and other Asian states, which fell short of formal alliances, can be considered limited hard balancing against China. Zhen Han and T. V. Paul, "China's Rise and Balance of Power Politics," *The Chinese Journal of International Politics* 13, no. 1 (Spring 2020), pp. 1–26. For other perspectives, see Rajesh Rajagopalan, "Evasive Balancing: India's Unviable Indo-Pacific Strategy," *International Affairs* 96, no. 1 (2020), pp. 75–93.

14. Tanvi Madan, *Managing China: Competitive Engagement, with Indian Characteristics* (Brookings, 2020).

15. Shivshankar Menon, "League of Nationalists: How Trump and Modi Refashioned the U.S.-Indian Relationship," *Foreign Affairs*, August 11, 2020.

16. As per annual goods trade data for 2018 to 2021, India's imports of approximately $500 billion were mainly from China (14–16 percent), Hong Kong (3.5–4 percent), other parts of Asia (17 percent), Europe (13–14 percent), the United States (7–8 percent), and oil-producing countries (about 20 percent). India's exports of approximately $300 billion were primarily to Europe (19 percent), the United States (16–18 percent), China (5–7 percent), Hong Kong (3.5–4 percent), and other parts of Asia (16 percent).

17. During the 2020 crisis, India deployed U.S.-supplied howitzers, Apache attack helicopters, P8I surveillance aircraft, as well as C-17 Globemaster, C-130 Super Hercules, and CH-47 Chinook helicopters, which ferried troops and equipment to the Ladakh region (the C-17 allowed for airlifting T-90 tanks). The Indian Air Force also drew upon non-U.S.-supplied Sukhoi and Mirage jets for patrols over Ladakh.

18. Mark Rosen and Douglas Jackson, *The U.S.-India Defense Relationship: Putting the Foundational Agreements in Perspective* (Arlington, VA: Center for Naval Analysis, February 2017).

19. Nilanthi Samaranayake, Michael Connell, and Satu Limaye, *The Future of U.S.-India Naval Relations* (Arlington, VA: Center for Naval Analysis, 2017).

20. In the 2010s, Tata group facilities in Hyderabad made 100 empennage assemblies for the Lockheed Martin C-130 aircraft and 150 cabin structures for the Sikorsky S-92 helicopter, while Hindustan Aeronautics Limited in Bangalore manufactured weapon bay doors for the F-18 and P-8I aircraft and wire harnesses for the F-18.

21. Cara Abercrombie, "Realizing the Potential: Mature Defense Cooperation and the U.S.-India Strategic Partnership," *Asia Policy* 14, no. 1 (January 2019).

22. Joshua White, *After the Foundational Agreements: An Agenda for U.S.-India Defense and Security Cooperation* (Brookings, 2021).

23. Robert Gates, "America's Security Role in the Asia-Pacific," Speech at the Eighth International Institute for Strategic Studies (IISS) Asia Security Summit, Shangri-La Dialogue, Singapore, May 30, 2009.

24. See Chidanand Rajghatta, "U.S. Cautions India Over S-400 deal with Russia, cites Strategic Partnership Choices," *Times of India*, June 15, 2019.

25. See "As U.S. Seeks Strategic Commitment from India, Top Diplomat Says Sanctions for Buying S-400 System Possible," *Times of India*, May 21, 2020.

26. Andrew Hanna, "The Broken Promise of Chabahar," *The Iran Primer* (U.S. Institute of Peace, October 8, 2019).

27. India's aid disbursements of $1.0–1.2 billion are calculated based on prevailing exchange rates, and these figures vary slightly across sources; still, these disbursements were much less than India's aid commitment of $2 billion,

which increased to $3 billion in 2016. Also, the purchasing power equivalent of Indian aid is higher than the disbursed amount by a factor of two to three for some components, such as scholarships and human capital assistance.

28. Larry Hanauer and Peter Chalk, *India's and Pakistan's Strategies in Afghanistan* (Santa Monica, CA: RAND Corporation, 2012).

29. See Ministry of External Affairs, Government of India, "Text of Agreement on Strategic Partnership between the Republic of India and the Islamic Republic of Afghanistan," October 4, 2011.

30. William Dalrymple, "A Deadly Triangle: Afghanistan, Pakistan, and India," The Brookings Essay (Brookings, June 25, 2013).

31. The main non-India factors driving or enabling Pakistan's pro-Taliban position were Pakistani military involvement in its foreign policy decisions, the links between Pakistan's military and Islamist networks, and Pakistan's contentious history with Afghanistan. These are discussed in Khalid Homayun Nadiri, "Old Habits, New Consequences: Pakistan's Posture toward Afghanistan since 2001," *International Security* 39, no. 2 (Fall 2012), pp. 132–68.

32. Carter Malkasian, "How the Good War Went Bad. America's Slow-Motion Failure in Afghanistan," *Foreign Affairs* 99, no. 2 (March/April 2020), pp. 77–91.

33. The White House, "Remarks by President Trump on the Strategy in Afghanistan and South Asia," August 21, 2017, https://trumpwhitehouse.archives .gov/briefings-statements/remarks-president-trump-strategy-afghanistan-south -asia/.

34. See, for example, John Allen, "The U.S.-Taliban Peace Deal: A Road to Nowhere," *Order from Chaos* (blog), Brookings, March 5, 2020.

35. Mujib Mashal, "How the Taliban Outlasted a Superpower," *New York Times*, May 26, 2020; Diaa Hadid, "The Key Role Pakistan Is Playing in U.S.-Taliban Talks," NPR, August 30, 2019.

36. Sebastien Roblin, "This is How the JF-17 Became the Backbone of Pakistan's Air Force," *The National Interest*, March 26, 2020.

37. Congressional Research Service, "Major U.S. Arms Sales and Grants to Pakistan since 2001," May 4, 2015.

38. In 2017, a Pakistani daily revealed a "long-term master plan," that highlighted sectors beyond energy and infrastructure. It envisioned Chinese investment in Pakistan's agriculture, fiberoptics and surveillance, and tourism sectors. See Khurram Husain, "Exclusive: CPEC Master Plan Revealed," *Dawn*, May 15, 2017.

39. These figures exclude projects worth $5–10 billion that were approved but not begun by 2020 (such as two hydropower plants valued at $4 billion), and they exclude two Chinese-supplied reactors in Karachi, valued at $10 billion, which were signed before CPEC and became operational in 2021.

40. Department of State, "Background Briefing with Senior State Department Officials on Security Assistance to Pakistan," January 4, 2018.

41. See "A Conversation with Ambassador Alice Wells on the China-Pakistan Economic Corridor," Woodrow Wilson Center, November 21, 2019.

42. Isaac Kardon, Conor Kennedy, and Peter Dutton, *Gwadar: China's Potential Strategic Strongpoint in Pakistan* (Newport, RI: China Maritime Studies Institute, U.S. Naval War College, 2020).

43. On these issues, see Feroz Hassan Khan, "Nuclear Security in Pakistan: Separating Myth from Reality," *Arms Control Today* (July/August 2009); Mark Fitzpatrick, *Overcoming Pakistan's Nuclear Dangers* (London: International Institute for Strategic Studies, 2014); and Naeem Salik and Kenneth Luongo, "Challenges for Pakistan's Nuclear Security," *Arms Control Today* (March 2013).

44. David Sanger and William Broad, "U.S. Secretly Aids Pakistan in Guarding Nuclear Arms," *New York Times*, November 18, 2007.

45. Paul K. Kerr and Mary Beth Nikitin, "Pakistan's Nuclear Weapons," Congressional Research Service, August 1, 2016.

46. Jeffrey Goldberg and Marc Ambinder, "Ally from Hell," *The Atlantic* (December 2011).

47. U.S. Department of State, Bureau of Counterterrorism, "Country Reports on Terrorism 2019: Pakistan," June 24, 2020, www.state.gov/reports/country-reports-on-terrorism-2019/pakistan/.

48. A similar argument is made by Sameer Lalwani and Heather Byrne, "Great Expectations: Asking Too Much of the U.S.-India Strategic Partnership," *Washington Quarterly* 42, no. 3 (2019), pp. 137–59.

THREE

Security Issues in Sino-Indian Relations

ŠUMIT GANGULY

From the standpoint of New Delhi, the People's Republic of China (PRC) constitutes the principal, long-term security threat to India. The threat stems from the unresolved border dispute, from the PRC's military capabilities, from its behavior in India's immediate environs, and finally from its hostility toward India in various international forums as well as India's growing ties with the United States. This chapter will outline and discuss these threats, as perceived from New Delhi. It will then discuss the likely future of the Sino-Indian security competition.

Historical Legacies

In considerable part, India's security concerns about the PRC stem from a long-standing, unresolved border dispute. The origins of this dispute have been discussed at considerable length elsewhere and do not need to be elaborated here.[1] Suffice to state that it stemmed from two important sources. At one level, it can be traced to the uncertain demarcation of the border in the Himalayan region.[2] At another, it can be attributed to the PRC's misgivings about India's interests in Tibet as well as its role as the principal successor state to the British Indian Empire in South Asia.[3]

This border dispute, which came to the fore in the late 1950s, was not resolved despite bilateral negotiations.[4] In the wake of the diplomatic deadlock, the PRC attacked India, resulting in a short, sharp, and brutal border war in October 1962.[5] The war proved to be an utter rout for the Indian Army, which was grossly unprepared to fight a war against a battle-hardened People's Liberation Army (PLA). India lost as much as 36,000 square kilometers of territory to the PRC in this conflict.[6] In the wake of this war, India embarked on a significant modernization of its conventional military capabilities to cope with this emergent threat from the PRC. Among other matters, it created ten new mountain divisions equipped and trained for high-altitude warfare.

India's security concerns about the PRC, of course, worsened in the wake of the Chinese nuclear test at Lop Nor in 1964. In fact, this contributed to an important debate within the country about how best to deal with this enhanced threat from the PRC.[7] In part, it also contributed to India's quest for and eventual acquisition of nuclear weapons. The border dispute, in the meanwhile, remained unresolved and led to an important clash in 1967 at Sebu La in Sikkim (which was then an Indian protectorate). On this occasion, a much better-armed and battle-ready Indian Army acquitted itself well.[8]

Later, in the 1980s, after fitful attempts, the two sides initiated a series of talks designed to address the border dispute. Over time the level of representation in the talks was steadily enhanced. Despite the enhanced diplomatic status of the talks, progress toward the resolution of the disputed border has proven to be altogether glacial. Even after twenty rounds of talks, little to nothing of substance has been accomplished. Furthermore, the PLA, on a series of occasions, has undertaken limited forays along the Line of Actual Control (LAC). The most significant of these took place during President Xi Jinping's visit to India in 2014. Given that an incursion occurred during his visit to India, Prime Minister Narendra Modi felt compelled to raise the matter with his guest, stating that "a little toothache can paralyze the entire body."[9]

Worse still, the PRC's attempts to build a road through disputed territory near the Bhutan-China-India trijunction led to a series of clashes in the summer of 2017. Bhutan, which lacked the military wherewithal to ward off the PLA's activities, felt compelled to seek Indian military assistance. The introduction of Indian military units into this area led to skirmishes between the Indian Army and the PLA. The standoff lasted several weeks before both sides agreed to disengage their forces.[10] However, the PLA did not formally renounce Chinese claims to this disputed area.

Subsequently, at a meeting in Wuhan on the sidelines of the Shanghai Cooperation Organization (SCO) conference in April 2018, the two sides reached a tentative *modus vivendi*. Among other matters, they agreed to provide suitable "strategic guidance" to their respective militaries to avoid a similar clash in the future.[11] However, there is little or no reason to believe that the underlying border tensions were seriously allayed.

In fact, given the Modi government's decision in August 2019 to abrogate the special status of the Indian-controlled section of the disputed state of Jammu and Kashmir,[12] it was reasonable to surmise that further problems on the border issue could well flare up, and this occurred in summer 2020.[13] The PRC, though preoccupied with protests in Hong Kong, nevertheless issued a number of strong statements about India's decision to revoke the state's special dispensation. Probably with a view toward assuaging Chinese concerns, shortly after the decision, India's minister for external affairs, Subrahmanyam Jaishankar, went to Beijing and made clear to his interlocutors that the change in Kashmir's status had no bearing on existing border arrangements with the PRC.[14]

Despite India's efforts to reassure the PRC, the situation along the border remained fraught. This became abundantly clear in May 2020, when the PLA made a series of incursions along the Line of Actual Control. These incursions took place at a number of different points along the border including the northern bank of Pangong Tso (Hot Springs) and in the Galwan Valley in the region of Ladakh. These incidents were of a different order than those that had taken place in the past. First, the PLA forces managed to seize as much as 40 to 60 square kilometers of territory that New Delhi deems to be its own. Second, they involved battalion-strength forces that were often armed with heavy weapons.[15]

Military Asymmetries

The growing military imbalance between India and the PRC is also a source of major misgiving in New Delhi. With its high rates of economic growth over the past several decades, the PRC has been able to devote significant resources to military modernization. India, on the other hand, has only made fitful investments in its military capabilities over a comparable time period. One obvious disparity is the respective sizes of the defense budgets of the two countries. The PRC spends close to $180 billion on defense, compared to India's approximately $50 billion.[16] More to the point, India is faced with adversaries on two different fronts, thereby placing greater demands on its extant military forces. India, as is well known, not only has to deal with the defense of the Indo-Pakistani border but since the early 1990s has had to cope with an ongoing insurgency in the disputed state of Jammu and Kashmir. Finally, at any given time, some of India's Armed Forces are also tied down in various other domestic counterinsurgency operations. All of these demands on the Indian Armed Forces, particularly the Indian Army, place it at a considerable disadvantage to the People's Liberation Army (PLA).

Given the threat that India faces along its 4,100 kilometer-long Himalayan border, it has, especially in recent years, been attempting to bolster its capabilities in the northeast. To that end, it has been enhancing its military capabilities along the border. Specifically, it has, especially in the wake of the Doklam incident, started to boost its road-building activities along the border.[17] It had also, in the 2010s, started to raise a new mountain strike corps to deal with the perceived threat in the northeast, where the PRC claims nearly 43,000 square kilometers of territory in the Indian state of Arunachal Pradesh.[18] Unfortunately, fiscal constraints forced India in 2016–2018 to pare down its more ambitious plans to expand the capabilities of the corps.[19]

Finally, while the possibility of an imminent conflict in this arena may not be likely, India also faces a significant capability threat from the PRC in the realm of nuclear weapons. Once again, the gap in the capabilities of the two states is significant. The PRC, as is well known, started its program as early as 1964. India's program, for all practical purposes, did not begin until the late 1960s and then proceeded in fits and starts, at best. Consequently, it lags considerably behind that of the PRC. Nevertheless, it is now developing forces that can bring significant segments of the PRC within the range of its missiles.[20] The PRC, on the other hand, has ballistic missiles that can cover all of the Indian subcontinent. More to the point, there is a significant gap in the number of nuclear warheads that the two sides can effectively deploy. The PRC has about 300 nuclear warheads in its arsenal.[21] India, on the other hand, has about 150 nuclear warheads, as per 2020 estimates.[22] Beyond these raw numbers, China's nuclear forces have undergone considerable modernization, their reach is considerably greater, and their accuracy exceeds that of their Indian counterparts. India, on the other hand, is fitfully boosting its missile capabilities to enable it to place important population centers within the PRC at risk.

Admittedly, the PRC sees the United States as its principal nuclear adversary, and its nuclear modernization drive, no doubt, is primarily focused elsewhere. Its capabilities nevertheless pose a significant threat to India. Furthermore, its long-term strategic link with Pakistan and its contribution to Pakistan's nuclear weapons program over decades has further complicated the Sino-Indian nuclear relationship.

Unfortunately, since the PRC does not recognize the legitimacy of India's nuclear weapons programs despite ongoing dialogues in other areas, the two parties have had no discussions about possible limits on deployments or force structures. Consequently, any possibility of a bilateral arms control regime remains stillborn. In the meanwhile, the possibility of inadvertent escalation along the border, though not on the horizon, remains present because of the unresolved border dispute.[23]

India and Its Environs

The PRC also poses a significant threat to India in its immediate environs. To begin with, the PRC has long had a robust security relationship with India's long-standing adversary, Pakistan. This security partnership was forged in the early 1960s in the wake of the disastrous Sino-Indian border war. Shortly after the conflict, Pakistan made important territorial concessions to the PRC in the disputed state of Jammu and Kashmir. Despite occasional vicissitudes, this partnership has proved to be quite enduring and robust.

Among other matters, the PRC has provided Pakistan with missile technology,[24] it may have aided the Pakistani nuclear weapons program,[25] and it has made the country a lynchpin of its Belt and Road Initiative. The China-Pakistan Economic Corridor (CPEC) under the aegis of the Belt and Road Initiative has been of particular concern to New Delhi because a segment of it passes through the disputed state of Jammu and Kashmir currently under Pakistan's control. In fact, when the PRC held a major conference on the subject in 2018, India, to express its displeasure about segments of the initiative that involve Pakistan, chose not to send a delegate to the meeting.[26] India's concerns were further heightened with the formal opening of the Gwadar Port facility on the Arabian Sea. This port, built with several billion dollars' worth of Chinese assistance, in the view of Indian naval planners, gives the PRC a foothold in a maritime domain that impinges on India's security.[27] Independent scholars have also commented on the potential security implications of this initiative.[28]

Beijing's pursuit of the Belt and Road Initiative in the South Asian region is also of considerable concern to India for two compelling and interrelated reasons. At one level, it would enable the PRC to expand its band of influence in the region. Simultaneously, Indian decisionmakers realize that they lack the necessary financial wherewithal to compete with the PRC in this endeavor.

The PRC has also steadfastly refused, until very recently, to place various Pakistan-based terrorists on the United Nations terrorist list.[29] These efforts have been designed to bolster Pakistan's military and economic capabilities and to enable it to serve as a strategic surrogate for the PRC in South Asia.

In 2019–2020, the PRC again demonstrated its willingness to unequivocally support Pakistan on the Kashmir dispute. This support came in the wake of India's decision in August 2019 to formally revoke the special status that the disputed state of Jammu and Kashmir had enjoyed since 1949. The termination of the state's special status, not unsurprisingly, generated considerable hostility in Pakistan. In turn, Pakistan chose to bring the matter to a closed session of the United Nations Security Council (UNSC).[30] The PRC quite predictably supported the Pakistani endeavor.[31] It is entirely reasonable to surmise that the PRC will continue to support Pakistan on this issue as it unfolds.

Beijing has also made significant inroads into the other, smaller countries abutting India, causing much concern in New Delhi. In several of these cases, it has been able to expand its footprint owing to far greater material capabilities and also by exploiting India's maladroit diplomacy on certain occasions. A brief discussion of its efforts to extend its influence in these nations is in order.

There is little or no question that the PRC was on the wrong side of history during the East Pakistan crisis, which led to the genesis of Bangladesh.[32] Furthermore, its very first use of the veto in the United Nations Security Council was against the proposed creation of Bangladesh.[33] Despite this early history of hostility toward the country, decades later Bangladesh has now emerged as a battleground for influence in the region between India and the PRC. The PRC has been able to make inroads into Bangladesh principally because of the two reasons adduced above. Furthermore, Dhaka has been more than willing to remind New Delhi that it can turn to the PRC as a viable alternative for both aid and security.

Sensing an opportunity to reduce Indian influence, the PRC has provided Bangladesh with significant economic and military assistance and has also expanded people-to-people contacts through the provision of scholarships and the like for Bangladeshi students. In recent years, the PRC has emerged as both the country's principal trade partner and its largest defense supplier. Bangladesh has also proven to be an eager participant in the Belt and Road Initiative.[34] Since the late 2010s, India has been even more concerned with reports that the PRC plans to construct a naval base in Pekua in the Bay of Bengal to house and service the submarines. Some Indian naval analysts have suggested that the construction of this naval station is part of the PRC's "string of pearls" strategy that is designed to create a naval stranglehold over India in the Indian Ocean littoral.[35]

Others, however, have argued that the PRC faces more formidable challenges in its attempts to establish a substantial naval presence in the Indian Ocean littoral. One prominent analyst has argued that India, not the PRC, is in a far better position to control vital chokepoints in the Indian Ocean. He, nevertheless, argues that the PRC is undertaking significant efforts to address these vulnerabilities.[36] Furthermore, other knowledgeable analysts have argued that the PRC is now planning on a "one and a half war" scenario, which would involve a conflict with India in the Indian Ocean.[37]

Long before its foray into Bangladesh, the PRC had developed a close working relationship with the military junta in Burma (Myanmar). In part, this was possible because India had, until the early 1990s, chosen consciously to distance itself from the regime, preferring to support the pro-democracy forces in the country. Only in the mid-1990s did India change its stance and seek to make up for lost ground.[38] However, in the meanwhile the presence of the PRC loomed large in the country.

In considerable part, the PRC had managed to secure a foothold in the country as it was willing to ignore the international community's attempts to isolate Myanmar owing to its abhorrent human rights record. However, in the early 1990s, two factors led to a significant shift in Indian policy. First, Indian policymakers concluded that they had to set aside their normative concerns about Myanmar in order to compete with the PRC's growing influence in the country. Second, and simultaneously, there was a significant overall shift in India's foreign policy orientation toward Southeast Asia, known as the "Look East" policy designed to engage the states of the region after decades of neglect. Since then four important objectives have driven India's policies toward the country: regional security, enhanced connectivity, economic development, and maritime concerns. However, the lack of policy coordination between a number of Indian ministries dealing with Myanmar has hindered policy coherence and has hobbled India's ability to play a more decisive role in the country.[39]

To India's dismay, despite the greater levels of cooperation that it has achieved with Myanmar, it still faces stiff competition from the PRC, which has relentlessly sought to bolster its presence in the country.[40] Nevertheless, India has persisted in its efforts to court Myanmar. This is evident from President Ram Nath Kovind's visit to the country in December 2018. His visit was deemed to be a success. However, it came a month after the PRC and Myanmar had agreed to build a new deep-sea port in Kyaukpyu on the Bay of Bengal.[41]

India's growing engagement with Myanmar has not been without costs. Like the PRC, it has maintained a near-deafening silence on the plight of the Rohingyas in Rakhine State. This minority community, as is well known, has faced significant persecution at the hands of the Myanmarese military forces. However, unlike in the past, when India both welcomed refugees from its neighborhood and stood up for human rights, in Myanmar it has scrupulously avoided any criticism of the regime's vicious treatment of its minority population. In considerable part its policies have stemmed both from the imperatives of Indian domestic politics as well as a clear-cut fear of losing further ground to the PRC in Myanmar.[42] Additionally, India is sensitive to the need for continued security cooperation with Myanmar so that it continues to deny sanctuary to rebels from northeastern India.

To India's further dismay, the PRC has also made significant inroads into Sri Lanka, a country where India had long played a dominant role. Two factors enabled the PRC to make substantial inroads into Sri Lanka. First, as the Sri Lankan civil war was at its peak, President Mahinda Rajapaksa sought military assistance from a variety of sources. Initially, India proved willing to provide some military supplies. However, after encountering opposition from Tamil politicians in the southern state of Tamil Nadu, it lost its enthusiasm for providing military assistance. Major Western powers, especially the United States, also proved unwilling to offer military aid because of rampant human rights abuses on the part of the Sri Lankan Armed Forces. The PRC readily stepped into this breach, providing substantial amounts of military assistance to the regime and thereby enabling it to bring an end to this sanguinary civil war, albeit at a substantial human cost.[43]

The PRC was able to wend its way into Sri Lanka largely because it was able to proffer large loans for major infrastructure projects in the country. This held considerable appeal for the regime of then Prime Minister Mahinda Rajapaksa. During his term in office, the PRC stepped in with offers of substantial highway, port, and power construction projects. The most prominent of these, of course, was the massive port of Hambantota in southern Sri Lanka.[44]

The new government of President Maithripala Sirisena, which assumed office in 2015, had some qualms about the country's excessive dependence on the PRC. Accordingly, it sought to distance itself from Beijing. However, the country's structural dependence on the PRC was great owing to the magnitude of the infrastructure projects started under the previous government as well as the very substantial loans it had taken. Unable to maintain its debt payments in December 2017, it was forced to hand over the port of Hambantota to a Chinese company on a ninety-nine-year lease.[45] This development was viewed with much concern in New Delhi. Worse still, in 2018, the Sri Lankan Navy chose to base its Southern Command at Hambantota Port. Sri Lankan assurances that the move would not compromise the security of its naval operations did little to reassure New Delhi.[46]

In the foreseeable future it is hard to see how India will be able to regain lost ground in Sri Lanka. Sri Lanka is now locked into a situation of structural dependence on the PRC because of the very substantial loans that it needs to service. More to the point, the PRC appears both able and willing to continue its arms assistance to the country. In 2018, for example, it provided the Sri Lankan Navy with a warship, thereby further strengthening its ties with the country's military.[47]

Maladroit Indian diplomacy, in considerable part, has enabled the PRC to significantly expand its role in the Himalayan state of Nepal, especially in recent years. India has long had a close relationship with Nepal and played no inconsiderable part in its democratization. It had, in fact, played a significant role in ending the Maoist-led civil war that had wracked the country for some time. Nevertheless, the small Himalayan kingdom has been extremely sensitive about guarding its sovereignty. In the wake of a disastrous earthquake in 2015, India responded with considerable alacrity.[48] The relief that it provided was considerable and generated much goodwill in Nepal. This bonhomie, however, would soon evaporate and redound to the advantage of the PRC.

The loss of Indian influence in Nepal stemmed from the decision of the first Narendra Modi government to get involved in its internal politics using rather blunt instruments. Specifically, Nepal had drafted a new constitution that in Indian eyes had failed to adequately take into account the concerns of a minority ethnic group, the Madhesis, who straddle the porous India-Nepal border. The Modi regime made its concerns known to the Nepalese authorities, but to little avail. Faced with what India deemed to be Nepalese intransigence, the Modi government instituted an informal blockade of the landlocked country.[49]

The consequences for Nepal were nothing short of devastating, as essential supplies such as petroleum and heating oil quickly dried up. Faced with acute shortage, it turned to the PRC, which proved more than willing under the circumstances to step into the breach. The very substantial goodwill that India had garnered owing to its historic role in the country as well as in the aftermath of the earthquake quickly dissipated. More to the point, Nepalese authorities concluded that they had now found a more reliable and willing economic partner in the PRC, which had also come to their assistance to ease the Indian blockade.

Even the small archipelagic state of Maldives has been the focus of the PRC's attention. Once again, the PRC made headway into this small nation through the promise of the development of major infrastructural projects. After warming to Chinese overtures and accepting substantial amounts of loan-based assistance, the Maldives, under a new government, has started to reconsider the putative benefits of Chinese investment.[50]

The PRC, it should be noted, has challenged the proposition that its attempts to obtain naval access in the Indian Ocean littoral has any significant security implications. Instead, it has argued that these efforts are directed to promote the PRC's economic interests as well as those of others in the region. To that end it has characterized its endeavors as the development of a "Maritime Silk Road." It is, according to Beijing, a complement to its Belt and Road Initiative. Specifically, it is designed to promote the development of infrastructure, including ports and free trade zones in Pakistan, Sri Lanka, and Bangladesh based upon Chinese financing.[51] Even if this argument can be taken at face value, there is little or no question that these projects will substantially enhance the influence of the PRC in these countries. Consequently, it is hardly surprising that New Delhi views them with some degree of alarm.

As the foregoing discussion has underscored, China's footprint across South Asia is now increasingly visible and substantial. The key question, of course, is the extent to which India can effectively respond to and counter the growth of Chinese influence in the region. Obviously, it has no chance whatsoever of inducing Pakistan to distance itself from the PRC. That strategic relationship has its own peculiar dynamic and India has no leverage over it.

With the other smaller nations, one of the possible issues that India can focus on in the immediate future is the sheer amount of indebtedness that these countries are taking on in their willingness to accept the PRC's infrastructural projects. Sri Lanka, as noted, has already been forced to lease out the port of Hambantota to the PRC. Other states may soon discover that the seeming largesse of the PRC is not without significant costs attached. Maldives, it is believed, has already developed misgivings about the extent of its indebtedness to the PRC.

India could also counter the influence of the PRC through the provision of more calibrated economic and technical assistance to all the smaller states. It could also assuage their concerns through more deft diplomatic efforts, including better access to India's markets—an issue of much concern to its smaller neighbors.

India, the International Order, the United States, and the PRC

The PRC has also been at odds with India in various global forums and has long viewed developments in Indo-U.S. relations with unease and hostility. India has for long sought to join the United Nations Security Council as a permanent member. While a number of major states have expressed their support, others have remained either noncommittal or unenthusiastic. The PRC, however, has maintained a distinctly equivocal position on India's inclusion in an expanded UNSC.[52] Obviously, without the support of the PRC, the prospect of India's ascension to this body is all but blocked. This is especially ironic, given that India was one of the most ardent supporters for seating the PRC as the proper representative of China from the outset.

The PRC also sought to undercut India's global interests in ensuring oil and natural gas supplies. On a number of occasions, the PRC managed to undermine India as it sought to ensure assured lines of supply. The most prominent of these cases involve India's attempts to obtain an oil block in Angola. Its state-owned enterprise, the Oil and Natural Gas Corporation (ONGC) found itself outbid by a Chinese firm. India faced a similar fate in Nigeria. These two instances can be deemed to be in the realm of competition for scarce resources.[53]

The PRC's attempts to induce India not to pursue natural gas deposits along the coast of Vietnam is a matter of a very different order. In 2018, it explicitly warned Vietnam against allowing India to continue its oil exploration efforts off the coast of Vietnam, asserting that the area was within China's maritime claims.[54] More recently, in an attempt to coerce both Vietnam and India, it dispatched a naval vessel near an ONGC offshore drilling site.[55] These threats do not amount to mere competition for resources as elsewhere. Instead, they constitute, for all practical purposes, attempts to undermine India's legitimate quest for energy security. This issue could escalate in the future, as India has long had excellent ties with Vietnam, it has made a significant investment in these offshore drilling projects and deems them to be crucial for ensuring its long-term energy needs.

In another context, the PRC has sought to hobble global acceptance of India as a de facto nuclear weapons state. This was evident from the moment India tested a series of five nuclear weapons in May 1998. Beijing forthrightly condemned the Indian tests and even coordinated its policies with the United States, as sanctions were imposed on India.[56] Subsequently, during the second George W. Bush administration, when the United States and India reached the U.S.-India Civil Nuclear Agreement in 2005, granting India de facto nuclear weapons status, the PRC made clear its objections. It contended that the deal would destroy nonproliferation efforts and that India should dismantle its nuclear weapons program and sign the Nuclear Nonproliferation Treaty (NPT).[57] When, despite its objections, the United States and India consummated the pact, China sought to grant Pakistan a similar nuclear deal.[58]

In the aftermath of the U.S.-India nuclear agreement, as India sought to enter the Nuclear Suppliers Group (NSG), an organization that regulates global commerce in nuclear materials, the PRC proved to be the principal impediment to its entry. It claimed that a consensus had to be forged first among the forty-eight members of the organization about admitting a non-NPT state into the organization, thereby effectively thwarting India's admission.[59]

Finally, the PRC expressed reservations about India's participation in a set of naval exercises with other members of the Quadrilateral Security Dialogue. Shinzo Abe, the Japanese prime minister, had originally proposed this four-way naval arrangement involving Australia, India, Japan, and the United States, with the ostensible goal of maintaining open sea lanes in the Indo-Pacific. The less overt goal of this entity, of course, was to counter the growing assertiveness of the PRC in the region. Given the PRC's obvious hostility toward this enterprise, India has been a hesitant participant in the project.[60]

Conclusions

It is not easy to envisage how a breakthrough could come about in the Sino-Indian security relationship. As long as the PRC can maintain its current levels of economic growth and sustain a degree of social stability, it is most unlikely to concede its claims on the disputed border. Furthermore, if Indo-U.S. interests continue to converge and defense cooperation proceeds apace, the PRC will view the relationship with growing concern. Under those circumstances, the PRC is likely to maintain its pressure on India in every possible arena. By the same token, no government in India can afford to make territorial concessions to the PRC. As a consequence, this territorial dispute, for the foreseeable future, is more than likely to remain frozen and competitive, if not conflictual.

Beyond the territorial dispute, any government in New Delhi is likely to remain extremely wary about the PRC's presence in South Asia. Beijing's efforts to broaden the scope of its influence in India's immediate environs will remain a source of grave concern to Indian policymakers. These misgivings are also likely to be reinforced with the expansion of the activities of the People's Liberation Army Navy (PLAN) in the Indian Ocean.

Additionally, as long as Sino-American relations remain troubled, the United States is likely to continue to court India as a viable strategic partner in Asia. Even though India's policymakers remain loath to fully repose their faith in the United States, they are nevertheless likely to follow a hedging strategy with the United States vis-à-vis-the PRC. This will necessarily entail bolstering the Indo-U.S. security partnership without entering into a formal alliance with the United States. Any growth in this strategic partnership, however, will inevitably attract the attention of Beijing. In turn, it is bound to raise suspicions about India's intentions and thereby contribute to its further distrust of New Delhi.

Of course, it is possible that if the economic, military, and diplomatic trajectories of the two states keep diverging, the Sino-Indian rivalry may just draw to a close. India and the PRC may well continue to have frosty relations, but India will no longer be in a competitive position vis-à-vis the PRC. Instead it may well find itself relegated to a position of permanent strategic inferiority in Asia, with its reach mostly confined, at best, to South Asia.

NOTES

1. Steven Hoffman, *India and the China Crisis* (University of California Press, 1990); John W. Garver, *Protracted Contest: Sino-Indian Rivalry in the Twentieth Century* (University of Washington Press, 2001).

2. Berenice Guyot-Rechard, *Shadow States: India, China and the Himalayas, 1910–1962* (Cambridge University Press, 2017).

3. Manjeet S. Pardesi, "Instability in Tibet and the Sino-Indian Rivalry: Do Domestic Politics Matter," in *Asian Rivalries: Conflict, Escalation and Limitations on Two-Level Games*, edited by Šumit Ganguly and William R. Thompson (Stanford University Press, 2011).

4. Srinath Raghavan, "A Missed Opportunity? The Nehru-Zhou Enlai Summit of 1960," in *India and the Cold War*, edited by Manu Bhagavan (University of North Carolina Press, 2019).

5. John W. Garver, "China's Decision for War with India in 1962," in *New Directions in the Study of Chinese Foreign Policy*, edited by Alastair Iain Johnston and Robert Ross (Stanford University Press, 2006).

6. Srinath Raghavan, "A Bad Knock: The War with China, 1962," in *A Military History of India and South Asia: From the East India Company to the Nuclear Era*, edited by Daniel P. Marston and Chandar S. Sundaram (Indiana University Press, 2007).

7. For a discussion of the debate, see Yogesh Joshi and Frank O'Donnell, *India and Nuclear Asia: Forces, Doctrine, and Dangers* (Georgetown University Press, 2019).

8. Ananth Krishnan, "The Last Sikkim Stand-Off: When India Gave China a Bloody Nose in 1967," *India Today*, June 30, 2017.

9. "Chinese Incursion in Ladakh: A Little Toothache Can Paralyze the Entire Body; Modi Tells Xi Jinping," *The Times of India*, September 2014.

10. Šumit Ganguly and Andrew Scobell, "The Himalayan Impasse: Sino-Indian Rivalry after Doklam," *The Washington Quarterly* 41, no. 3 (September 2019), pp. 177–90.

11. Ananth Krishnan, "Modi-Xi Bonhomie 2.0: All That Happened during the 'Informal' Wuhan Summit," *India Today*, April 28, 2018.

12. Šumit Ganguly, "Modi Crosses the Rubicon in Kashmir," *Foreign Affairs*, August 8, 2019, www.foreignaffairs.com/articles/india/2019-08-08/modi-crosses-rubicon-kashmir.

13. On this point, see Shaiba Rather, "India and China Border Briefer: The Shadow of Article 370's Revocation," *Lawfare Blog*, November 23, 2020, www.lawfareblog.com/india-and-china-border-briefer-shadow-article-370s-revocation. Also see: Sushant Singh, "Can India Transcend Its Two-Front Challenge," *War on the Rocks*, September 14, 2020, https://warontherocks.com/2020/09/can-india-transcend-its-two-front-challenge/.

14. Sutirtho Patranobis, "J-K Decision an Internal Issue, Says Jaishankar in China Talks," *The Hindustan Times*, August 13, 2019.

15. Ashley J. Tellis, *Hustling in the Himalayas: The Sino-Indian Border Confrontation* (Washington, DC: Carnegie Endowment for International Peace, 2020).

16. PTI (Press Trust of India), "China Hikes Defense Budget by 7.5%; It's Over Three Times of India's," *Business Today*, March 5, 2019; Vivek Raghuvanshi, "India's New Defense Budget Falls Way Short of Modernization Plans," *Defense News*, February 5, 2019.

17. Vasudevan Sridharan, "India Bolsters Defence on Border with China by Building 44 New Roads," *South China Morning Post*, January 17, 2019.

18. SCMP Reporters, "The China-India Border Dispute: Its Origins and Its Impact," *The South China Morning Post*, July 29, 2020, www.scmp.com/news/china/diplomacy/article/3094884/china-india-border-dispute-its-origins-and-impact.

19. Sandeep Unnithan, "The Mountain Is Now a Molehill," *India Today*, February 24, 2016.

20. Frank O'Donnell and Yogesh Joshi, *India and Nuclear Asia: Forces, Doctrine and Dangers* (Georgetown University Press, 2018).

21. Arms Control Association, "Nuclear Weapons: Who Has What at a Glance," July 2019, www.armscontrol.org/factsheets/Nuclearweaponswhohaswhat.

22. Hans M. Kristensen and Matt Korda, "Indian Nuclear Forces, 2018," *Bulletin of the Atomic Scientists* 74, no. 6 (2018), pp. 361–66.

23. For a thoughtful discussion, see Rajesh Basrur, "India and China: A Gathering Nuclear Storm?" *ORF Issue Brief*, July 18, 2018.

24. Evan S. Medeiros, *Reluctant Restraint: The Evolution of China's Nonproliferation Policies and Practices, 1980–2004* (Stanford University Press, 2007).

25. Julian Schofield, "Chinese Nuclear Assistance to Pakistan and North Korea," in *Strategic Nuclear Sharing*, edited by Julian Schofield (London: Palgrave Macmillan, 2014).

26. PTI, "India to Skip China's New Silk Road Forum," *The Economic Times*, July 12, 2018.

27. PTI, "Pakistan's Strategic Gwadar Port Opens China-Pakistan Economic Corridor," *The New Indian Express*, November 16, 2018.

28. Filippo Boni, "Protecting the Belt and Road Initiative: China's Cooperation with Pakistan to Secure CPEC," in "Where the Belt Meets the Road;

Security in a Contested South Asia," edited by Nadege Rolland, Filippo Boni, Meia Nouwens, Nilanthi Samarananayke, Gurpreet Khurana, and Arzan Tarapore, *Asia Policy* 14, no. 2 (April 2019), pp. 1–41.

29. Sarah Zheng, "Why China Dropped Its Opposition to UN Blacklisting of Pakistan-Based Terror Chief Masood Azhar," *South China Morning Post*, May 2, 2019.

30. Foster Klug/AP, "Pakistan PM Warns of War with India over Disputed Kashmir," *Washington Post*, September 24, 2019.

31. PTI, "China Raises Kashmir Issue at UN," *The Hindu*, September 28, 2019.

32. Gary J. Bass, "The Indian Way of Humanitarian Intervention," *Yale Journal of International Law* 40, no. 2 (2015).

33. Robert Alden, "China's First U.N. Veto Bars Bangladesh," *New York Times*, August 26, 1972.

34. Joyeeta Bhattacharjee, "Decoding China-Bangladesh Relationship," Observer Research Foundation, June 27, 2018, www.orfonline.org/expert-speak/41935-decoding-china-bangladesh-relationship/.

35. Arshad Mahmud, "New Bangladesh Sub Base Could Revive India Tensions," *Asia Times*, July 23, 2019, www.asiatimes.com/2019/07/article/new-bangladesh-submarine-base-could-revive-tensions-with-india/.

36. David Brewster, "An Indian Ocean Dilemma: Sino-Indian Rivalry and China's Strategic Vulnerability in the Indian Ocean," *Journal of the Indian Ocean Region* 11, no. 1 (February 2015), pp. 48–59.

37. You Ji, "The Indian Ocean: A Grand Sino-Indian Game of 'G,'" in *India and China at Sea: Competition for Naval Dominance in the Indian Ocean*, edited by David Brewster (Oxford University Press, 2018).

38. Andrew Selth, "Burma and the Strategic Competition between China and India," *Journal of Strategic Studies* 19, no. 2 (1996), pp. 213–30.

39. See the discussion in Sunniva Engh, "India's Mynamar Policy and the 'Sino-Indian Great Game,'" *Asian Affairs* 47, no. 1 (2016), pp. 32–58.

40. Kingling Lo, "China Eyes Closer Military Cooperation with Myanmar as It Looks to Expand Sphere of Influence Near India's Borders," *South China Morning Post*, November 23, 2017.

41. Debarshi Dasgupta, "With China on Its Mind, India Deepens Engagement with Myanmar," *The Straits Times*, December 16, 2018.

42. Subir Bhaumik, "Why Do China, India Back Myanmar over the Rohingya Crisis," *South China Morning Post*, October 18, 2017.

43. Peter Popham, How Beijing Won Sri Lanka's Civil War," *The Independent*, May 23, 2010.

44. Jason Burke, "Chinese-Built Port in Sri Lanka Fuels Indian Fears Beijing Is Encircling Them," *The Guardian*, November 18, 2010.

45. Reuters, "Sri Lanka Hands Over Running Hambantota Port to Chinese Company," *South China Morning Post*, December 10, 2017.

46. Agence France-Press, "Sri Lanka to Base Navy's Southern Command at Chinese-Run Port," *South China Morning Post*, June 30, 2018.

47. Christopher Woody, "China Is Giving Away a Warship, and It's the Latest Sign of the Growing Rivalry between Asia's 2 Most Powerful Militaries," *Business Insider*, July 27, 2018, www.businessinsider.com/chinas-warship-gift-to-sri-lanka-amid-growing-competition-with-india-2018-7.

48. Smriti Kak Ramachandran, "India, Other Countries Continue to Send Help to Nepal," *The Hindu*, August 26, 2015.

49. Hemant Ojha, "The India-Nepal Crisis," *The Diplomat*, November 27, 2015, thediplomat.com/2015/11/the-india-nepal-crisis/.

50. IANS (Indo-Asian News Service), "China, Maldives Clash over Mounting Debt as India Warms Up to Male," *Economic Times*, July 8, 2019.

51. David Brewster, "Silk Roads and String of Pearls: The Strategic Geography of China's New Pathways in the Indian Ocean," *Geopolitics* 22, no. 2 (2017), pp. 269–91.

52. Vinay Kaura, "China on India's UNSC Bid: Neither Yes nor No," *The Diplomat*, June 3, 2015.

53. Raj Verma, "China Outperforms India in Oil Industry in Angola and Nigeria," *India Review* 17, no. 4 (2018), pp. 372–96.

54. IANS, "China Slams Vietnam for Inviting India to Invest in South China Sea," *The Hindustan Times*, January 11, 2018.

55. Rudroneel Ghosh and Sanjay Dutta, "In Tussle with Vietnam, China Parks Vessels Near ONGC Videsh Site," *The Times of India*, August 21, 2019.

56. Srikanth Kondapalli, "China's Response to Indian Nuclear Tests," *Strategic Analysis* 22, no. 3 (1998), pp. 493–94.

57. Mohan Malik, "China Responds to the US-India Nuclear Deal," *China Brief*, the Jamestown Foundation, May 29, 2006, https://jamestown.org/program/china-responds-to-the-u-s-india-nuclear-deal/.

58. James Acton, "China-Pakistan Nuclear Deal," *Arms Control Wonk*, October 22, 2008, armscontrolwonk.com/archive/602066/china-pakistan-nuclear-deal/.

59. PTI, "China Blocks India's Bid to Enter NSG," *The New Indian Express*, June 21, 2019.

60. James Power, "Billed as a Counter to a Rising China, the Quad Has Yet to Find a Purpose," *South China Morning Post*, November 23, 2018.

FOUR

Governance Challenges: Legitimacy and Citizenship in China and India

EDWARD KOLODZIEJ

The Challenge of Legitimacy: The Global Context

The connectedness and interdependence of the peoples and states of the world have created a global society in which all are implicated and on which humankind depends for its survival.[1] The dilemma confronting the world's diverse and inextricably entangled populations is that, although they increasingly depend on each other for the realization of their social and personal security and welfare, there is no global government to ensure these objectives. The deeply flawed responses of state and nonstate actors to the coronavirus crisis exposed the debilitating absence of a universal government to address this and other scourges.

Global governance reverts by default to the anarchy of the nation-state system into which the world's populations are dispersed. Among the central issues of governance confronting the world's population is evaluating the claims of legitimacy that are the foundation for regimes in control of a state's authority and monopoly of power. It is difficult to overestimate the importance of assessing these claims. Whereas the issue of legitimate rule was restricted by geography and by limited means of transportation and communication between peoples, it is no longer a localized concern. Each national population can weigh the worth of its regime's legitimacy against the example and experience of others, if they are not otherwise constrained from doing so by an oppressive regime. Legitimacy has also become a crucial interest of contending regimes as a determinant factor of whether they will survive and thrive.

The Chinese and Indian Challenges to Liberal Democratic Legitimacy

At risk for the foreseeable future is the viability of liberal democratic government. It confronts two formidable opponents, the Chinese Communist Party's (CCP) conception of legitimacy and a growing number of illiberal populist majoritarian democratic states, including India under the regime of the Bharatiya Janata Party (BJP). The transparency of free and open democratic regimes and the accountability of elected officials have opened, ironically, these regimes to close examination and criticism by their opponents. The CCP attacks liberal democratic regimes as both ineffective and illegitimate: ineffective, because they fail to address the public's concerns —poverty, inequality, epidemics, sustainable economic growth, and so forth; illegitimate, because the inherent political divisions and polarization within a free society result inevitably in chronic social disorder. The CCP insists that only a centralized democratic Leninist Party, possessing a monopoly of power, can be the voice of *all* the Chinese people; can more effectively address their security and welfare needs than a liberal democratic regime; and can ensure domestic order. The CCP promotes its rule as a model for other antidemocratic states and regimes to adopt. As Bret Stephens perceptively notes, the CCP seeks to dethrone "liberal democracy as the dominant political model of the twenty-first century."[2]

The other formidable opponent of liberal democracy arises from within the liberal democracies themselves, what Joseph Conrad might have termed democracy's "Secret Sharer." James Madison's celebrated essay, No. 10 of the *Federalist Papers*, cautioned that a determined majority could destroy a democratic government by imposing its will on a minority.[3] What Madison could not envision was that this flaw of democratic rule would lead to majority support for a fascist regime in Mussolini's Italy and a totalitarian regime in Hitler's Germany.[4] In contrast to the CCP's coercive solution to legitimacy, illiberal regimes and their supreme leaders rely on the ballot box to claim that they alone speak for the people.[5]

Until recently, India has been considered the world's largest multicultural and multireligious liberal democracy. The successive and decisive national election victories of the BJP since 2014 are challenging India's status as a secular democracy. In the aftermath of its 2019 electoral victory, the BJP has taken a number of steps that put India on the road to becoming an illiberal democracy. India could be at the cusp of joining the ranks of a growing number of populist illiberal democracies, prominent among them being Belarus, Egypt, Hungary, the Philippines, Poland, Russia, Turkey, and Venezuela. These populist regimes are governed by an antiliberal democratic party in the thrall of an authoritarian leader.[6]

What would be threatened if these authoritarian and illiberal democratic regimes become the norm for what passes for global governance? What do free peoples forfeit in supporting these regimes? In a nutshell, these principles define liberal democratic rule and its promise: that all humans are free and equal; one person, one vote to undergird majoritarian rule qualified by the protection of minority rights; state support of human rights and civil liberties—free speech, press, religion, and rights of assembly and petition; and the rule of law, administered by an independent judiciary. The CCP and populist regimes ignore, circumvent, or suppress these principles.[7] Comprising 36 percent of the world's population,[8] China and India will have a powerful say in whether the peoples and states of the global society will pursue a liberal democratic or an autocratic path.

Defining Legitimacy and Citizenship in the People's Republic of China

To understand the role of legitimacy in governing 1.4 billion Chinese, a sharp distinction must be made between the Chinese Communist Party, on the one hand, and the Chinese state and civil society, on the other. Legitimacy applies only to the CCP. Mao Zedong defined legitimacy for the CCP early in its formation. It is built on two Maoist principles: that "political power grows out of the barrel of a gun" and that "the Party commands the gun, and the gun must never be allowed to command the Party."[9] Survival, not legitimacy, is the CCP's primary objective. The People's Liberation Army (PLA) and a vast array of Chinese internal security forces are the CCP's "guns" to control the Chinese state and civil society.

Since the CCP's formation in 1921 to the present, the CCP has rejected the Rousseauian notion of legitimacy as a social contract resting on the consent of the public, expressed through free and unfettered elections. The CCP will never subject itself to a vote of the Chinese people. The exercise of a monopoly of power by a centralist Leninist Party, as the self-proclaimed vanguard of a global socialist revolution, is sufficient for the CCP to justify its unquestioned rule. China's social contract is a contract of the CCP with itself. The power of the gun, which the CCP unconditionally controls, confers legitimacy.

Marxist doctrine provides a malleable ideological rationale to sanction contradictory claims of legitimacy by successive CCP leadership cadres since the CCP took control of the Chinese mainland in 1949. Mao molded Marxism into an ideological tool to rationalize the changing power requirements of CCP rule. Early in the formation of the CCP, he recognized that "the great strength of Marxism-Leninism lies precisely in its integration with the concrete revolutionary practice of all countries. For the Chinese Communist Party, it is a matter of learning to apply the theory of Marxism-Leninism to the specific circumstances of China. . . . [A]ny talk about Marxism in isolation from China's characteristics is merely Marxism in the abstract, Marxism in a vacuum."[10] Marxism for Mao and for his successors is what the CCP and the leadership say it is.

Mao turned classical Marxism upside down in relying on China's peasantry rather than a purported revolutionary proletariat to gain control of the mainland and end all foreign occupation by 1949. Despite tens of millions having died from hunger or weakened from malnutrition in the "Great Leap Forward" (1958–1962), Mao's hold on the CCP, state, and civil society never wavered. When the party apparatus threatened to undermine his control of the CCP, he launched the Cultural Revolution against the party bureaucracy in 1966, prevailing as the head of the CCP until his death a decade later. Tens of thousands again died, were imprisoned, or sent to work in peasant communities for so-called reeducation in Mao's brand of Marxism. A global revolutionary ideology was domesticated to serve his power needs.

CCP reformers, led by Deng Xiaoping, recognized that Mao's imposition of an autarchic economic system on China was a disaster. It threatened the CCP's control of the Chinese population. To revive the Chinese economy and ensure CCP rule, Marxist doctrine was again torqued and tortured to justify China's entry into the Western global market system. China now became a socialist system with capitalistic characteristics.

The Chinese economy grew exponentially (at annual rates of 8 to 14 percent in the 1990s and 2000s) with the introduction of economic liberalization, including market pricing, the return to family farming, and foreign investment and technology. These reforms paved the way for

China's emergence as the workshop of the world. In 2014 China, alone, produced approximately 12 billion pairs of shoes and enough toys for the world market to provide almost two pairs of shoes and one or two toys to every member of the human race.[11] In drawing hundreds of millions of Chinese out of poverty, an unprecedented accomplishment, Deng's reforms moved the world economy, as William Overholt concludes, "into the post-industrial age. . . . This is an Adam Smith public good."[12] China is now the epicenter of a complex network of global supply chains under multinational corporate direction, domestic and foreign, for the production of goods and services for all of the world's populations.

A Faustian bargain was struck between the CCP and the Chinese population. The CCP would foster economic growth and technological development and promote China as a global power in return for popular submission to unconditional CCP rule. It is important to note that this bargain was not between the CCP and the Chinese people. The party alone defines the terms of the contract. Like the broader social contract, this Faustian bargain is a bargain with the CCP itself for survival on terms defined by the party.

The greater economic freedom accorded the Chinese people and corporations was never intended to weaken the CCP's monopoly of power. Deng Xiaoping's use of the PLA to violently suppress the Tiananmen Square student-led uprising in 1989 reaffirmed the party's unquestioned rule. The temporary political setback in world public opinion was the price to pay for party survival.[13] The price was not great either economically or politically as the Western democracies welcomed China into the World Trade Organization in 2001. They continued to harbor the illusion that economic reforms and China's integration in the Western market system would lead eventually to political reforms, following the model of the liberal democratic states.

That illusion was sustained for much of the first decade of the twenty-first century. During this period Deng's successors progressively imposed tighter political controls over Chinese civil society. Many of the liberal reformers who signed the Charter 08 Manifesto, calling for greater political freedom, were arrested.[14] Others died in prison, including the 2010 Nobel Peace Prize Laureate Lui Xiaobo. Throughout this period, Deng's strategy to foster China's rise as a global power was adopted: that China "cope with affairs calmly, hide our capacities and bide our time, be good at maintaining a low profile, and never claim leadership."[15] China kept a low external political profile during Hu Jintao's tenure as party secretary (2002–2012). His term focused on internal economic growth without raising alarms in Western capitals about China's geopolitical aspirations.

The choice of Xi Jinping as party secretary in 2012 provoked what Elizabeth Economy characterizes as a "Third Revolution" in party rule.[16] His ascension to undisputed power marked a profound change in party governance, in the CCP's control over the Chinese state and civil society, and a sharp break from Deng's cautionary low profile in foreign affairs. High on Xi's agenda was China's sustained economic growth; its leadership in key technologies, like information and communications technology (ICT) and aerospace, by 2025;[17] modernization of the PLA;[18] launching of an ambitious financial plan to increase Chinese influence around the globe under the aegis of the Belt and Road Initiative (BRI) and a revised Maritime Silk Road;[19] the aggressive assertion of Chinese sovereignty over large portions of the East and South China Seas;[20] the affirmation of China as a global power with a say on all issues of regional and global concern to the CCP and China; and the promotion of CCP rule and its economic policies as models for other states to adopt.[21]

Gaining control of the CCP was among Xi's first priorities. He quickly added the posts of president and chair of the powerful Central Military Commission to his position as party secretary general. He also chaired nine other leading policy groups.[22] Among these are the Leading Group on Overall Reform, the newly established National Security Commission, and Foreign Affairs and Taiwan.

Besides chairing the Central Military Commission, Xi has also assumed the rank of commander in chief of the PLA Joint Operations Command Center. His reach then goes deep down within PLA operations. The military reports directly to Xi, whereas Mao had to negotiate with his generals, who enjoyed considerable prestige in having distinguished themselves in the civil war and in the CCP's capture of the Chinese state. Xi also controls a vast complement of internal security forces whose mission is to maintain the CCP's monopoly of power. Since 2011 spending on internal police and security forces actually exceeded spending on the military.[23] The centralization of power in the post of the secretary general affords him access to enormous policy and coercive power to control the party, the state, and civil society.

In securing these commanding heights, Xi systematically eliminated his rivals and worked diligently to bend party members—approximately 90 million—to his command. Powerful party members, Politburo member Bo Xilai and the security czar Zhou Yongkang, were convicted of corruption and imprisoned. More than a hundred generals and admirals were also swept up in the anticorruption campaign. By the time of the Nineteenth National Congress in 2017, the CCP's Discipline Commission, which Xi chairs, initiated the investigation and punishment of 1.4 million party members for various infractions of conduct. Since corruption is endemic to authoritarian rule, campaigns to weed out corruption are welcomed by the Chinese public, however skeptically, in light of past failures to cleanse the system.[24]

Xi obliged all party members to pledge loyalty to the party and, accordingly, to his own leadership.[25] He also urged party members to criticize their own failures and those of others. Compliance with this expectation effectively exposes would-be opponents and frustrates their efforts to organize against Xi's rule.[26] Whistleblowing is institutionalized on a national scale. It has the effect not only of exposing corruption but also of increasing Xi's power, while stifling criticism of the CCP and Xi's failures.

Party members have to be wary of each other. Fear of being denounced works to the advantage of Xi's control of the party. The psychology of Xi-induced whistleblowing places party members in a dilemma. If they do not denounce their peers and corruption is exposed, they face punishment for their silence and implied complicity. If they denounce their faults, however petty, they risk exposing themselves to censure, not praise. Remember Mao's 1957 campaign to let a hundred flowers bloom: "Letting a hundred flowers blossom and a hundred schools of thought contend is the policy for promoting progress in the arts and the sciences and a flourishing socialist culture in our land."[27] When party members and intellectuals critical of Mao's CCP rose to the bait, they exposed themselves as enemies of the regime and were punished for their candor; some were even executed.

Xi enjoys dictatorial political and economic control over China. He replaced the collective leadership of the Deng and Hu Jintao eras with his personal rule. Going further, he also dictated that the National People's Congress eliminate limits on how long he can serve as secretary general and president. In pursuit of his "dream" of an economically strong and prosperous China and a militarily powerful PLA, eventually at parity with the United States and the West, Xi has also wrapped himself ideologically around the contradictory definitions of Marxist-Leninist ideology to strengthen his personal power. He exemplified the CCP leadership's capacity for cognitive dissonance in his remarks to the Nineteenth National Congress of the CCP: "Our Party has been guided by Marxism-Leninism,

Mao Zedong Thought, Deng Xiaoping Theory, the Theory of Three Represents,[28] the Scientific Outlook on Development."[29] Xi added his own confusion to these quarrelsome interpretations of Marxist-Leninist ideology. He had inserted in the Chinese Constitution "Xi Jinping's Thought on Socialism with Chinese Characteristics for the New Era."[30] What is remarkable about CCP leadership is its cynical reliance on alternative and mutually exclusive interpretations of Marxist ideology to justify its legitimacy. Coherence is scarcely a valued commodity. Alternative facts suborn reality and truth to protect the CCP's self-created world.

CCP rule under President Xi is shifting from a highly controlled authoritarian state to what Hannah Arendt would describe as totalitarian rule.[31] Knowing what 1.4 billion Chinese citizens are thinking, doing, and saying is a top priority of the regime. The CCP is rapidly increasing its surveillance of all Chinese citizens. By 2017 China had installed 176 million surveillance cameras across the country, and this number increased to about 400 million by 2021, according to an IHS Markit report. To complement its surveillance system, a Social Credit System has also been created to determine the social credit scores of all Chinese citizens, measuring such behavior as payment of taxes, traffic violations, personal finances, and online media commentary. Those scores determine whether one can purchase travel tickets, acquire personal loans, get a job and other amenities as well as avoid direct state oversight and supervision.

A "Great Firewall" has also been erected to control information reaching the Chinese population. The CCP has hired over two million investigators to report violating websites at odds with party guidelines of what is acceptable posted material. Specially trained internet police interrogate authors of websites that do not comply with official party narratives. Their websites are eliminated or amended and some errant website authors are punished. The party also controls the dissemination of favorable narratives in support of governmental policies through its direction of state broadcaster CCTV, the official news agency Xinhua, the *People's Daily*, and the *Global Times*. In a February 2016 videoconference with Chinese journalists in the United States, President Xi instructed that "All news media run by the party must work to speak for the party's will and its propositions, and protect the party's authority and unity."[32]

The CCP will brook no criticism from either domestic or foreign sources. For example, in 2020 dissidents like Ren Zhiqiang, a rich property owner, and Xu Zhiyong, a distinguished law professor, were taken into police custody for advocating political reforms.[33] Booksellers in Hong

Kong have been arrested for publishing materials critical of the CCP.[34] Protesters are also harassed or jailed in the thousands.

In 2020, China adopted a law to ban treason, secession, sedition, and subversion to apply specifically to Hong Kong. Hong Kong had been guaranteed autonomy, including freedom of speech and assembly, under the treaty ceding British control of Hong Kong to China in 1997. The National People's Congress justified its proposal of the law as necessary to preserve the "One Country, Two Systems" principle and to preclude any Hong Kong moves toward independence. The law severely restricts Hong Kong's autonomy and increasingly subjects the enclave to CCP rule. Under the law, protests would be curbed, personal freedoms curtailed, criticisms of the CCP would not be permitted, and violators would be punished and face imprisonment for subversion. In late 2020, some leading pro-democracy supporters were arrested under the law.

A number of provisional conclusions can be drawn from this brief discussion of the CCP's conception of legitimacy and its claim to a monopoly of power. The CCP and the regime of President Xi Jinping have clearly established their overwhelming power to control the Chinese state and civil society. In CCP-speak, legitimacy and power are distinctions without a difference. Second, the CCP has demonstrated that an authoritarian regime, rapidly tilting toward totalitarianism, can achieve remarkable economic growth and technological development without instituting liberal political reforms. Third, the CCP's claim to be a model for other authoritarian systems and a guide for how the peoples of the world should be ruled threatens liberal democracy.[35]

There are ample flaws in the CCP's record and rising doubts about its future prospects. Among the most pertinent, first, there are too many forces for the CCP to control within and outside China. These range from increasing inequality in China to climate and environmental calamity and pandemics. Second, it is problematic that a tightly centralized political system will have the flexibility to sustain economic growth and technological development at a level to keep its bargain with the Chinese population. Finally, there is the pushback from Western liberal states and the compelling message at the foundation of these regimes that all humans are created free and equal and have a right to determine what regime should rule them. No one can predict whether the CCP can surmount these challenges and a host of others. These are amply developed in Xu Zhiyong's lengthy critique of the CCP and, specifically, of President Xi Jinping's policy failures.[36]

Defining Legitimacy and Citizenship in India

The challenges confronting the Indian people and their leaders at independence in 1947 were vastly more formidable than China's at the time of the CCP's takeover of the Chinese mainland in 1949. How could a unified nation and state be fashioned out of a multicolored quilt comprising multiple religious, cultural, and linguistic social identities, further differentiated by regions, caste, class, and gender? How could a united nation and state be fashioned out of these disparate but intertwined parts?

The problem of defining legitimacy and citizenship resolved itself into two opposed solutions. At issue, as Scott Hibbard defined the dilemma, "is whether that national community ought to be defined inclusively—with membership extended to all members of the population—or whether full membership should be reserved for those of the dominant community. In other words, should the nation be defined along religious or secular lines."[37] In the three-quarters of a century since independence, the Indian people have oscillated between these two end points in defining legitimate rule and Indian citizenship.[38]

The BJP's actions after its 2019 electoral victory incorporated the lessons of India's first prime minister, Jawaharlal Nehru, on the use of political power to advance its party's objectives; the BJP's actions moved India in the direction of a Hindu state. Conversely, Mahatma Gandhi provided the spiritual inspiration for Nehru's cosmopolitan move to stamp India as a secular state. Gandhi's religious and intellectual journey to advocate a secular solution for India's government was embedded, paradoxically, in his profound understanding of the Hindu religion's long, historical tradition of tolerance for diversity.[39]

For purposes of this discussion, the trajectory of Indian history since independence can be viewed, telescopically, as an unrelenting struggle, still very much ongoing, heated and deadly, between two clashing visions of India, of the legitimacy of India's government and the identity of Indian citizens. The first, a secular India, is necessarily diverse and pluralist, a mirror of the social complexity of its peoples. A secular India is founded on the equality of each citizen without reference to the social identities of each individual. Democratic government, universal suffrage, the protection of civil liberties and human rights, and equality before the law are fundamental principles of secular legitimate rule.

In contrast to the United States, which places a wall between the state and religion in the First Amendment of the Constitution, the secular

Indian state, in accordance with the Indian Constitution whose preamble declares India as a secular state,[40] fuses religion and public space. The state is obliged not only to protect and defend religious practices but also to remain neutral in its relations with all religions.[41] Indian secularism is designed to strengthen religious freedom and the equality of citizenship. As Rajeev Bhargava, a professor at Jawaharlal Nehru University (JNU), observed, the state must ensure "that the relation between religious and political institutions be guided by nonsectarian principles that remain consistent with a set of values constitutive of a life of equal dignity for all."[42]

The Hindu national vision seeks a Hindu state and the promotion of Hindu culture as its idea of India. Since just over 80 percent of India's 1.4 billion people are Hindus, the Hindu nationalist would essentially invest all Indian citizens with *Hindutva* or "Hinduness" in a metaphorical sense. A secular state is rejected because it is viewed as denigrating and diminishing the overwhelming weight and importance of India's dominant community. The realization of India's authentic communal identity and the identity of each citizen lies in India as a Hindu state.

The extreme version of this vision casts nearly 200 million Muslims, who comprise 14 percent of India's population, as foreigners and as a threat to India as a Hindu state.[43] Hindu nationalist conformity to its conception of *Hindutva* extends beyond religion to those who speak a language other than Hindi. The Indian Constitution identifies twenty-two "scheduled" languages, including Hindi. While India has no official national language, the Constituent Assembly in 1949 designated Hindi, which is spoken by approximately 40 percent of the population, as the Union's official language. In a speech in September 2019, Home Minister Amit Shah complained that the Constitution's protection of India's language diversity is an impediment to the communal integration of all persons in a common language and culture: "It is very important to have a language of the whole country which should become the identity of India in the world."[44] Diversity and pluralism were given short shrift.

Actions taken by the BJP since its reelection in May 2019 further threatened India as a secular democratic state and undermined the prescriptions of legitimate rule and citizen identity embedded in the Indian Constitution. Three moves are especially important in tilting India toward the BJP vision: the annulment of the statehood of Jammu and Kashmir; the passage of the Citizenship Amendment Act (CAA); and the renewed and energetic application of the National Register of Citizens (NRC) to Assam as a prelude to its national extension.[45]

For years the BJP had proclaimed its intention to end the special status of Jammu and Kashmir, the only Indian state comprising a Muslim majority.[46] On August 5, 2019, the BJP government annulled Articles 370 and 35A of the Constitution. These articles created a "special" status for Jammu and Kashmir, conferring authority on the state to make its own laws and preventing outsiders from purchasing land in the state, as an economic protection for all its citizens. Henceforward two Union Territories, directly ruled and administered by New Delhi, would be formed, Jammu and Kashmir being one and Ladakh the other.

There was no advanced notice of this move and only a rushed two-day debate in Parliament, where the legislation passed with a vote of 351–72 in the Lower House (Lok Sabha) and 125–61 in the Upper House (Rajya Sabha). Nor was there any consultation with the Legislative Assembly of Jammu and Kashmir, as required by Article 370. To prevent a backlash, a lockdown was imposed on the Kashmir Valley, enforced by hundreds of thousands of security forces, most of whom were already stationed in the region; phone and internet communications were temporarily cut off; and political leaders were held in detention for several months.

While the abrupt end to the constitutional "special" status of Kashmir prompted opposition, it was muted in light of the decades of violence, which had put the region into permanent upheaval. Since 1990 there have been more than 40,000 fatalities in the region—about half this number were militants, one-sixth security forces, and about one-third civilians who were killed either by militants or in cross fire or clashes with security forces.

The passage of the Citizenship Amendment Act (CAA) in December 2019 did not meet with the same reluctant acceptance. The CAA bill passed by a vote of 311-80 in the Lok Sabha and 125-105 in the Rajya Sabha. The bill provides immigrants of six religions from three countries with legal status, if they lack it, and a path to citizenship. The deliberate exclusion of Muslims marked the first time in independent India's history that a religious test was added to the nation's naturalization process. It directly contradicts Articles 14 and 15 of the Constitution, which guarantee every citizen equality before the law (Article 14) and prohibit the state from discriminating "against any citizen on grounds only of religion, race, caste, sex, place of birth" (Article 15).[47]

The Modi government argues that the CAA promotes the free expression of religion since it targets immigrants, not Indian citizens, who experienced persecution in three predominantly Muslim countries, that is, Afghanistan,

Bangladesh, and Pakistan. Yet immigrants from other religiously based states—Buddhist Sri Lanka and Burma—which discriminate against Muslims are excluded. Similarly, Muslim minority communities, like Pakistan's Ahmadis and Shias, enjoy no protection under the CAA. President Donald Trump's Orwellian-speak validation of the Modi government as a champion of religious liberty, during his visit to India in February 2020,[48] reflected the president's support for illiberal democratic regimes.

The third attack on secular rule concerns the government's accelerated implementation of the National Register of Citizens (NRC). First applied to Assam's 33 million residents, the NRC required them to prove that they or their ancestors were Indian citizens before March 25, 1971 (when the Pakistan Army began a crackdown, prompting large numbers of Bengalis in East Pakistan to cross into India, culminating in Bangladesh's independence from Pakistan). The final citizenship list published in August 2019 omitted 1.9 million residents. More than half are ethnic Bengalis and more than one-third are Muslims. Those without valid citizenship documentation are rendered stateless. Those who are unable to convince tribunals established to review petitions of citizenship are relegated to newly built detention camps.[49] The Modi government included funds in its annual budget to scale the Assam experience to a national level.

What is particularly disquieting about these assaults on Muslims' rights and on human rights, more generally, is the violence associated with these actions. The lockdown and heavy security force presence quelled resistance to the abrogation of Jammu and Kashmir statehood. The same heavy hand characterized the government's reaction to widespread national opposition to the CAA. The government called out security forces, imposed curfews, and stood aside as police beat protestors.[50] When riots again broke out between Hindus and Muslims in February 2020, the government failed to intervene to prevent police brutality and mob violence linked to over twenty-five deaths.[51] In March–April 2020, at the outset of the coronavirus in India, anti-Muslim sentiment was on display when a Muslim organization and its conference, which was attended by hundreds of overseas participants, were blamed as the source of the COVID-19 pandemic.[52]

It should be recalled that Hindu nationalists, supported by BJP leaders, were deeply involved in riots related to Ayodhya in 1992 and Gujarat in 2002.[53] Ayodhya concerned the destruction of the Babri Masjid (mosque), built on the site Hindu nationalists claimed was the birthplace of the Hindu god Rama. In that episode, thousands died in riots in several cities. The issue, which was raised early on in the Nehru government, was not resolved legally until November 2019, when the Indian Supreme Court granted the right to build a Hindu temple on the Babri Masjid site, while assigning several acres elsewhere for a mosque. A decade later the Gujarat riots targeted at Muslims resulted in about one thousand deaths. The state government, then under the direction of BJP chief minister Narendra Modi, made no effort to curb the violence.

These incidents highlight the most dramatic episodes of sectarian violence promoted by Hindu nationalists. They do not convey the continuing threats posed to religious minorities, journalists, and intellectuals who have exposed governmental failures to protect religious liberties not only by ignoring vigilante attacks on non-Hindu communities but also by actively employing the state to intimidate critics and activists opposed to state violation of civil liberties and human rights.[54]

Transforming India into a Hindu state has potentially adverse implications for managing the ongoing Pakistani-Indian conflict. Formerly, that conflict was rooted in rival claims of religious and secular legitimacy. The BJP reframed that conflict as a religious struggle between a Muslim and a Hindu state. There is typically space, within an open democratic secular state and between that state and religiously constituted communities, for discussion, negotiation, and compromise. Fervent religious loyalties and unassailable religious doctrines are less disposed to compromise. There is the danger that, in any future clash between Pakistan and India, the regimes of two religiously grounded states would find it difficult to manage the rift short of a military confrontation.

How Can the Trend toward Chinese Authoritarian Rule and Indian Illiberal Democracy Be Arrested?

No quick solution can be offered in the brief space of this evaluation of China and India to arrest antidemocratic trends in these two states. The Chinese Communist Party solved the problem of legitimate rule to its satisfaction simply by acquiring a monopoly of power to rule the Chinese people. Citizens are consigned to unquestioned loyalty to the CCP and to obedience to its unconditional rule.

The CCP rules by law, which it alone determines, not by the rule of law to which it would also be subject and accountable. The Tiananmen Square massacre testifies to the CCP's resolve to survive even at the expense of its own citizens. The coercive tools available to the CCP to remain in power make any outside efforts to reform what is now progressively totalitarian rule all but impossible: the scope and depth of the CCP's surveillance of the Chinese population; the impressive police and military resources at its disposal; its control of communications, media, and the internet to ensure only its narrative reaches the Chinese public; its willingness to quash even the smallest instances of criticism with imprisonment and death; and the ease with which it is ready to violate treaty obligations in rejecting the policy of "One China and Two Systems" by crushing dissent in Hong Kong.

There is more hope in checking the trend toward illiberal majoritarian rule in India, where there are several sources of pushback.[55] Most of the work will depend on the Indian people. First, India's civil society remains vigorous and its communities are jealous of their freedoms and independence.[56] As per 2018 data, there were over 17,000 newspapers and about one million magazines registered in the Office of the Registrar of Newspapers in India and 178 TV stations, as well as countless websites in dozens of languages. The government can of course suppress or harass some of these outlets. It can also bribe media outlets with attractive state contracts or the blandishment of access to influence and power in return for favorable media coverage of its policies. Any Indian government will still be hard-pressed to match the CCP's control of Chinese civil society. There are also countless numbers of nongovernmental organizations (NGOs), which can be expected to resist subordination to a Hindu state.

Second, Indian governments, both Hindu nationalist and secular-oriented, depend for their survival on favorable economic growth and the increasing distribution of welfare to the Indian population. An economic downturn could diminish the electoral prospects of the Hindu nationalists and their supporters in the BJP. The May 2021 election victories of BJP opponents in three states, notably in West Bengal (India's fourth most populous state), suggest that many who may be sympathetic to *Hindutva* also want an effective government besides the bolstering of their Hindu identity. Newspaper reports suggest that the BJP's inability to prevail in Bengal was in part the result of the Modi government's mismanagement of the coronavirus pandemic.[57] Fostering the cause of Hindu identity may have strengthened the BJP's hold on India, but it must also produce effective government to retain its grip on India's identity.

Third, and closely associated with the previous constraint, is the BJP's tenuous hold on lower-caste support. Despite its Hindu nationalist message and a politics of religious division, it has limited support from this group.

Fourth, the social complexity of Indian society, described earlier, is among the most formidable obstacles to the permanent implantation of a

Hindu majoritarian state on the Indian population. India's federalist system can also check movement toward an illiberal democracy. Nine states, for example, declared that they would not implement either the CAA or the NRC.[58] The BJP and Hindu nationalists also encounter formidable pushback from those opposed to relinquishing their native tongues and the imposition of Hindi.

Fifth, foreign pressures should not be discounted as potentially significant in the struggle to maintain India as a secular society. This includes sustained criticism of violations of human rights from international NGOs, and from the United Nations, which are important. They put pressure on Indian governments to observe human rights, and they provide support and encouragement for domestic groups opposed to a Hindu nationalist state and for strengthening secularism at state and societal levels.

There are also the criticisms and condemnations from the liberal democracies. Both the CCP and Hindu nationalist-oriented regimes in India are keen to be recognized as legitimate. In no case should liberal democracies extend legitimacy to these regimes. During his visit to India, President Trump uncritically embraced the Modi government as a champion of religious liberties; such actions obviously run counter to what is needed to weaken the trend toward a discriminating Hindu-majoritarian state. It was also not helpful that the U.S. president provided his imprimatur for President Xi Jinping's construction of concentration camps to hold more than a million Uighur Muslims in western China.[59]

If criticism will not move Hindu nationalists and the CCP, the liberal democracies have the resources to put pressures on their leaders, including sanctions on their financial holdings, much like those imposed on Russian oligarchs. Western corporations can be induced to decrease investment in India's economic development, a move that would weaken a Hindu nationalist government's ability to maintain economic growth and its electoral majority.

It is also odd that the Muslim states have not been fully engaged in objecting to the discrimination toward Muslims both in China and India. One would have thought that they would actively support a movement of "Muslim Lives Matter." The liberal democracies might well shame the Muslim states to join the international chorus of protest. If words will not move either China or India to respect human rights, the oil-rich Muslim states might consider embargoing oil shipments to these energy-poor states.

This brings the discussion to the question posed at the start. Which path will the peoples of the global society choose—or be forced to choose:

the freedom and equality offered by the liberal democracies or the road either to the authoritarian rule of the CCP or to illiberal majoritarianism, represented by partisans of a Hindu nationalist state? Preserving and extending open, tolerant societies around the world will be difficult. Whether that enterprise will succeed will depend on whether countless citizens are willing to make the sacrifices necessary to ensure that government of, by, and for the people will not perish from the earth.

NOTES

1. For connectedness, see Parag Khanna, *Connectography: Mapping the Future Global Civilization* (New York: Random House, 2016); for interdependence, see Jared Diamond, *The Third Chimpanzee: The Evolution and Future of the Human Animal* (New York: Harper Perennial, 1992), and Jared Diamond, *Guns, Germs, and Steel: The Fates of Human Societies* (New York: W. W. Norton, 1997). Consult Edward A. Kolodziej, *Global Governance: Challenges for Democracy and Global Society* (New York: Rowman and Littlefield, 2016), pp. 11–68 for characteristics of the global society.

2. Bret Stephens, "China and the Rhineland Moment," *New York Times*, May 29, 2020, www.nytimes.com/2020/05/29/opinion/china-hong-kong.html.

3. Alexander Hamilton, James Madison, and John Jay, *The Federalist Papers* (Mineola, NY: Dover Publications, 2014), pp. 41–47.

4. Peter Fritzsche, *Hitler's First Hundred Days: When Germans Embraced the Third Reich* (New York: Basic Books, 2020).

5. Federico Finchelstein, *From Fascism to Populism in History* (University of California Press, 2019); and Jan-Werner Müller, *What Is Populism?* (University of Pennsylvania Press, 2016).

6. Freedom House scores for these regimes on a 100-point scale, from low to high levels of political freedom, are as follows: China (10), Russia (20), Egypt (21), Venezuela (21), Turkey (32), Belarus (38), the Philippines (59), Hungary (70), and Poland (84). These scores vary across years. In 2018 India was scored at 76; in 2019 its score was 71. See https://freedomhouse.org/countries/freedom-world/scores.

7. It is useful to review the principles of liberal democratic rule to gain perspective about the threat that authoritarian and illiberal democratic regimes pose for free government. Among the most systematic, penetrating, and comprehensive efforts to present the democratic case is Robert A. Dahl, *Democracy and Its Critics* (Yale University Press, 1989).

8. As per data for 2019, China had approximately 18.3 percent of the world's population (1.43 billion), India 17.6 percent (1.37 billion).

9. See Mao Zedong, *Problems of War and Strategy,* Speech delivered at the Sixth Plenary Session of the Sixth Central Committee of the Party, November 6, 1938, www.marxists.org/reference/archive/mao/selected-works/volume-2/mswv2_12.htm.

10. Mao Tse-Tung, *Selected Readings from the Works of Mao Tse-Tung* (Peking: Foreign Languages Press, 1967), p. 126.

11. William H. Overholt, "China and the Evolution of the World Economy," *China Economic Review* 40 (September 2016), pp. 267–71.

12. Ibid.

13. William H. Overholt, *China's Crisis of Success* (Cambridge University Press, 2018).

14. "Charter 08," *Foreign Policy*, October 8, 2010, https://foreignpolicy.com/2010/10/08/charter-08/.

15. Quoted in the Chinese state newspaper, Huang Youyi, "Context, Not History, Matters for Deng's Famous Phrase," *Global Times*, June 15, 2011, www.globaltimes.cn/content/661734.shtml.

16. Elizabeth C. Economy, *The Third Revolution: Xi Jinping and the New Chinese State* (Oxford University Press, 2018).

17. For more on Xi's agenda, see www.abc.net.au/news/2018-10-06/china-plans.

18. See Defense Intelligence Agency, *China Military Power: Modernizing A Force to Fight and Win* (Washington, DC: Defense Intelligence Agency, 2019).

19. Sarwar A. Kashmeri, *China's Grand Strategy: Weaving a New Silk Road to Global Primacy* (Santa Barbara, CA: Praeger, 2019).

20. Bill Hayton, *The South China Sea: The Struggle for Power in Asia* (Yale University Press, 2014); and Klaus Heinrich Raditio, *Understanding China's Behaviour in the South China Sea: A Defensive Realist Perspective* (Singapore: Palgrave MacMillan, 2019).

21. Elizabeth Economy, "Yes, Virginia, China Is Exporting Its Model," *Asia Unbound* (blog), Council on Foreign Relations, December 11, 2019, www.cfr.org/blog/yes-virginia-china-exporting-its-model.

22. Frank Dikotter, *The Cultural Revolution: A People's History, 1962–1976* (New York: Bloomsbury Publishing, 2016), pp. 12–13 lists these posts.

23. Bruce J. Dickson, *The Dictator's Dilemma* (Oxford University Press, 2016), p. 43.

24. Yuen Yuen Ang, *China's Golden Age: The Paradox of Economic Boom and Vast Corruption* (Cambridge University Press, 2020); Minxin Pei, *China's Crony Capitalism* (Harvard University Press, 2016); and Andrew Wedeman, *Double Paradox: Rapid Growth and Rising Corruption in China* (Cornell University Press, 2012).

25. Javier C. Hernandez, "At 'Sacred' Lake, Chinese Declare Love for Xi and Communist Party," *New York Times*, January 8, 2020. Nanhu Lake in eastern China is the cradle of the CCP and the shrine the faithful are encouraged to visit to pledge their loyalty to the party.

26. Susan L. Shirk, "China in Xi's 'New Era': The Return to Personalistic Rule," *Journal of Democracy* 29, no. 2 (April 2018), pp. 21–33.

27. On Mao's 1957 campaign to let a hundred flowers bloom, see www.phrases.org.uk/meanings/226950.html.

28. The "Three Represents" refers to the program of former party president Jiang Zemin to recruit entrepreneurs and other socioeconomic actors to become members of the CCP.

29. President Xi Jinping's address to the Nineteenth National Congress of the CCP, November 3, 2017, www.xinhuanet.com/english/special/2017-11/03/c_136725942.htm, p. 15.

30. Shirk, "China in Xi's 'New Era,'" p. 26. In his speech commemorating the seventieth anniversary of the CCP's victory in 1949, Xi repeated his gratitude for the thought of his predecessors and implied that his new thinking, as an addition to this pantheon, squares with theirs as the "core" of the CCP's leadership of the Chinese people (www.fmprc.gov.cn/mfa_eng/topics_665678/).

31. Hannah Arendt, *The Origins of Totalitarianism* (New York: Harcourt, Brace and Company, 1951).

32. Edward Wong, "Xi Jinping's News Alert: Chinese Media Must Serve the Party," *New York Times,* February 22, 2016.

33. For an account of Ren's incarceration, see Li Yuan, "A Loyal Chinese Critic Vanishes, in a Blow to the Nation's Future," *New York Times*, March 31, 2020. For Professor Xu's profound critique of the CCP's rule and his call for reform, see his "Viral Alarm: When Fury Overcomes Fear," translated by Geremie R. Barmé, February 10, 2020, www.chinafile.com/reporting-opinion/viewpoint/viral-alarm-when-fury-overcomes-fear.

34. Anthony Kuhn, "A Chilling Effect As Hong Kong's Missing Bookseller Cases Go Unresolved," NPR, February 23, 2016, www.npr.org/sections/parallels/2016/02/23/467787873/a-chilling-effect-as-hong-kongs-missing-bookseller-cases-go-unresolved.

35. See Kashmeri, *China's Grand Strategy*.

36. See Shirk, "China in Xi's 'New Era."

37. Scott Hibbard, *Religious Politics and Secular States* (Columbia University Press, 2010), p. 116.

38. Ibid., pp. 115–76. Hibbard provides a brief and trenchant history of this struggle between the years after independence and the first decade of the twenty-first century.

39. Ibid., pp. 121–22.

40. Ainslie T. Embree, "Religion in Public Space: Two Centuries of a Problem in Governance in Modern India," *India Review* 1, no. 1 (January 2002), p. 52.

41. Gurpreet Mahajan, "Secularism as Religious Non-Discrimination: The Universal and the Particular in the Indian Context," *India Review* 1, no. 1 (January 2002), pp. 33–51. I have relied on Mahajan's in-depth presentation of the relations between the state and religion. Also helpful is Rajeev Bhargava, "What Is Indian Secularism and What Is It For?" *India Review* 1, no. 1 (January 2002), pp. 1–32, as well as Embree, "Religion in Public Space," pp. 52–76.

42. Bhargava, "What Is Indian Secularism," p. 26.

43. Karan Deep Singh and Suhasini Raj, "'Muslims Are Foreigners': Inside India's Campaign to Decide Who Is a Citizen," *New York Times*, April 4, 2020;

"They Are Manufacturing Foreigners," *New York Times*, September 15, 2021.

44. Quoted in Šumit Ganguly, "An Illiberal India?" *Journal of Democracy* 31, no. 1 (January 2020), p. 196.

45. For clarification, some political parties that do not subscribe to the BJP's vision voted for legislation on these issues. The BJP and most of its coalition partners voted for, the Congress Party and its coalition partners voted against, and other political parties were split in their votes on the relevant bills.

46. Ganguly, "An Illiberal India?", pp. 197–98.

47. Congressional Research Service, "In Focus: Changes to India's Citizenship Laws," December 18, 2019. The six religions are Hindus, Sikhs, Buddhists, Jains, Parsees, and Christians.

48. Peter Baker, Michael Crowley, and Jeffrey Gettleman, "Trump Sees Commitment to Religious Freedom in India as Riots Break Out," *New York Times*, February 27, 2020.

49. The *New York Times* reports on these camps in its August 17, 2019 issue.

50. Jeffrey Gettleman and Maria Abi-Habib, "As Protests Rage on Citizenship Bill, Is India Becoming a Hindu Nation?" *New York Times*, December 16, 2019.

51. Jeffrey Gettleman and Suhasini Raj, "As New Delhi Counts the Dead, Questions Swirl about Police Response," *New York Times*, February 27, 2020.

52. See Jeffrey Gettleman, Kai Schultz, and Suhasini Raj, "In India, Coronavirus Fans Religious Hatred," *New York Times*, April 12, 2020; and Siddharth Varadarajan, "In India a Pandemic of Prejudice and Repression," *New York Times*, April 21, 2020.

53. Hibbard, *Religious Politics and Secular States*, pp. 164–73 covers both riots. Hibbard's tracing of the rise and fall of secularism in India, pp. 115–76, implicates the Congress Party in this process. The temptation to seek votes among Hindu nationalists by successive Congress Party leaders was too strong to resist, implicitly lending legitimacy to the BJP quest for a Hindu state.

54. See Ganguly, "An Illiberal India?" pp. 192–202, and Šumit Ganguly, "India under Modi: Threats to Pluralism," *Journal of Democracy* 30, no. 1 (January, 2019), pp. 83–90.

55. I draw the first four of these from Ganguly, "An Illiberal India?" pp. 200–201.

56. The Office of the Registrar of Newspapers in India and Press in India provides extensive data about media outlets in India (rni.nic.in/all_page/press_india.aspx).

57. Jeffrey Gettleman and Hari Kumar, "With India Drowning in Crisis, Modi's Party Loses Big in a Key Election," *New York Times*, May 2, 2021.

58. "Nine states that have refused to implement NRC and CAA," CNBC TV18, December 25, 2019.

59. David Choi and Sonam Sheth, "Trump Told China's President That Building Concentration Camps for Millions of Uighur Muslims Was 'Exactly the Right Thing to Do,' Former Adviser Says," *Business Insider*, June 17, 2020.

FIVE

Cooperation and Defection Cycles in India-Pakistan Relations

KANTI BAJPAI

Why do India and Pakistan go through alternations of cooperation and defection? This chapter attempts to provide an explanation not of discord, which is well documented, nor of outright collaboration, which is receiving increasing attention. It focuses instead on cycles of cooperation and defection in the period 1996–2016, after which cooperative efforts largely stopped. Beyond normal diplomatic intercourse, India and Pakistan cooperate in a range of ways including "talks about talks," confidence-building and other stabilizing measures, high-level summits, military restraint in the face of provocations, signaling accommodation on "core issues," and actual dispute settlement. Their defections from cooperation include canceling meetings, reneging on commitments and agreements, reverting to well-worn hard-line positions on core issues, public threats and accusations, and military actions all the way to war. The chapter suggests that a set of systemic and domestic incentives consistently pushed the two countries toward cooperation while other domestic factors produced defection. At base, the key internal challenge was: Could Pakistan truly end terrorism if a Kashmir settlement were reached, and could India truly shift toward a Kashmir settlement if the threat of terrorism were removed?

The chapter begins by examining key recent writings on India-Pakistan relations for answers. It then proceeds to present three chronologies of cooperation-defection and asks what drove the two governments to cooperate and defect. In conclusion, it offers some thoughts on the commitment problems that dogged negotiations and, briefly, on the United States' role in helping sustain cooperation.

Explaining the Cooperation-Defection Cycle

Most of the academic literature on India-Pakistan relations focuses on explaining conflict, including war. It can be divided into two streams: the monadic, which sees the Pakistani state as the root cause; and the dyadic, which posits the nature of bilateral interactions as causative.[1] Monadic explanations include Pakistan as a revisionist "greedy state," as susceptible to "false optimism," as prone to managing the power asymmetry in a provocative way (cultivating alliances, supporting terrorism and insurgency behind the shield of nuclear deterrence), and as psychologically obsessed with India.[2] Dyadic explanations ascribe conflict to the structural features of the relationship: power asymmetry, religious animosities, and differences in political values and identity. In his last major book, Stephen Cohen synthesized these explanations in his formulation of a "paired minority conflict," where each side regards itself as "the threatened, weaker party, under attack from the other."[3] The cooperation literature is smaller, but explanations here invoke international and dyadic factors: the influence of "international society" practices; the imperatives of dialogue arising from the sundering of territory, identity, and citizenship after 1947; dedicated negotiating after a conflict becomes "ripe" for negotiation; and the need for military stability under the shadow of nuclear weapons.[4]

While insightful, neither the conflict nor the cooperation literature on India-Pakistan relations offers an integrated explanation of the cyclical nature of India-Pakistan relations. Cooperation-defection cyclicality has received little attention, especially in scholarly writings on South Asia. Practitioners, though, have been more acute. For example, former Indian foreign secretary Shyam Saran describes India-Pakistan relations in terms of "dialogue-disruption-dialogue," which "repeat[s] itself in endless cycles."[5] Among academics, Ashley Tellis notes "the cycle of interrupted diplomatic engagement and the exchange of military threats."[6] Pallavi Raghavan argues that while India and Pakistan have had wars, skirmishes, and diplomatic spats and allocate considerable sums to defense, "[t]he dialogue process moves along in fits and starts."[7]

What accounts for the cyclicality? The conventional explanation is intermittent terrorist attacks on India.[8] T. C. A. Raghavan, however, traces it to "doves" and "hawks," who by turns "fade in importance."[9] Pallavi Raghavan argues that, from 1947 to 1952, India and Pakistan had to negotiate on administrative and legal matters arising from partition. Negotiation produced conflict but was also "the best instrument for defining the extent of the sovereignty and jurisdiction of both states."[10] Rajesh Basrur attributes cooperation and conflict to systemic and domestic factors. Systemically, nuclear weaponization plus economic globalization encourage cooperation. Domestically, political debates and processes can lead to defection. India's inclusive, secular, and decentralized democracy and Pakistan's majoritarian, religious, and hybrid democracy make cooperation difficult. Internal political maneuvering and outbidding complicate bilateral negotiations further.[11]

These writings suggest that the causes of the cooperation-defection cycle are to be found in systemic and domestic factors. First, systemic factors including nuclear weaponization, economic globalization, and great power diplomacy could encourage cooperation. As the United States and Soviet Union discovered, managing nuclear deterrence and stability requires cooperation. India and Pakistan must likewise manage the risk of nuclear war despite their quarrels. Economic opportunities arising out of globalization could encourage cooperation too. Integrating into global value chains and attracting investors is helped by peace and stability, not war and confrontation. Cooperation may also result from great power interventions: external powers for various reasons may want peace and stability in regions. Other systemic factors may encourage conflict. For instance, nuclear weaponization has also created the conditions for subconventional violence. Cross-border terrorism against India has occurred because Pakistan's nuclear weapons have made Indian military retaliation infeasible for fear of escalation. In addition, both militaries hold that limited war may be plausible thanks to nuclear weapons. The Pakistani ingress into Kargil in 1999 and India's threat of a "Cold Start" retaliation is indicative of this calculation.[12]

Second, domestic politics matter. Internal differences over political identity and values as well as the cut and thrust of everyday politics could lead to domestic "outbidding" and hypernationalist opposition to cooperation. When hawks are in the ascendant in the strategic community, with a mindset that values strategic "greediness," false optimism, asymmetric warfare, and revanchism, cooperative efforts may be painted as appeasement. However, internal economic or political conditions could also cause leaders to seek cooperation—to allow them the time and resources to deal with domestic stresses and strains. If doves are in the ascendant in the strategic community and can portray negotiations as rational problem-solving, cooperation may advance. Terrorism could push India and Pakistan apart, but it could push them closer too. Cross-border terrorism puts Indian leaders under pressure to retaliate against Pakistan, which in the shadow of nuclear weapons risks escalation. To reduce the domestic pressure to retaliate, dialogue with Pakistan might act as a buffer against precipitate action.[13] In Pakistan, terrorism has grown into a chronic internal challenge. Negotiating with India toward a settlement of key disputes might reduce the political support at home for terrorism.

The essay analyzes the cooperation-defection cycles in India-Pakistan relations against the background of systemic and domestic factors. Two points are in order. First, accounts of decisionmaking on both sides are still scarce. This analysis is therefore a "plausibility probe." Second, an alternative explanation of India-Pakistan dynamics is that cooperative acts are mere "performances" playing to international and domestic audiences and that defection is equally cynical and narrowly political. Playing to the international gallery was intermittently a factor in 1996–2016, and personal political motives can never be altogether discounted. However, the testimony of decisionmakers and insightful commentators suggest that the two governments genuinely sought cooperation and that defection was not "mere politics."

Vajpayee, Sharif, Musharraf: Lahore, Kargil, Agra

The first cycle of cooperation-defection began during the 1996 Pakistani election campaign in which prime ministerial candidate Nawaz Sharif stated that if reelected, he would open negotiations on Kashmir and improve relations with India. This led the two countries in 1997 to initiate the "six-plus-two" Composite Dialogue. After the nuclear tests of May 1998, Indian Prime Minister Atal Behari Vajpayee suggested that the two leaders meet at the United Nations General Assembly (UNGA) in September. At the meeting, they agreed to a summit in Pakistan, with Vajpayee to journey on the inaugural bus between Amritsar and Lahore.[14] The initiative soon ran into "complex inter-agency wrangling" and was watered down to have Vajpayee flag off the bus instead. Unhappy with that modification, Sharif telephoned Vajpayee to urge reverting to the original plan. To circumvent bureaucratic opposition, they agreed Sharif would give *Indian Express* editor Shekhar Gupta an interview in which he would invite Vajpayee. In the interview, Sharif kept his word. Vajpayee immediately accepted the invitation.[15]

At the summit on February 20–21, 1999, the two sides signed the Lahore Declaration. In the aftermath of the nuclear tests of May 1998, the declaration dealt largely with bilateral consultations on security concepts and nuclear doctrine; military stabilizing measures; and future bilateral consultations on security, disarmament, and nonproliferation.[16] More importantly, Vajpayee visited the Minar-e-Pakistan, where the Muslim League had called for the partition of the subcontinent. In the visitor's book he underlined India's support for the Pakistani state, writing, "A stable, secure and prosperous Pakistan is in India's interest. Let no one in Pakistan be in doubt. India sincerely wishes Pakistan well."[17] The two leaders also agreed, in confidence, to start back-channel talks on Kashmir.[18] The subsequent back-channel discussions may have included delineating an international border to replace the Line of Control (LOC) dividing the state.[19] A posting on the Indian Ministry of External Affairs website notes that a "broad understanding the two sides arrived at was to discard all proposals unacceptable to either side and take an intense look at potential solutions that might be acceptable to both."[20] Just weeks later, India discovered the infiltration of Pakistani troops into its side of the LOC in Kargil, leading to a fourth war between them. A promising if limited initiative for greater engagement and stability was ended by a chain of events it was intended to prevent.

What led Sharif and Vajpayee to cooperate? First, international pressures to stabilize relations after the nuclear tests was a systemic-level factor operating on both sides. Hours after Pakistan's matching nuclear tests, Islamabad had called in the high commissioner of India to warn against a putative Indian strike on Pakistani nuclear installations.[21] In this situation, Vajpayee calculated that high-level bilateral discussions would calm nerves and demonstrate that New Delhi and Islamabad could manage their post-nuclear relationship. India's high commissioner at the time explained Vajpayee's thinking: "We had to get rid of that international pressure. And what better way to tell the world . . . 'okay I am going to meet Nawaz.' . . . We don't need all the international mediation. We will manage our affairs with Pakistan."[22]

Sharif felt the international pressure too but had another motivation for cooperation. For some years, he had advocated more normal economic ties to loosen the grip of the Pakistani military in domestic affairs and give his party a stronger hold on political power. In his interview with Shekhar Gupta, he suggested that a Kashmir settlement, nuclear and conventional military stability, and, in particular, economic interactions were vital: "I'd like to say, Vajpayee Sahib, let's solve the Kashmir problem, let's solve the other problems, so that we can also move on like the rest of the world . . . there are such great prospects for our cooperation in business and investment. You are busy making weapons, and so are we, because we are competing against India. Some rivalry this is!"[23]

Given these systemic and domestic factors for cooperation, what swung the pendulum to war? The operation in Kargil was likely planned before the Lahore summit—perhaps as early as 1986—but was formally approved by General Pervez Musharraf sometime between January and March 1999.[24] Sharif was briefed but probably did not comprehend the extent and significance of the operation.[25] Musharraf appears to have had several motives. His account emphasizes a response to India's provocations in Siachen.[26] Most analysts refer to other objectives: to reclaim Siachen by cutting off supply lines to Indian troops at the glacier; to increase the military pressure on Indian forces in Kashmir; to revive the insurgency; to prevent Sharif from downplaying Kashmir in his peace efforts with India; to force Delhi to open negotiations on Kashmir; and to refocus waning international attention on the Kashmir dispute.[27] At any rate, Pakistan's internal political contradictions caused the Vajpayee-Sharif initiative to fail. The elected Pakistani prime minister was unable to control his military. A seemingly low-risk asymmetric challenge to India's control of Siachen turned into outright war.

After the war, India-Pakistan relations once again deteriorated. In October 1999, Musharraf overthrew the Sharif government. In December, the hijacking of an Indian passenger flight, first to Lahore and eventually to Kandahar, led to further worsening. Yet by 2000, the two governments had sought to resurrect cooperation. In July 2000, the Kashmiri militant group, Hizbul Mujahideen, from its base in Pakistan, offered Delhi a cease-fire. While this was withdrawn two weeks later, Vajpayee reciprocated with a six-month cease-fire from November 2000 to May 2001. In January 2001, Pakistan provided humanitarian supplies to India after the Bhuj earthquake there. And on May 24, 2001, Vajpayee invited Musharraf to Agra to disentangle the relationship. The summit, on July 14–16, failed to produce an agreement and was followed by crisis. After terrorists attacked the Kashmir Legislative Assembly in October and the Indian Parliament in December, Vajpayee ordered a military mobilization, which led to a seven-month confrontation. The confrontation ended after Musharraf's televised speech in January 2002, in which he condemned terrorism.

Why did India and Pakistan seek to cooperate just months after war? First, the broad systemic factor that impacted both countries—to demonstrate responsibility internationally—continued to operate, indeed it had been reinforced and magnified by Kargil: the world could well conclude that South Asians, and particularly Pakistan, could not be trusted with nuclear weapons. Minister of Home Affairs L. K. Advani, in nudging Vajpayee to hold the Agra summit, reasoned that Musharraf wanted a meeting to end Pakistan's "isolation" after the war, India needed to "test the mind" of the new leader, and, most important from the perspective of this chapter, India would gain internationally by reaching out to its adversary.[28] Musharraf, who had led Pakistan into war, was under even greater pressure to reassure the international community. As noted earlier, Pakistani actions in Kargil were widely criticized abroad, with even China failing to support Islamabad.[29] In addition, having overthrown Sharif, Musharraf was under scrutiny for his usurpation of power.

For India, beyond the systemic factor, terrorism in Kashmir played a part in the outreach to Pakistan. Defense Minister Jaswant Singh, who with Advani had instigated the Agra summit, recollects that the Kashmiri militants' response to the Vajpayee cease-fire had been "disappointing." If so, working with Pakistan to curb terrorism and perhaps strike a deal on Kashmir was the alternative.[30] Musharraf's motives, too, were domestic. After 9/11, Pakistan-based terrorism would become a factor in his desire for cooperation, but at this stage his concern was different, as he explains in his memoirs: "[M]y focus was mainly on internal consolidation and socioeconomic uplift [in Pakistan]."[31] In relation to India, he notes: "The Indo-Pakistan dispute is a hindrance to socioeconomic cooperation and development in south Asia. . . . There is no military solution to our [India and Pakistan's] problems. The way forward is through diplomacy. . . . As early as 2001, I believed the time had come to turn over a new leaf."[32] This translated into his offer of help in the Bhuj earthquake, in Gujarat State, in January 2001, which he claims "broke the ice and led to an invitation for me to visit India."[33]

Why then did Agra fail? Essentially, the two sides were unable to agree on the relative importance of Kashmir and terrorism. Advani objected to

Musharraf's strident insistence on the centrality of Kashmir, his discounting of cross-border terrorism, and his dismissiveness toward the Simla and Lahore accords—all of which the Pakistani president vented to the Indian media during the summit, to the anger of the Indian leadership. In the end, while Vajpayee and Jaswant Singh may have been willing to accept a statement that would have emphasized the Kashmir dispute, the mood turned against an accord. Musharraf claims that the final version of the draft statement had balanced Kashmir and terrorism. Since the document is not public it is hard to know, but the Indian decision to walk away was based not just on the language in the proposed statement; it increasingly drew on Musharraf's public statements, which were blunt about where Pakistan saw the balance between the two issues.[34] Clearly, both sides regarded Kashmir as integral to conceptions of nationhood. But while India came to accept that discussing Kashmir was acceptable up to a point, it would not concede that terrorism was legitimate in any way: if terrorism ended, a (limited) Kashmir settlement might be reached. For Pakistan, discussing Kashmir was not merely acceptable but rather was central, and terrorism as "freedom fighting" was legitimate up to a point: if Kashmir were settled, terrorism/freedom-fighting would no longer have a rationale.

Manmohan and Musharraf: Breakthrough and Opportunity Lost

The Lahore to Agra cycles of cooperation-defection were followed by the most ambitious effort at cooperation since the 1972 Simla Agreement, this time by Prime Minister Manmohan Singh and Musharraf, between 2004 and 2007. At the heart of the cooperative effort were public statements by the two leaders on the nature of a possible Kashmir agreement and a secret but steady back-channel negotiation encompassing two dozen meetings.[35]

In an interview days after coming to power in May 2004, Manmohan suggested that "soft borders" might be part of a Kashmir solution and that "Short of succession [secession], short of redrawing boundaries, the Indian establishment can live with anything."[36] He and Musharraf met in New York in September. Building on back-channel discussions, Musharraf in his UNGA speech omitted Pakistan's perennial mention of the Kashmir dispute. Manmohan in turn pledged to continue bilateral negotiations. The two leaders then met face-to-face, discussed confidence-building measures (CBMs), and addressed a joint press conference.

The following month, Musharraf suggested that a plebiscite was no longer the way forward in Kashmir. Instead, New Delhi and Islamabad should identify regions on either side of the LOC that could be demilitarized. These regions could be given independence, put under joint India-Pakistan control, or placed under the UN.[37] In response, in November 2004, Manmohan reduced troops in the state and offered to open talks with separatists. In February 2005, bus service between the two Kashmiri capitals began. In April, Musharraf attended an India-Pakistan cricket match in New Delhi. A third round of the Composite Dialogue was held in January 2006. India further reduced troops in Kashmir, and in March 2006 offered Pakistan a treaty of peace, security, and friendship. In response, Pakistan insisted that Kashmir was the central issue. Disagreement notwithstanding, they agreed to more nuclear CBMs and continued talks on resolving the Siachen and Sir Creek disputes.[38]

In September 2006, Manmohan and Musharraf met in Havana at the nonaligned summit, where they endorsed progress in Kashmir talks, proposed a joint mechanism on counterterrorism, and agreed to speed up resolution of Siachen and Sir Creek. Based on statements by Manmohan and back-channel discussions, in early December Musharraf outlined "four points" toward a Kashmir settlement: identify the contested parts of Kashmir; demilitarize those regions and curb the militancy there; bring self-governance or self-rule to those regions; and evolve a joint management mechanism that would monitor self-governance and residual common subjects.[39] In March 2007, the Composite Dialogue discussed the demilitarization of Kashmir, a Siachen deal, and the liberalization of visas. Most importantly, the two sides reputedly came close to a Kashmir settlement.[40] Since Manmohan had insisted that there was "no question of redrawing boundaries," India suggested instead that the LOC could be made irrelevant. Drawing on Musharraf's four points, it therefore proposed soft borders so that people could "move freely from one side to the other." In addition, the two sides of Kashmir would evolve parallel forms of local self-government and joint governance through a "cooperative, consultative mechanism" to deal with issues such as tourism, travel, religious pilgrimages, trade, health, education, and culture but with defense and foreign policy in Indian and Pakistani hands. Finally, if all the other elements were in place, there would be a phased withdrawal of troops.[41] Just weeks later, however, it was clear that the proposed summit in Pakistan to unveil at least the broad principles of the agreement had failed to materialize.[42] When Musharraf left office in August 2008, the possibility of a breakthrough receded further.

Why did the two sides move toward the most intense and ambitious process of cooperation, and why ultimately did they fail to produce a single major agreement? The evidence suggests that a combination of systemic and domestic factors pushed negotiations.

First, at the systemic level, both India and Pakistan recognized the limits of violence, particularly with nuclear weapons on both sides. This was not a lesson that was cast-iron or accepted uniformly across their strategic communities. Clearly, though, India's military mobilization in 2001–2002 had produced mixed results: some Pakistani concessions on terrorism (which soon petered out), but more importantly, loss of men and matériel without a shot being fired.[43] Underlining the limits of coercion, Satinder Lambah, the Indian back-channel envoy, noted in a speech in May 2014 that "the past six decades have clearly shown, the Kashmir issue cannot be settled by war, force or violence."[44] As for Pakistan's Kargil intrusion, it had ended with military withdrawal and international isolation.[45] Nor had terrorism loosened India's grip on Kashmir or affected its image in the international system—indeed, in the wake of the 9/11 attacks in the United States, New Delhi's complaints about Islamabad's role in terrorism had gained credibility. Both Kargil and the 2001–2002 confrontation had also carried a risk of escalation, including to the nuclear level. As Pakistani foreign minister Khurshid Kasuri concluded: "Pakistan had become a nuclear power. War was no longer an option for either side." As for Kashmir, he told Pakistani generals, "Put your hand here—on your heart—and tell me that Kashmir will gain freedom" without an understanding with India.[46]

A second systemic factor nudging the two sides toward cooperation was U.S. diplomatic cajoling. From the Kargil War onward, Washington had begun to play a greater role in South Asia. During Kargil, this was to prevent military escalation. After 9/11, it was to enlist Pakistan in the war on terror. During the 2001–2002 mobilization crisis, the United States sought once again to prevent escalation. It nudged both countries to resume bilateral negotiations, including over terrorism and Kashmir; conveyed information and assessments to both sides; and in Pakistan's case, exerted pressures to diminish confrontation with India. Beyond crisis prevention and management, Washington's influence with New Delhi may have come from negotiations over the "Next Steps in Strategic Partnership" accord (2004) and the U.S.-India Civil Nuclear Agreement (2005). In Islamabad's case, Washington was holding discussions on declaring Pakistan a "Major Non-NATO Ally" and resuming supplies of embargoed F-16 aircraft. Pakistani leaders also hoped that their country might qualify for a nuclear deal parallel to India's.[47] It could hardly be lost on New Delhi or Islamabad that it was important for the U.S. government to show that India and Pakistan were making efforts to promote regional stability. For the administration to sell the deals at home, it needed to reassure influential American legislators and commentators that the two powers were trying to mend fences.

Third, India and Pakistan sought cooperation in the service of an economic agenda with implications not just for social welfare but also for geopolitical advantage. India in particular, by the late 1990s, had enjoyed a decade of high economic growth. Indian leaders sensed that the country could at last establish itself as an influential geopolitical player. This required not just sustained economic growth but also a stable region: India could not play a larger role if it were locked into conflict with a lesser power. Explaining the rationale for the putative Kashmir agreement, back-channel envoy Lambah noted: "It [the agreement] could provide a boost to the Indian economy . . . open a market with one of the world's largest populations, restore our historical links to Central Asia and Eurasia and contribute to enhancing our energy security. . . . Above all, it will herald a new era of peace and prosperity for the entire region."[48] Peace and prosperity in the region would in turn "enable India to focus more on the rapidly emerging geopolitical challenges."[49] Recounting Manmohan Singh's thinking on relations with Pakistan and India's South Asian neighbors, Sanjaya Baru, the prime minister's media adviser, writes: "Dr. [Manmohan] Singh was convinced that destiny was on India's side and India's rise as the world's largest democracy and an economic power would only be slowed down by an unsettled neighbourhood."[50]

In Pakistan, too, there was new thinking on economic growth and the link to geopolitics. In his memoirs, Musharraf notes that when he assumed power, Pakistan "stood at the brink of being declared a failed state, a defaulted state, or even a terrorist state." Later, he concludes: "The twenty-first century will be driven by geoeconomics more than by geostrategy or geopolitics."[51] Journalist Steve Coll, in his account of the India-Pakistan back channel, reports that in addressing his senior generals "Musharraf talked about how a peace settlement might produce economic benefits that could strengthen Pakistan—and its military. The Army had a fifteen-year development plan; the generals knew that the plan would be difficult to pay for without rapid growth."[52] Khurshid Kasuri, Musharraf's foreign minister recalls: "I was very happy to see how much focus there was on the economy among the Army's officers." Mahmud Durrani, a retired general and Pakistan's ambassador in Washington at the time, describes the thinking of senior officers: "Can my economy support me? Can my foreign policy support me? What does the world think of us?" Kasuri's chief of staff attests to the changing attitude: "[T]he feeling that the world is changing and that we have to change."[53]

Fourth, the specter of chronic terrorism in India and Pakistan encouraged diplomatic engagement. In India, it became clear that violence and political instability in Kashmir could not be contained through counterterrorism operations and negotiations with separatist leaders. Involving Islamabad in discussions on Kashmir seemed sensible. After the 2001–2002 crisis, Pakistan's crackdown on extremist groups had helped create the right atmosphere.[54] Indian calculations now were that a Kashmir agreement with Islamabad would "hopefully strengthen its ability to turn the tide on terrorism and radical militancy."[55] In Pakistan, Musharraf was attacked twice in 2003 and narrowly escaped with his life: as former Pakistani ambassador to the United States Maleeha Lodhi notes, "This [the attacks] is what turns him decisively."[56] Religious radicalism, which fed off various causes including hatred of India and resentment over Kashmir, was therefore not just New Delhi's problem. To deal with it required Islamabad to reduce tensions with India so as to reduce support for extremism.

Why then did cooperation fail? Negotiations in 2004–2007 reflected an understanding that it was necessary to engage not just on confidence-building but also on core issues, Kashmir in particular. The conventional view is that the window of opportunity that opened with Vajpayee and Sharif closed after the November 26, 2008, terror attacks in Mumbai. In fact, though, it was domestic developments in both countries that led to failure well before the Mumbai attacks.

In India, Manmohan Singh dithered over the Kashmir agreement. His worries related to the opposition Bharatiya Janata Party (BJP), but more so his own Congress Party. Senior colleagues including Defense Minister A. K. Antony, External Affairs Minister Pranab Mukherjee, and Minister of Home Affairs Shivraj Patil balked at crucial moments. They were joined by Chief of Army J. J. Singh and National Security Adviser M. K. Narayanan. All four in varying degrees opposed the Siachen accord and in all likelihood were opposed to the larger Kashmir accord as well.[57] While there was support to "normalize relations with Pakistan," these senior figures probably found the Kashmir agreement unworkable. As Foreign Secretary Saran writes: "There was no doubt in my mind that any understanding on Kashmir had to be part and parcel of a larger peace process," that is, one that included control of terrorism.[58] Here again was the problem that unraveled Agra: the balance between discussions—and actions—on Kashmir and terrorism.

In Pakistan, too, Musharraf failed to commit to the emerging accords, as he dealt with a series of domestic challenges. His handling of these challenges compounded the mistakes he made with the military. Crucial was his failure to sufficiently consult his corps commanders on antimilitant operations in the Federally Administered Tribal Areas (FATA).[59] This proved decisive when internal problems escalated, primarily the Lal Masjid takeover by militants and the opposition of the Supreme Court and Pakistani lawyers to his moves against the judiciary. The police action against the *masjid* in March 2007 led to 100 deaths, and the tangle with the judiciary and lawyers raised serious questions about Musharraf's continuance in office.[60] The killing of the Baloch leader Nawab Bugti by the army and Benazir Bhutto's assassination further undermined the president's position. In August 2008, he finally resigned when the military failed to back him.

As a result of the hesitations on both sides on the Kashmir agreement, the momentum dissipated. Pakistani foreign minister Kasuri urged a postponement of the proposed 2007 summit with Manmohan. Pakistan, he reasoned, "should not waste" the draft agreement, given Musharraf's travails at home; it was better to wait for a more propitious time. Islamabad therefore asked Delhi to hold on the summit. India was in any case in the midst of state elections. Moreover, Manmohan and his team had developed doubts on Pakistan's commitment to the agreement once Musharraf departed the political stage. They also harbored a suspicion that the negotiations had been a "ploy to buy time and win favor in Washington while continuing to support the jihadis." Finally, New Delhi's decisionmakers wondered about their own ability to carry through against domestic opposition, even violence.[61]

Despite Musharraf's departure and the Mumbai terror attacks in November 2008, cooperation-defection continued. Manmohan Singh met Pakistani president Asif Ali Zardari at the Shanghai Cooperation Organization (SCO) in June 2009 and the Pakistani prime minister Yousaf Raza Gilani at the nonaligned summit in Sharm el-Sheikh, Egypt, in July 2009. Their shared concerns over terrorism and desire for economic payoffs from cooperation, so evident in the Manmohan-Musharraf negotiations, drove engagement. Yet, defection continued to undermine their cooperative efforts. For instance, the Pakistani prime minister criticized India for interfering in restive Baluchistan, undermining Manmohan and Zardari's dovish stance.⁶² Nevertheless, New Delhi and Islamabad persisted with economic cooperation. The two sides finally signed the Turkmenistan-Afghanistan-Pakistan-India (TAPI) energy pipeline agreement in December 2010. In April 2012, Islamabad announced it would give India Most Favored Nation (MFN) status, and India lifted restrictions on Pakistani foreign direct investment. In July, Pakistan urged that the two dust off agreements on Siachen and Sir Creek. This was followed by a meeting of the foreign ministers in September 2012. In November 2012, the chief ministers of the two Punjabs met to discuss economic, energy, and cultural links. However, by December, domestic politics had once again intervened. Under pressure from agriculture lobbies and right-wing extremists, Islamabad edged away from MFN. Increasing cease-fire violations in 2012 and 2013 caused further harm.⁶³ In sum, despite efforts at cooperation, Pakistan periodically defected, and instability along the border undermined the diplomatic environment.

Modi and Sharif: Comprehensive Dialogue and the Joint Investigation Team Fiasco

With Prime Minister Narendra Modi in power, India and Pakistan went through three rapid cooperation-defection cycles. After the Uri terrorist attack in September 2016 and India's "surgical strike" in response, the cycles ended. In fact cooperation had already petered out in March 2016 after the formation of the Joint Investigation Team (JIT), which India had convened as a response to the Pathankot terrorist attack in January 2016.

The first cooperation-defection cycle began with Modi inviting Nawaz Sharif to his inauguration. During the visit, India reminded Pakistan to act against terrorism. By contrast, Sharif chose not to mention Kashmir.⁶⁴ Weeks later, the two sides announced they would hold foreign secretary–level "talks about talks" in August. This positive start ended when the Pakistani high commissioner in New Delhi invited the Kashmiri separatist group, Hurriyat, to his country's Independence Day celebrations on August 14. Previous Indian governments had allowed the Hurriyat to attend the event. Modi's government responded to the invitation by canceling the impending talks.⁶⁵

A second cooperation-defection cycle began in March 2015, when the foreign secretaries met in Islamabad. This was followed by the Modi-Sharif talks at the Ufa (Russia) SCO Summit in early July, where they agreed they would "discuss all outstanding issues," the national security advisers (NSAs) would meet on terrorism, the Mumbai terrorist trials would be speeded up, and Modi would attend the South Asian Association for Regional Cooperation (SAARC) summit in Islamabad later in 2015.[66] Under fire at home for the omission of Kashmir from the joint statement, Sharif now insisted that Kashmir must be part of the discussions and that his NSA would meet the Hurriyat in New Delhi during the talks. India reacted by threatening to cancel the NSA talks, though finally it was Pakistan that canceled.[67] In the meantime, terrorists struck in Gurdaspur on July 27 and Udhampur on August 5.

The third cooperation-defection cycle began with the Modi-Sharif meeting at the Paris Climate Change Conference in November 2015, where they announced the resumption of dialogue. A week later, the two NSAs met in neutral Bangkok.[68] Two days after Bangkok, when Foreign Minister Sushma Swaraj attended the "Heart of Asia" conference in Islamabad, it was agreed that a Comprehensive Dialogue would replace the Composite Dialogue but with a near-identical remit—peace and security (read terrorism), Kashmir, and six other issue areas.[69] On Christmas Day, on his way back from Afghanistan, Modi suddenly dropped in to see Sharif in Lahore, during which the two agreed that the foreign secretaries would meet in January 2016.

Before the foreign secretaries could meet, terrorists attacked in Pathankot. Nonetheless, New Delhi exercised restraint, offering to organize a Joint Investigation Team with Pakistani officials. More cooperation followed. In early March 2016, Pakistan informed India of a possible terror attack in Gujarat during the Shivratri religious festival.[70] On March 23, New Delhi now permitted the separatist Hurriyat to attend Pakistan Day celebrations at the High Commission. The JIT visited Pathankot on March 27. However, almost immediately, Pakistan defected. Upon the return of its JIT members, Islamabad accused India of "stage managing" the Pathankot attack. It also called off the return visit of the Indian members of the JIT, and on April 7 it canceled the Comprehensive Dialogue.[71] The terrorist attack on Uri in September put an end to dialogue. In response to the attack, India threatened to revise the Indus Waters Treaty, canceled its participation in the SAARC summit in Islamabad, and on September 28, retaliated in a "surgical strike" across the LOC.

Why did Modi and Sharif repeatedly try to cooperate, at least until 2016? The need to avoid direct, large-scale conventional military conflict under the shadow of nuclear weapons was a systemic factor that neither side could ignore. Days after Foreign Minister Sushma Swaraj's return from the "Heart of Asia" conference in Islamabad, she insisted in parliament that "war is not an option" and that the two governments had "decided that through talks we will resolve the issue of terrorism."[72] U.S. nudges to both countries may have also contributed to cooperative engagement. On Modi's unexpected trip to Lahore, Reuters reported that the United States had urged both countries, and particularly Pakistan, to resume talks after the Gurdaspur terror attacks in July 2015. Washington's influence over Islamabad may have strengthened due to a putative nuclear deal with Pakistan. As a result, General Raheel Sharif, chief of army, apparently supported the outreach to India.[73]

Beyond this, Sharif's motives as in the past were likely economic and narrowly political. What about Modi? Prior to coming to power, he had often criticized the Congress government for appeasing Pakistan. Why then did he opt for cooperation? The answer, first of all, is that he was probably responding to a systemic factor, namely, a leader's need to obtain and maintain a degree of international legitimacy. After the 2002 Gujarat riots, Modi had become a diplomatic pariah in the United States and in other Western democracies. This shunning necessarily ended with his coming to power in 2014. Buoyed by a decisive electoral victory, he turned to winning hearts and minds abroad.[74]

Inviting his South Asian counterparts to his inauguration was one part of Modi's drive for external legitimation. The more important part was engaging a range of consequential and friendly powers. In his first eight months in office, Modi visited Australia, Bhutan, Brazil, Fiji, Japan, Myanmar, Nepal, and the United States. He also hosted Vladimir Putin of Russia, Tony Abbott of Australia, Nguyen Tan Dung of Vietnam, and Tony Tan of Singapore. From 2004 to 2013, Manmohan Singh had made sixty-seven visits abroad. In 2015, Modi made twenty-seven visits abroad, for a total of thirty-five foreign trips in his first *twenty months* in office—half the number of trips Manmohan had made over the course of *nine years*. Of the eighty foreign trips Modi made from May 2014 to April 2019, roughly 44 percent were in his initial months in office.[75]

Commentators have claimed this frenetic diplomacy was needed in order to refurbish India's image after Manmohan's supposedly lackluster tenure; but reaching out to Pakistan was probably also Modi's attempt to convey to the world that he was a responsible leader. Responding to criticism of his outreach to Islamabad, he suggested that after the Uri and Pathankot terror attacks, it became easier to persuade the world that the difficulties with Pakistan came from across the border: his meetings with

Sharif had shown that Indian actions were not the cause of South Asia's instabilities.[76] While his initiatives may have helped Indian diplomacy, Modi's engagement with Pakistan can also be regarded as a way of polishing his image and establishing his international bona fides.

What then led to the collapse of cooperation by 2016? Despite the systemic factors that encouraged engagement, India was unable to commit firmly to Kashmir discussions, and Pakistan equally was unwilling to commit to a dialogue on terrorism. New Delhi's insistence that it would only discuss terrorism and its reluctance to discuss Kashmir meant that in the first two cycles the Pakistani leadership found itself unable to cooperate: it simply could not sell the idea at home. It was only after India agreed that the new Comprehensive Dialogue would include Kashmir that Sharif was able to countenance serious engagement. However, immediately after announcing this concession, in her "war is not an option" statement in parliament, India's foreign minister Swaraj again focused exclusively on terrorism.[77] When New Delhi invited Pakistan to jointly investigate the Pathankot strike, this showed restraint. The gesture should have promoted engagement. Instead, Islamabad accused India of manipulating the JIT visit and putting Kashmir on the backburner. It then canceled the JIT and Comprehensive Dialogue.[78]

Conclusion

From 1996 to 2016, India-Pakistan relations went through three key cooperation-defection phases. Significant cooperation had not resumed at the time of writing this chapter in late 2020. A combination of systemic and domestic factors encouraged cooperation. The systemic factors pushing cooperation included the need for military stability in the shadow of nuclear weapons, demonstrating international responsibility in the aftermath of the nuclear tests, a desire for international legitimacy (especially for Musharraf and Modi), and U.S. cajoling. The domestic factors pushing cooperation included an economic growth agenda in both countries, but especially in Pakistan, and the specter of chronic terrorism. Specific terrorist incidents, so often blamed for the collapse of cooperative initiatives, were not usually the reason cooperation failed. While some domestic factors were positive for cooperation, others were negative. The Vajpayee-Sharif effort was undone by a faction of the Pakistan Army that was working against the initiatives of their own prime minister. The Manmohan-Musharraf negotiations foundered on high-level opposition in India in the ruling party and the spread of unrest in Pakistan (unrelated to the negotiations). Modi and Sharif's attempts at cooperation unraveled over India's unwillingness to seriously engage the Kashmir dispute and Pakistan's inability to soft-pedal Kashmir.

Ultimately, as analysts of India-Pakistan relations have noted, domestic debates over political identity/political values seem to set limits on peace and stability. Having said that, what derailed cooperation in this period was a difference over political sequencing: a Kashmir settlement before the end of terrorism; or the end of terrorism before a Kashmir settlement. Put slightly differently, the questions confronting negotiators were, would a Kashmir settlement truly end terrorism, or would the end of terrorism deliver a Kashmir settlement? Neither side could produce a convincing answer, one that would be credible at home to a larger public. And further, even if they could, what was to stop future leaderships and publics reneging on an agreement? In short, a fundamental commitment problem led to defection after defection even as systemic factors encouraged cooperation.[79]

Finally, what are the lessons for U.S. policy? First, U.S. engagement periodically nudged India and Pakistan toward cooperation, but the United States was not in a position to do much more. India and Pakistan played to the U.S. gallery and to world opinion, but not enough to set aside their deeper differences. Second, while this chapter does not deal with the United States' role in the Kargil War and the 2001–2002 confrontation, those episodes suggest Washington is most effective in staving off hostilities and escalation rather than in fundamental dispute settlement. Third, if a commitment problem is what stops India and Pakistan from actual dispute settlement, it is tempting to think an outside power could increase confidence that agreements will be implemented. The truth is that the United States simply does not have the capacity to ensure that Indian and Pakistani promises to each other will be honored. Even more fundamentally, given its many global responsibilities and the growing feeling its primary worries are domestic, it probably also does not have the motivation to step into the breach. Much more central to its international agenda are relations with China and with allies in Europe and East Asia as well as conflicts in the Middle East. Dispute settlement in South Asia has never figured high in U.S. grand strategy, and its role in the region has been intermittent at best. In effect, the United States, like its South Asian partners, has a commitment problem.

NOTES

1. Thanks to Rohan Mukherjee for the terms.

2. Šumit Ganguly, *Deadly Impasse: Indo-Pakistani Relations at the Dawn of a New Century* (Cambridge University Press, 2016), pp. 21–22; Šumit Ganguly, *Conflicts Unending; India-Pakistan Tensions since 1947* (Oxford University Press, 2001); T. V. Paul, "Causes of the India-Pakistan Enduring Rivalry," in *The India-Pakistan Conflict: An Enduring Rivalry*, edited by T. V. Paul (Cambridge University Press, 2005), pp. 3–24; Husain Haqqani, *India vs. Pakistan: Why Can't We Just Be Friends* (New Delhi: Juggernaut, 2016), pp. 7, 10.

3. Stephen P. Cohen, *Shooting for a Century: Finding Answers to the India-Pakistan Conundrum* (New Delhi: HarperCollins, 2013), pp. 119–38; Šumit Ganguly, *Origins of War in South Asia* (Boulder, CO: Westview, 1986); and Rajesh Basrur, "India-Pakistan Relations: Between War and Peace," in *India's Foreign Policy: Retrospect and Prospect*, edited by Šumit Ganguly (Oxford University Press, 2010), pp. 11–31.

4. Šumit Ganguly, "Discord and Cooperation in India-Pakistan Relations," in *Interpreting World Politics*, edited by Kanti P. Bajpai and Harish C. Shukul (New Delhi: Sage, 1995), pp. 400–412; Pallavi Raghavan, *Animosity at Bay: An Alternative History of the India-Pakistan Relationship, 1947–1952* (New Delhi: HarperCollins, 2020); Ashutosh Mishra, *India-Pakistan: Coming to Terms* (New York: Palgrave Macmillan, 2010); P. R. Chair, Pervez Cheema, and Stephen P. Cohen, *Four Crises and a Peace Process: American Engagement in South Asia* (Brookings, 2007); and Sameer Lalwani and Hannah Haegeland, eds., *Investigating Crises: South Asia's Lessons, Evolving Dynamics, and Trajectories* (Washington, D.C.: The Stimson Center, 2018).

5. Shyam Saran, *How India Sees the World: Kautilya to the 21st Century* (New Delhi: Juggernaut, 2017), p. 80. See also Shivshankar Menon, *Choices: Inside the Making of India's Foreign Policy* (New Delhi: Allen Lane/Penguin Random House India, 2016), pp. 114–15, and T. C. A. Raghavan, *The People Next Door: The Curious History of India's Relations with Pakistan* (New Delhi: HarperCollins, 2017), p. 303.

6. Ashley J. Tellis, *Are India-Pakistan Peace Talks Worth a Damn?* (Washington, D.C.: Carnegie Endowment for International Peace, 2017), p. 7.

7. Raghavan, *Animosity at Bay*, p. 4.

8. Saran, *How India Sees the World*, p. 80; Menon, *Choices*, p. 115; and Haqqani, *India vs. Pakistan*, p. 6.

9. Raghavan, *People Next Door*, p. 303.

10. Raghavan, *Animosity at Bay*, p. 184.

11. Basrur, "India-Pakistan Relations: Between War and Peace," pp. 11–22.

12. On India's Cold Start idea, see Walter S. Ladwig, "A Cold Start for Hot Wars? The Indian Army's New Limited War Doctrine," *International Security* 32, no. 3 (2007/8), pp. 158–90.

13. Lalwani and Haegeland, *Investigating Crises*, p. 54. For a skeptical view

of the dialogue, see Tellis, *Are India-Pakistan Peace Talks Worth a Damn?* pp. 1–93.

14. Srijan Shukla and Sajid Ali, "The Bus Ride That Almost Helped Vajpayee, Sharif Rewrite History of South Asia," *The Print*, July 1, 2019, https://theprint.in/past-forward/the-bus-ride-that-almost-helped-vajpayee-sharif-rewrite-history-of-south-asia/255250/; Shekhar Gupta, "Indians Are Shy about Accepting Truths about Wars, Irrespective of Results" *India Today*, July 31, 2014, www.indiatoday.in/magazine/national-interest/story/20140811-shekhar-gupta-kargil-war-anniversary-atal-bihari-vajpayee-nawaz-sharif-804780-2014-07-31; and former intelligence chief, A. S. Dulat's *Kashmir: The Vajpayee Years* (New Delhi: HarperCollins, 2017), pp. 15–16.

15. Shukla and Ali, "The Bus Ride That Almost Helped Vajpayee."

16. "Lahore Declaration 1999," Ministry of External Affairs, Government of India, https://mea.gov.in/in-focus-article.htm?18997/Lahore+Declaration+February+1999.

17. Quoted in Dulat, *Kashmir*, p. 17.

18. Raghavan, *People Next Door*, p. 231.

19. Ganguly, *Deadly Impasse*, p. 33.

20. "Back Channel: The Promise and Peril," Ministry of External Affairs, Government of India, May 23, 2003, www.mea.gov.in/articles-in-indian-media.htm?dtl/13817/Back+channel+the+promise+and+peril. This appears to be a media article that the ministry uploaded.

21. Raghavan, *People Next Door*, p. 227.

22. Shukla and Ali, "The Bus Ride That Almost Helped Vajpayee, Sharif."

23. Quoted in Celia W. Dugger, "Indian Leader Accepts Pakistani Offer,' *New York Times*, February 4, 1999, www.nytimes.com/1999/02/04/world/indian-leader-accepts-pakistani-offer-to-take-a-ride-to-lahore.html.

24. On the various origins of the Kargil War, see Nasim Zehra, *From Kargil to the Coup: Events That Shook Pakistan* (Lahore: Sang-e-Meel, 2019), pp. 42–47; Owen Bennett Jones, *Pakistan: Eye of the Storm* 3rd ed. (Yale University Press, 2009), pp. 107–23; and Ganguly, *Deadly Impasse*, p. 35.

25. Ganguly, *Deadly Impasse*, p. 34.

26. Pervez Musharraf, *In the Line of Fire: A Memoir* (New York: The Free Press, 2006), pp. 87–90.

27. Zehra, *From Kargil to the Coup*, pp. 120–23; and Ganguly, *Deadly Impasse*, pp. 35–36. C. Christine Fair, *Fighting to the End: The Pakistan Army's Way of War* (Oxford University Press, 2014; ppb. ed. 2018), pp. 151–52, adds that revenge for 1971, India's occupation of Siachen, and Indian provocations and shelling along the LOC were also motives.

28. L. K. Advani, *My Country, My Life* (New Delhi: Rupa, 2008; ppb. ed. 2010), pp. 696–97; Dulat, *Kashmir*, pp. 223–27; and Raghavan, *People Next Door*, p. 249.

29. Zehra, *From Kargil to the Coup*, pp. 273–76; and Ashley J. Tellis, C.

Christine Fair, and Jamison Jo Medby, *Limited Conflicts under the Nuclear Umbrella: Indian and Pakistani Lessons from the Kargil Crisis* (Santa Monica, CA: RAND Corporation, 2001), pp. 8–11, www.rand.org/pubs/monograph_reports/MR1450.html.

30. Jaswant Singh, *India at Risk: Mistakes, Misperceptions, and Misadventures of Security Policy* (New Delhi: Rupa, 2013), pp. 218–19; and Raghavan, *People Next Door*, pp. 247–49.

31. Musharraf, *In the Line of Fire*, p. 297.

32. Ibid., p. 299.

33. Ibid.

34. Dulat, *Kashmir*, pp. 224–27; Ganguly, *Deadly Impasse*, pp. 59–61; and Khurshid Mahmud Kasuri, *Neither a Hawk nor a Dove: An Insider's Account of Pakistan's Foreign Relations Including Details of the Kashmir Framework* (Oxford University Press, 2015), pp. 159–60 suggest that Vajpayee and Jaswant may have been amenable to a softer view. For India's official view, see Advani, *My Country, My Life*, pp. 698–707; Jaswant Singh, *India at Risk*, pp. 221–29; and Myra Macdonald, *Defeat Is an Orphan: How Pakistan Lost the Great South Asian War* (London: Hurst, 2017), pp. 78–82. See also J. N. Dixit, *India and Regional Developments: Through the Prism of Indo-Pak Relations* (New Delhi: Gyan Publishing, 2004), pp. 15–17 on Musharraf's public statements prior to the summit on the primacy of Kashmir.

35. Steve Coll, "The Back Channel," *The New Yorker*, February 22, 2009, p. 20, http://newyorker.com/magazine/2009/03/02/the-back-channel.

36. Jonathan Power, "India's New Leader: Singh Talks of Peace and a War on Poverty," *International Herald Tribune*, May 24, 2004, www.nytimes.com/2004/05/24/opinion/IHT-indias-new-leader-singh-talks-of-peace-and-a-war-on-poverty.html?auth=login-email&login=email.

37. K. J. M. Varma, "Oppn Condemns Pervez's Formula on Kashmir," *The Tribune*, October 27, 2004, www.tribuneindia.com/2004/20041027/world.htm#1.

38. Ganguly, *Deadly Impasse*, pp. 92–93.

39. Musharraf, *In the Line of Fire*, pp. 304–305.

40. Ganguly, *Deadly Impasse*, p. 96.

41. Satinder K. Lambah, "A Possible Outline of a Solution," *Outlook*, May 14, 2014, www.outlookindia.com/website/story/a-possible-outline-of-a-solution/290718; Sanjaya Baru, *The Accidental Prime Minister* (Gurgaon, India: Penguin, 2014), pp. 186–87; and Coll, "The Back Channel," pp. 21–22.

42. Coll, "The Back Channel," p. 3.

43. Myra Macdonald, *Defeat Is an Orphan*, p. 140 notes 800 military deaths, including 176 from "mines, mishandling ammunition and explosives, and traffic accidents." See also Raghavan, *People Next Door*, p. 263.

44. Lambah, "A Possible Outline of a Solution."

45. Khurshid Mahmud Kasuri, *Neither a Hawk*, p. 424.

46. Quoted in Coll, "The Back Channel," p. 2.

47. MacDonald, *Defeat Is an Orphan*, pp. 74–75, pp. 137–49, and pp. 176–79; and Kasuri, *Neither a Hawk*, pp. 181–85 for an account of the United States' role.
48. Lambah, "A Possible Outline of a Solution."
49. Ibid.
50. See Baru, *Accidental Prime Minister*, p. 195.
51. Musharraf, *In the Line of Fire*, pp. 139, 308.
52. Coll, "The Back Channel," pp. 19–20.
53. Quoted in Coll, "Back Channel," p. 20. See also Kasuri, *Neither a Hawk*, pp. 117, 320.
54. Raghavan, *People Next Door*, p. 275.
55. Lambah, "A Possible Outline of a Solution."
56. Quoted in Coll, "The Back Channel," p. 19. See also Musharraf, *In the Line of Fire*, p. 2: "[T]he events of December 2003 put me in the front line of the war on terror."
57. Baru, *Accidental Prime Minister*, pp. 181–89; and Saran, *How India Sees the World*, pp. 90–92, on opposition to the Siachen accord.
58. Saran, *How India Sees the World*, p. 96.
59. Macdonald, *Defeat Is an Orphan*, p. 185, on Musharraf's problems with the Corps Commanders. On the other hand, his foreign minister states that they were on board on negotiations with India: see Coll, "The Back Channel," pp. 2–3 and pp. 19–20.
60. Macdonald, *Defeat Is an Orphan*, pp. 186–87; and Raghavan, *People Next Door*, pp. 287–90, on the internal disorders.
61. This paragraph draws on Coll, "The Back Channel," pp. 3–4 and p. 22.
62. "India Interfering in Baluchistan," *Times of India*, July 18, 2009, https://timesofindia.indiatimes.com/world/pakistan/India-interfering-in-Balochistan-Gilani/articleshow/4793302.cms.
63. Kalbe Ali, "MFN Status for India on Backburner," *Dawn*, December 29, 2012, www.dawn.com/news/774729/mfn-status-for-india-on-backburner; and Raghavan, *People Next Door*, p. 296.
64. On Sharif's return, his NSA Sartaj Aziz insisted that Kashmir was discussed: "Modi, Sharif Discussed Kashmir during Meeting, Says Top Pakistan Official," *India Today*, May 28, 2014, www.indiatoday.in/india/story/narendra-modi-nawaz-sharif-kashmir-issue-india-pakistan-sartaj-aziz-194816-2014-05-28.
65. "India Cancels Talks with Pakistan over Kashmir Row," BBC News, August 19, 2014, www.bbc.com/news/world-asia-28832477.
66. "Full Text of India-Pakistan Joint Statement on PM Narendra Modi-Nawaz Sharif Talks in Russia," *The Hindu*, July 10, 2015, www.thehindu.com/news/resources/full-text-of-the-joint-statement-by-the-foreign-secretaries-of-india-and-pakistan-in-russia/article10566559.ece?ref=relatedNews.
67. Baqir Sajjad Syed, "NSAs' Talks Cancelled over Indian Conditions," *Dawn*, August 23, 2015, www.dawn.com/news/1202269.
68. Suhasini Haider, "India, Pakistan NSAs Meet in Bangkok," *The Hindu*,

December 6, 2015, www.thehindu.com/news/national/national-security-advisers-of-india-and-pakistan-meeting-in-bangkok/article7955001.ece.

69. Baqir Sajjad Syed, "Breakthrough at 'Heart of Asia': Pakistan, India to Resume 'Comprehensive' Talks," *Dawn*, December 10, 2015, www.dawn.com/news/1225402/breakthrough-at-heart-of-asia-pakistan-india-to-resume-comprehensive-talks.

70. Haqqani, *India v. Pakistan*, p. 105.

71. Ankit Panda, "Back to Square One: Pakistan Calls Off Peace Talks with India," *The Diplomat*, April 9, 2016, https://thediplomat.com/2016/04/back-to-square-one-pakistan-calls-off-peace-talks-with-india/.

72. RSTV Bureau, "War with Pakistan Is Not an Option, Sushma Tells Parl," Rajya Sabha TV (RSTV), December 16, 2015, https://rstv.nic.in/war-pakistan-not-optionsushma-tells-parliament.html.

73. Mehreen Zahra-Mallik, "Behind the Scenes, Pakistan's Military Helped Revive Talks with India," Reuters, December 27, 2015, www.reuters.com/article/india-pakistan-modi-nawaz-military-idUSKBN0U90EQ20151226; and Ankit Panda, "Making Sense of Modi's Surprise Stopover in Lahore," *The Diplomat*, December 29, 2015, https://thediplomat.com/2015/12/making-sense-of-modis-surprise-stopover-in-lahore/.

74. Ian Hall, *Modi and the Reinvention of Indian Foreign Policy* (Bristol University Press, 2019), p. 153.

75. Computed from "Prime Minister Visits," Ministry of External Affairs, Government of India, April 23, 2020, www.mea.gov.in/prime-minister-visits.htm.

76. Modi noted in the interview that after the Pathankot and Uri strikes "the world realized that Modi is truthful [about terrorism] . . . he made the effort [to reassure Pakistan]": see "PM Modi Tells about His Visit to Pakistan," India TV (YouTube), author's translation, May 5, 2019, www.youtube.com/watch?v=3-uiS5b4FE0.

77. RSTV Bureau, "War with Pakistan Is Not an Option."

78. Panda, "Back to Square One."

79. On the commitment problem, see James D. Fearon, "Rationalist Explanations for War," *International Organization* 49, no. 3 (1995), pp. 379–414; and James D. Fearon, "Bargaining, Enforcement, and International Cooperation," *International Organization* 52, no. 2 (1998), pp. 269–305.

SIX

Nuclear Stability in South Asia

DINSHAW MISTRY

In its 2019 *Worldwide Threat Assessment*, the U.S. intelligence community stated that "The continued growth and development of Pakistan and India's nuclear weapons programs increase the risk of a nuclear security incident in South Asia," and that "new types of nuclear weapons will introduce new risks for escalation dynamics and security in the region."[1] Similar to other governmental and nongovernmental analyses, this assessment suggested that there are three main nuclear challenges in South Asia. First, how secure are Pakistan's nuclear assets from theft and unauthorized transfer to other states and nonstate actors? Second, to what extent is there crisis stability in the region? Could a military crisis between India and Pakistan escalate into one or both sides using nuclear weapons? Third, is there a nuclear arms race in the region, and how will this impact deterrence stability? The first issue was examined in chapter 2. This chapter examines the second and third issues.

The chapter begins with basic information on nuclear forces in South Asia, and then discusses crisis stability and arms buildups. It notes that India-Pakistan military crises in the late 2010s were much less severe than those in 1999–2002, and therefore the prospect of escalation to the nuclear level was, in hindsight, negligible in these later crises. Still, compared to some restraint in the late 2000s, both sides ratcheted up their planned and actual military behavior during crises in the late 2010s. These developments, and India's military strike plans, Pakistan's retaliatory inclinations, its tactical nuclear weapons, and the ambiguity between certain nuclear and conventional missiles, all increase the risks of an India-Pakistan nuclear exchange in a future crisis. On arms buildups, India and Pakistan enlarged their nuclear arsenals at a modest rather than huge rate in the 2000s and 2010s. This did not, and future similar rates of growth would not necessarily, undermine basic deterrence stability. However, new types of weapons (such as tactical nuclear systems) and doctrines could undermine crisis stability, and larger arsenals could also have negative implications for nuclear security. Finally, the India-China dyad is more crisis-stable compared to the India-Pakistan dyad.

Nuclear Forces in India and Pakistan

In 1998, when they carried out nuclear tests and declared themselves to be nuclear weapons states, India and Pakistan had small and rudimentary nuclear arsenals. Pakistan had about twenty nuclear weapons and India perhaps thirty (though with fissile material for sixty to ninety). Each state had few combat aircraft modified for nuclear delivery, and just one type of short-range and one type of medium-range missile. By 2020, their strategic forces were considerably larger.[2] Each had an estimated 150 nuclear warheads, as well as eight to ten types of short-range, medium-range, and (for India) intermediate-range missiles. Their missiles had also been extensively tested—each type of missile was typically tested every two to three years, and inducted into service after about three successful developmental tests. In terms of their warheads, India had 12–20 kiloton warheads for its short-range systems and 40 kiloton boosted-fission or thermonuclear warheads for medium-range missiles (in 1998, India announced testing a 43 kiloton device that could be scaled up to 200 kilotons); Pakistan had 5–12 kiloton warheads for its short-range and 10–40 kiloton warheads for its medium-range systems.

Pakistan and India also improved their command and control mechanisms, and their nuclear postures became somewhat clearer. Pakistan adopted an asymmetric escalation posture, so that its nuclear weapons aimed to deter a conventional attack from India, but also any nuclear use by India. India, with a no-first-use policy, opted for an assured retaliation posture, seeking a sufficiently large and survivable arsenal to deter nuclear use by China and Pakistan. Further, there was a "catalytic" element in Pakistan's nuclear strategy and India's conventional strategy during crises. Pakistan's nuclear weapons, and India's conventional military plans, which the United States feared could lead to nuclear use by Pakistan, induced (catalyzed) the United States to intervene in regional crises, and both states assumed that U.S. intervention would benefit their respective positions.

Crisis Stability and Nuclear Use Possibilities
Was There a Risk of Nuclear Use in India-Pakistan Crises?

India and Pakistan were involved in two major military crises in 1999 and 2001–2002, and three less severe crisis episodes in 2008, 2016, and 2019.[3] All involved a substantial Pakistan-linked provocation against India—a cross-border military incursion in 1999, and high-impact terrorist attacks in the other cases. U.S. officials were concerned that a forceful Indian military response could have led to larger-scale conventional military clashes that, in turn, could have escalated to the use of nuclear weapons. Accordingly, the United States diplomatically intervened, often at the senior-most levels of government, to convince each antagonist to descend down the escalation ladder.[4] It sought to persuade Pakistan to reverse its military intrusion (in 1999) or act against terrorist groups (in the other cases), and it urged India to hold back on military action. In 1999 and 2001–2002, the two sides came close to substantial conventional military battles—but the extent of this possible next level of conventional warfare, and whether it could have spilled over into nuclear use, cannot be definitively determined. In the other cases, they remained far from such escalation. And the importance of the U.S. role relative to that of the governments of India and Pakistan in crisis-de-escalation also cannot be definitively determined, since, in the end, a combination of U.S. diplomacy and certain decisions by India and Pakistan helped ease the crises.

In 1999, India and Pakistan engaged in three months of combat along the Line of Control in the Kargil region of Kashmir, resulting in about 500 Indian and several hundred Pakistani military fatalities. India's political leadership sought to keep hostilities localized, and restricted its air force from crossing the Line of Control. Yet eventually, faced with high casualties, they warned of military operations against Pakistan, beyond the Kashmir sector, if Pakistani forces did not withdraw to their side of the Line of Control. India also prepared four Prithvi missiles and one Agni missile for a nuclear contingency.[5] Pakistan signaled its nuclear intentions to deter Indian military escalation. These signals included the display of Ghauri missiles and statements by Pakistan's prime minister and other officials conveying deterrent threats.[6] In the end, the crisis eased when India's military evicted Pakistani intruders from much of the terrain they had occupied, and because Prime Minister Nawaz Sharif, after a meeting with President Bill Clinton, agreed to withdraw Pakistani forces from the remaining areas in their control.

The 2001–2002 crisis was triggered by a December 2001 terrorist attack on India's Parliament, and compounded by a May 2002 terrorist strike on an Indian Army camp in Jammu. From December 2001 to October 2002, although they held back from military combat, both sides mobilized several hundred thousand troops for a war going beyond the Kashmir sector. India's Army mobilized not just its defensive holding corps but also all its three strike corps—this was an exercise in coercive diplomacy against Pakistan, which also kept the United States engaged in pressuring Pakistan, as well as a preparation for military action if Pakistan did not act against terrorist groups.

To deter Indian military attacks, Pakistan repeatedly signaled its nuclear intentions—in messages and letters to world leaders, and in a statement by the director of Pakistan's Strategic Plans Division. These spelled out Pakistan's "red lines" that would trigger nuclear use—India's imposing an economic or sea blockade, a military threat in the plains, meddling in Pakistani politics, or cutting off Indus River waters. Pakistan also signaled its deterrent in missile movements in December–January and May–June, and via missile tests on May 25–28.

India was seriously contemplating military action in January and in May–June. One Indian plan involved military operations in Pakistan-held Kashmir. Another envisioned a strike corps drawing in and tying down Pakistan's Army Reserve North, and India was confident that its three strike corps would prevail over Pakistan in any battle of attrition.[7] Prime Minister Atal Bihari Vajpayee noted that India could risk a nuclear strike to halt years of Pakistan-sponsored terrorism (terrorist attacks in Kashmir had killed 500–600 Indian security personnel annually in 1999–2001, 200–300 in the mid-1990s, and 100–200 in the early 1990s).[8] Also, in late December 2001 and early January 2002, India's political and military leadership stated that India could absorb and massively retaliate against any Pakistani nuclear strike.[9]

Eventually, U.S. and international diplomacy—including visits to the region by Secretary of State Colin Powell and U.K. Prime Minister Tony

Blair, and phone calls by President George W. Bush—secured strong Pakistani pledges and some action to curb militants, and this restrained India from military strikes.

The 2008, 2016, and 2019 crises involved very minor or no military skirmishes, and since significant conventional military escalation did not occur, both sides remained some distance from the next—nuclear—level of escalation. These crises occurred in the context of continuing terrorist attacks against India, albeit on a lesser scale than in the early 2000s (Indian security force fatalities due to terrorist strikes in Kashmir were near 100 annually in the late 2000s; near 50 in the mid 2010s; and 80–90 in 2016–2019).

In late 2008, after the November 26 terrorist attack killing 160 civilians in Mumbai, there was genuine concern about Indian military retaliation against Pakistan, but this did not occur. Neither side mobilized its armed forces (though India placed its air force, and Pakistan placed all three branches of its military, on alert); and there was no nuclear rhetoric or posturing such as missile tests. Still, analysts noted that India had set a one-month deadline for Pakistan to act against militants, and could have undertaken military operations if the crisis had not eased.[10] Intense U.S. engagement helped resolve the crisis. The United States lessened India's justifications for military action by pressing Pakistan to act against militants, confirming the absence of direct Pakistani state involvement in the terrorist attacks, and highlighting Pakistan's investigation of terrorist groups.[11]

In September 2016, ten days after militants killed eighteen soldiers in Kashmir, India announced that it had conducted "surgical strikes" against terrorist launch pads across the Line of Control. In a press conference hours after the operation, India's director general of military operations framed the action as preemptive strikes against impending terrorist infiltration. He added that, just before the press briefing, he had informed his Pakistani counterpart about the strikes; and that India did "not have any plans for continuation of further operations" but was ready for any reaction from the Pakistan side.

Overall, India's very limited military operations lasted just a few hours. Small groups of special forces, collectively numbering about 100–200 persons, struck four to five launch pads, each only one to two miles across the Line of Control, albeit spread along a front of some 100 miles. Pakistan cast doubt on India's action and did not militarily respond. Still, India's Air Force and Navy had been instructed to keep their forces on alert, and villages along the Line of Control and international border had been evacuated, to prepare for possible Pakistani retaliation. And the strategic and political significance of the strikes was greater than the military dimensions. This was the first time India publicly declared that its forces had breached the Line of Control. India aimed to retaliate against, inflict damage upon, humiliate, and deter future attacks by Pakistan-based terrorist groups—all while keeping military action very limited.[12]

In February 2019, twelve days after a militant attack killing forty-one Indian paramilitary personnel in Kashmir, India retaliated with an air raid. Sixteen Indian Mirage-2000s were in Pakistan-controlled airspace for only about twenty minutes, firing air-to-surface weapons from over Pakistan-held Kashmir at a terrorist camp about five miles inside Pakistan's Khyber province. India framed this as a defensive preemptive operation—saying it had "credible intelligence" about an impending terrorist attack, and that, "in the face of imminent danger," it "struck the biggest training camp of JeM [Jaish-e-Mohammed terrorist group]."[13] Later, Indian officials noted that "The choice of target and execution came with a lot of planning and intelligence inputs. It was important to send a message to Pakistan that India will not tolerate any more [terrorist] attacks."[14]

Pakistan claimed that Indian jets bombed an empty hillside. The next day, it responded with an airstrike at what it said were "non-military target[s]" at short distances across the Line of Control, to demonstrate its "right, will and capability for self defence."[15] It also noted that "We have no intention of escalation, but are fully prepared to do so if forced into that paradigm." While it is not clear whether the Pakistani aircraft struck Indian ground targets, Pakistani jets shot down an Indian MiG-21 that engaged them, but Pakistan then released the pilot, thus gradually easing the crisis. The Indian national security adviser and intelligence chief spoke with their Pakistani counterparts via hotlines, indicating that India would respond strongly if the pilot was harmed or not released.

The United States helped in crisis management. The secretary of state, national security adviser, chairman of the Joint Chiefs of Staff, and heads of Central Command and Pacific Command spoke with their counterparts in India and Pakistan, focusing on getting Pakistan to quickly release the Indian pilot and on obtaining assurances that India would not fire conventional missiles at Pakistan, which it had reportedly threatened.[16]

Ultimately, although this crisis quickly eased, it should be noted that both sides had heightened the alert status of their militaries; they increased troop deployments and movements along the border; India reportedly asked its armed forces to ready Prithvi missiles in the Rajasthan sector; and the Indian Navy deployed three dozen vessels (that were on an existing exercise) in the North Arabian Sea, including its aircraft carrier and conventional submarines, apparently influencing the Pakistan Navy to not venture into the open ocean. India's nuclear-armed submarine was also reportedly on patrol at this time.

To summarize, in this case, Pakistan and India both resorted to military action to signal their resolve—India to indicate that it would respond to terrorism, and Pakistan to demonstrate a response to India. And while they kept their actual military strikes very limited to prevent escalation, one, albeit small, round of escalation nevertheless occurred. Significantly, this was the first time since the 1971 war that either state's air force attacked targets across the border.

Crisis Stability Concerns

India-Pakistan military skirmishes in the late 2010s were much less severe than their military crises of 1999 and 2001–2002. Still, analysts and policymakers raised several concerns about military escalation, including to the nuclear level, in both past and future crises.

First, India and Pakistan developed plans for, and undertook military exercises simulating, limited war scenarios, and each side affirmed its retaliatory intentions against the other. Such limited encounters could escalate to more substantial military clashes if either side crossed the other's ambiguous "red lines."

In 2001–2002, India's Armed Forces were fully mobilized for military action, and India's leadership believed they could avert nuclear exchanges by not crossing Pakistan's red lines. Subsequently, because of the lengthy time (two to three weeks) for large-scale mobilization of its strike corps, India developed a "Cold Start" strategy. This involved quickly mobilizing some armored divisions—perhaps eight brigades with 30,000–50,000 troops—for limited strikes at Pakistan. Yet, because both sides' red lines are unclear, a series of reciprocal, even if limited, escalating military operations could result in one side crossing the other's ambiguous lines. Illustrating this, in 1999, Pakistan's military moved its missiles as per (what it later claimed was) standard defensive process during a crisis, but these movements were considered to be threatening by Washington and New Delhi. As another example, in 2002, an Indian military commander moved his forces across a canal and ominously close to the border, which greatly raised U.S. and Pakistani concerns about impending Indian military action. To take a third example, in 2019, about a week after Pakistan released the Indian pilot and thus appeared to de-escalate the crisis, it stated that it detected an Indian conventional Scorpène-class submarine off its coast, but to avoid escalation, it had not targeted the vessel.[17]

More generally, during a crisis, misperception, poor intelligence, and command and control limitations all compound the blurred nature of red lines and make them susceptible to being crossed. Also, existing crisis management structures within a national bureaucracy may fall short. Thus, during the 2008 and 2016 crises, India's institutionalized response mechanism was not mobilized or fell short of its intended objectives, and India instead opted for ad hoc responses with limited coordination among relevant actors both within and outside the central government.[18]

India's shifting inclinations toward limited war should also be noted. In the 1999 and 2001–2002 crises (under a Bharatiya Janata Party [BJP] government), India was strongly considering substantial military action against Pakistan. In contrast, in 2008 (under a Congress-led government), India demonstrated strategic restraint—it was prepared for limited military strikes but eventually held back. Thereafter, however, in 2016 and 2019 (under a BJP government), India upgraded its military response plans, albeit to a much lesser level than its military plans in the 2002 crisis. Some observers suggest that the international community's tacit acceptance of India's cross-border attacks in 2016 and 2019 embolden it to maintain, and incrementally expand, such limited military options in future crises.[19]

Pakistan repeatedly affirmed its intentions to respond to Indian attacks, and also ratcheted up its retaliatory options. For example, during the 2008 crisis, Pakistani officials informed their U.S. counterparts that no Pakistani government could survive inaction to an Indian military attack, and therefore Pakistan would respond with force, even at the cost of expanding the conflict.[20] To take another example, in the late 2010s, Pakistan indicated that it would militarily retaliate to an extent equivalent to, or slightly greater than, any Indian military action. Illustrating this, during the 2019 crisis, when Indian officials reportedly noted that they could fire six missiles at Pakistan, Pakistan responded that it would retaliate with three times as many.[21] While the numbers in such rhetoric may be inaccurate, and both sides were referring to conventional rather than nuclear missiles, the rhetoric nevertheless indicated Pakistan's thinking about retaliating to a level greater than India's military action. Confirming this, Pakistani officials later noted, "Pakistan's policy in a limited conflict is quid pro quo *plus* [emphasis added] . . . we will not take any act of aggression lying down."[22]

Second, military escalation could quickly involve nuclear use by Pakistan because it does not have a no-first-use policy and because it specifically developed tactical nuclear weapons to respond to India's limited war plans. Pakistan made the case that Indian military planners had found a space, between Pakistan's strategic nuclear forces and its conventional forces, for limited conventional war, and that its tactical missile, the Nasr, filled this gap in Pakistan's deterrence against Indian conventional forces.[23] Tactical nuclear weapons are thus conceptualized as one layer of Pakistan's three-layered deterrence: deterrence at a tactical level against limited Indian military incursions, at the operational level to deter a sizable Indian military offensive, and at a strategic level to prevent an Indian nuclear attack or large-scale war. Still, forward-deployed tactical weapons are more likely to be subject to attack, and more likely to be used when they come under attack, or when field commanders perceive an imminent attack.

Third, because short-range ballistic missiles and cruise missiles could be either nuclear or conventionally armed, this ambiguity increases the chances of nuclear use. In the fog of war, if one side detects missile launches or launch preparations by its rival (such as a real or false radar indication of an incoming missile strike), it could assume it is facing a nuclear strike even if the incoming missiles are conventional. And the presumably stricter control over authorizing nuclear use could ease in this situation, so that the target state fires its nuclear missiles rather than risk losing them.

It should be clarified that pressures to quickly use nuclear weapons are more likely for countries without no-first-use (Pakistan) than for those with no-first-use (India). But even with its no-first-use policy, a situation of nuclear ambiguity could influence India to use nuclear missiles when the nuclear threshold has already been breached, or if India eases this policy in war—as discussed below.

Fourth, India could reconsider or refine its no-first-use policy as well as its massive retaliation approach to deterrence. On no-first-use, senior past and serving Indian security officials have stated that India's no-first-use policy implies *no first initiation of use*.[24] This approach could permit Indian nuclear use if it believes an adversary has initiated planning for a nuclear strike—and, in theory, such planning could range from missile launch preparations to conventional force movements to communications between civilian and military officials in the nuclear command chain.

India could also reconsider its "massive retaliation" approach to deterrence. India's official nuclear doctrine threatens massive nuclear retaliation against any limited nuclear use by Pakistan, but domestic and international observers question the credibility of this approach. Thus, India's security establishment has considered proportional or calibrated nuclear retaliation against targets such as Pakistani military bases, and this approach would make nuclear use more likely during any India-Pakistan war.

Fifth, India could seriously consider counterforce operations that draw upon its space assets, precision munitions, and medium-range missiles.[25] India has satellite capabilities to detect a substantial portion of Pakistan's nuclear assets in real time. India's drones with ranges of several hundred kilometers (km) could also track Pakistan's mobile missiles. Thus, in a conventional counterforce operation, Indian aircraft with precision-guided munitions could target Pakistan's mobile missiles, while conventional missiles could target Pakistan's airfields and command and control sites. In a nuclear counterforce strike, India could use some nuclear-armed missiles to destroy much of Pakistan's strategic missile forces at or near their bases or operating zones.

India's acquisition of capable missile defenses could make it more likely to contemplate counterforce strikes. It would then not have to destroy all of Pakistan's nuclear forces—which is very difficult—to have confidence about a counterforce mission. Instead, it would aim to eliminate about 80–90 percent of Pakistan's retaliatory nuclear capability against major Indian cities (i.e., Pakistan's medium-range missiles, aircraft at known airfields, and one to two sea-based platforms), with the assumption that missile defenses could counter retaliation from Pakistan's very few remaining medium-range missiles.

Three developments could offset India's counterforce temptations. First, India may have difficulty finding specific Pakistani nuclear assets. In the 2019 crisis, India used its surveillance aircraft and satellites to keep track of Pakistan's naval forces but could not detect one submarine for nearly three weeks. Second, if Pakistan acquires an enlarged arsenal of 200–250 nuclear weapons, so that it has about 150 warheads on medium-range ballistic missiles (including MIRVed systems), cruise missiles, and possibly sea-based systems, it could at least partly overcome Indian missile defenses. In this situation, even if two-thirds of these assets are destroyed in an Indian attack, and half the surviving forces are countered by Indian missile defenses, the remaining systems (about twenty-five) could still inflict punitive retaliation against Indian cities—making India less confident about undertaking counterforce operations. To be sure, beyond just an increase in numbers, Pakistan would also have to better disperse or conceal its nuclear forces so that they survive any Indian first strike. However, this wider dispersal of forces can increase command and control problems and undermine crisis stability.

Third, India may not acquire effective missile defenses. India's indigenous missile defense system—based on an interceptor derived from its short-range Prithvi missile—was undergoing testing in the 2010s and remained unproven as of the early 2020s. Further, while India may acquire Russian-supplied S-400 air defense systems, these have not been tested for India-relevant missile defense operations, and their effectiveness for such missions is unclear. Moreover, India had not sought or obtained more mature missile defenses, such as American Patriot-3, Aegis-ashore, and Thaad systems or Israel's Arrow.

To summarize, factors related to India's limited war plans and Pakistan's retaliatory inclinations increase the risks of conventional military escalation in an India-Pakistan crisis. And additional factors—Pakistan's tactical nuclear weapons, the ambiguity between certain nuclear and conventional missiles, India's reconsideration of its nuclear doctrine, and India's counterforce temptations—increase the risks of an India-Pakistan nuclear exchange in an escalating crisis.

Nuclear Force Expansion and Deterrence Stability

In just over two decades after their nuclear tests, between 1998 and 2020, Pakistan and India each increased their nuclear arsenals from around 20–30 to 150. This addition of about 120–130 nuclear weapons in twenty-two years represents a low-to-moderate rather than massive rate of growth. If their nuclear arsenals continue to grow at a similar rate, then basic deterrence stability may not be undermined, in the sense that gradually growing nuclear forces would not give either country a first-strike capability against the other. Still, Pakistan and India developed many new types of delivery systems, and some raise concerns. While their medium-range systems can enhance deterrence stability, their short-range systems, cruise missiles, and naval systems could, under certain circumstances, undermine crisis stability.

Nuclear Force Capabilities

To begin with, the range of India and Pakistan's delivery systems and their relevance to each state's deterrent should be clarified. Pakistan's short-range systems—the 80–100 km range Nasr, 200 km range Abdali, and 300 km range Ghaznavi—cannot strike the major Indian cities of New Delhi, which is 350 km, and Mumbai, which is 600 km, from the border. Its short-to-medium-range systems—the 700 km range Shaheen-1 and 900 km range Shaheen-1A—give Pakistan countervalue capabilities against these and other cities in north and west India, and thereby enhance Pakistan's deterrent. Pakistan's medium-range missiles—the 1,300 km range Ghauri, 1,500 km range Shaheen-2, and 2,200 km range possibly multiple-warhead Ababil—give Pakistan even better countervalue options. They can strike north and west Indian cities from considerable strategic depth within Pakistan (i.e., a few hundred kilometers from the Indian border); alternatively, they could strike south and east India from the same launching sites that the Shaheen-1 could reach north and west India. And the 2,700 km range Shaheen-3 can reach India's Andaman Islands, which are beyond the range of all other Pakistani missiles, and where Pakistan assumes India could locate some nuclear forces.

Pakistan has also fielded two nuclear-armed cruise missiles: the 700 km range ground-launched Babur and the 350 km range air-launched Raad. Further, a sea-launched Babur was tested from an underwater platform in 2017 and 2018.

As for India, its short-range (250–350 km range) Prithvi missile has to be deployed in less secure border areas to strike major Pakistani targets. The 700 km range Agni-1 enables India to cover most of Pakistan when launched some distance from the border, and gives India a credible deterrent versus Pakistan. The 1,000–2,000 km range Agni-P that was first tested in 2021 will eventually replace the Agni-1. The 2,000 km range Agni-2 can cover all Pakistani targets from secure launch points far from the border. It can also strike military, industrial, and urban centers in central and western China, but cannot reach China's major eastern cities, Shanghai and Beijing. These are 2,500 km from northeast India (where Indian missiles may be somewhat vulnerable to Chinese strikes), 3,500 km from east India, and 5,000 km from central and south India's more secure launch sites. The 3,000 km range Agni-3, 4,000 km range Agni-4, and 5,000 km range Agni-5 can strike these targets, and thus give India a better deterrent against China when they are fielded in sufficient numbers.

The Agni-3 and Agni-5 have wider diameters and are capable of carrying multiple warheads; and the canisterized Agni-P and Agni-5 can be rapidly fired without lengthy launch preparation.

India also has two submarine-launched missiles, the 700 km range K-15 and the 3,500 km range K-4. The first operational patrol of its nuclear-powered submarine took place in 2018, and its second such submarine completed sea trials in 2019. In addition, India developed two cruise missiles that were not assigned to its nuclear Strategic Force Command, and so were not believed to be nuclear-armed, though they could be—these are the 290 km range Brahmos and the 700 km range Nirbhay.

Nuclear Growth Rates

During the 2020s, Pakistan and India's nuclear arsenals could expand at a moderate rate of five to ten deployable weapons annually. These estimates are based on the projected growth rates of fissile material; they assume that most fissile material added each year is weaponized (i.e., used in warheads), and that the growth of missile delivery systems matches the increase in warheads.

In 2020, India had a 100 megawatt (MW) heavy water reactor that produces weapons-grade plutonium for five weapons per year, and reportedly planned a second such reactor. Thus, by 2025, it could have 175 (if only one reactor was operational) to 225 (if its previously unweaponized plutonium stock is used) nuclear weapons. By 2030, it could have 200 (if only one reactor was operational), 225 (if a second reactor starts operating in 2025), or 250–300 (if its prior plutonium stock is used) nuclear weapons.

Two other plutonium sources could add to this inventory, but are not included in these estimates. India's breeder reactor, if it commences operations in the mid-2020s, could add fifty additional nuclear weapons to India's inventory by 2030. And India's reactor-grade plutonium, derived from its unsafeguarded heavy-water reactors, could be used for several tens to a few hundred nuclear weapons. Yet little to no breeder-derived or reactor-grade plutonium may be weaponized if these are needed as fuel for India's future breeder reactors.

Pakistan's nuclear rate of growth could be comparable to or greater than India's. As per maximalist estimates, Pakistan's enrichment plants could produce high-enriched uranium (HEU) for ten to fifteen nuclear weapons per year; and its four heavy-water reactors (rated at 30–40 MW for the first, 40–50 MW for the second and third, and 50–70 MW for the fourth) could collectively produce plutonium for sixteen weapons per year.[26] Somewhat lower estimates suggest that Pakistan annually produces fissile material for four uranium-based and six to eight plutonium-based weapons.[27] Thus, assuming linear growth of ten warheads per year, fissile material for fourteen warheads/year, adequate reprocessing capability, and no uranium shortage, Pakistan could have 200 nuclear weapons (and fissile material for 220) by 2025, and 250 nuclear weapons (and fissile material for 300) by 2030.

To summarize, as per low-end projections, India could have 200–225 and Pakistan may have 250 nuclear weapons by 2030. As per maximalist projections, each side could have around 300 nuclear weapons by 2030 and 400 by 2035.

Deterrence Stability and Arms Buildups

As Pakistan and India gradually enlarge their nuclear forces, how would these strengthen their deterrents? Could these larger forces give one side first-strike capabilities against the other, thereby undermining basic deterrence stability? Could larger forces undermine crisis stability?

The impact of India's growing nuclear forces on deterrence stability can be assessed by analyzing their distribution, as shown in table 6-1. In 2020, India's 150 nuclear weapons were believed to be allocated for deployment on aircraft (fifty); short-range Prithvi missiles (thirty); medium-range missiles (fifty)—comprising the Pakistan-focused Agni-1 (twenty), dual China- and Pakistan-focused Agni-2 (ten), and China-focused Agni-3 (ten) and Agni-4 (ten), with the Agni-5 having almost completed testing but not inducted into the strategic forces; and rudimentary naval platforms (twenty).[28] Thus, India had only about twenty warheads on capable China-focused missiles, and therefore did not have a credible deterrent against China. Its 100 warheads on Pakistan-focused delivery systems gave it adequate countervalue capabilities versus Pakistan.

With a larger inventory of 200–250 nuclear warheads, India could have 100–120 nuclear weapons on Pakistan-focused delivery systems, twenty to thirty on dual China- and Pakistan-focused land-based missiles, forty to sixty on China-focused land-based missiles, and thirty on perhaps two submarines, directed at both Pakistan and China. These countervalue capabilities would give India a more capable deterrent versus China, with a caveat. India's 700 km range K-15 and 3,500 km range K-4 submarine-launched missiles cannot hit China's major eastern cities from secure

TABLE 6-1. Possible Distribution of India's Nuclear Forces (Warheads Deployed on Each System)[a]

	2020	Projection 2025	Projection 2030	Higher projected level with Pakistan focus	Higher projected level with China & sea focus	Further higher level with Pakistan focus	Further higher level with China & sea focus
Aircraft	50	50	50	50	50	50	50
Prithvi SRBM[b]	30						
Possible New SRBM		30	30	**60**	30	**80**	40
Cruise missiles		0	10	**30**	10	**30**	10
Agni-1 SR/MRBM[c], replaced by Agni-P	20	30	30	40	30	50	30
Agni-2 MRBM[d]	10	20	**30**	30	30	30	30
Agni-3-4-5 IRBM[e]	20	**40**	**60**	60	**80**	60	**90**
SLBM[f]	20	30	30	30	**70**	50	**100**
Total	150	200	250	300	300	350	350

[a] **Bold** indicates main increase from prior period.
[b] SRBM: Short-range ballistic missile, range below 300 km.
[c] SR/MRBM: Short-to-medium-range ballistic missile, range 500–1,000 km.
[d] MRBM: Medium-range ballistic missile, range 1,000–3,000 km.
[e] IRBM: Intermediate-range ballistic missile, range 3,000–5,500 km.
[f] SLBM: Submarine-launched ballistic missile.

coastal bastions in the Bay of Bengal. For these targets, India is developing 5,000–6,000 km range K-5 missiles, to be carried on up to four nuclear-powered submarines.

With an inventory of 300–350 nuclear warheads, India could develop additional forces directed either toward Pakistan or toward China and with more sea-launched systems. A Pakistan-focused inventory would comprise more short-range tactical missiles (sixty to eighty) and nuclear-armed cruise missiles (about thirty). For reasons outlined in the previous section, short-range tactical nuclear systems are more likely to be used in a crisis, and therefore India's induction of such systems would worsen crisis stability. Further, since Pakistan's strategy involves responding to India at every rung of the escalation ladder, India's short-range nuclear deployments could influence Pakistan to respond in kind—thereby resulting in a tactical nuclear arms race. Pakistan may not necessarily expand the overall size of its arsenal, especially if it has fissile material constraints. Instead, Pakistan could use its limited fissile material for short-range systems rather than medium-range systems, or, alternatively, could allocate medium-range systems for tactical operations.

A China-focused Indian nuclear inventory could have seventy to one hundred warheads on submarines and eighty to ninety on land-based intermediate-range missiles. These substantial countervalue capabilities would provide India with a stronger deterrent versus China. They would still be insufficient for credible first-strike options against China.

Pakistan's 2020 inventory of about 150 nuclear weapons (shown in table 6-2) were assumed to be allocated mostly for less-destabilizing countervalue systems—short-to-medium and medium-range ballistic missiles (sixty) and aircraft (forty).[29] Still, some were allocated for tactical missiles (twenty-four), short-range missiles that cannot reach India's major cities (sixteen), or cruise missiles (twelve), and, as mentioned previously, these systems undermine crisis stability.

A larger Pakistani arsenal of 200–250 warheads could have mixed impacts on deterrence. First, Pakistan could have more warheads (perhaps thirty to forty) on very short-range tactical nuclear missiles, which would worsen crisis stability. Second, as noted previously, Pakistan could have a larger inventory of countervalue medium-range missiles (about 150), which would strengthen its deterrent versus India, decrease India's counterforce temptations, and thereby enhance deterrence stability. Third, Pakistan could have twenty to thirty air-launched or ground-launched cruise missiles and ten to thirty sea-launched cruise missiles, and these could

TABLE 6-2. **Pakistan's Projected Nuclear Forces**
(Warheads Deployed on Each System)

	2020	Projections for 2025*	Subsequent higher level, possibly in 2030[a]
Aircraft	40	40	40
Nasr tactical SRBM[b]	24	30	35
Ghaznavi SRBM	16	25	35
Shaheen-1 SR/MRBM[c]	16	25	35
Ghauri, Shaheen-2 &-3 MRBM[d]	40	50	55
Cruise missiles (air- or land-based)	12	20	30
SLCM[e]		10	20
Total	150	200	250

[a] These assume that the overall increase over the prior level (prior column) is distributed approximately equally among Pakistan's several types of ballistic and cruise missiles.
[b] SRBM: Short-range ballistic missile, range below 300 km.
[c] SR/MRBM: Short-to-medium-range ballistic missile, range 500–1,000 km.
[d] MRBM: Medium-range ballistic missile, range 1,000–3,000 km.
[e] SLCM: Sea-launched cruise missile.

have mixed effects. The numerical increase in weapons could further enhance Pakistan's resilience against an Indian first strike, thus adding to deterrence stability. Still, cruise missiles could aggravate the problem of nuclear ambiguity, thereby undermining crisis stability.

As for Pakistan's ten to thirty naval nuclear warheads—which could be deployed either on surface vessels or on two to four Chinese-supplied (but not nuclear-powered) submarines—these could have mixed effects on deterrence.[30] On the positive side, submarine-based systems are more survivable, and therefore strengthen Pakistan's overall deterrent against India. On the other hand, naval systems in both Pakistan and India give rise to command and control concerns. The communication and control mechanisms between national authorities and nuclear assets are far less developed for their sea-based forces compared to land-based forces. Also, sea-based nuclear weapons would presumably not permit warheads to be maintained separately from launchers. This separation, and the consequent longer timeline required for launch readiness, provides Pakistan and India with valuable space for signaling, monitoring, and crisis management; without such a separation, crisis stability worsens.[31] Thus, command and control limitations with naval nuclear forces could undermine crisis stability between India and Pakistan.

Crisis Stability Issues in the China-India Dyad

China and India have not been involved in severe militarized crises on the scale of the 1999 and 2002 India-Pakistan crises. Their most significant standoffs, in 2017 at Doklam and 2020 in Ladakh, were largely localized encounters, confined to a limited geographic area, and did not involve armed combat or the exchange of fire. There was little tactical or strategic necessity for significant further conventional escalation. The scope of military operations did not come anywhere near either side's red lines, which could have triggered nuclear use. Even then, however, localized incidents could have somewhat escalated. India's Northern Command chief noted that in August 2020—when India and China sought to disengage months after the Galwan valley clashes in June—India moved some forces and tanks onto certain mountain heights, and China mobilized tanks and troops in the same area. This generated concerns about a major conventional battle if either side fired at opposing forces appearing to advance toward their location.[32]

More generally, the nuclear deterrence dimension is not central to, and has limited salience in, the bilateral China-India relationship, and their disputed territorial area is far from their strategic heartlands and from major population and economic centers.[33] For these reasons, the risks of military escalation to the nuclear level in future China-India crises appear very limited, though not negligible.

One concern is that potential skirmishes between Indian and Chinese naval forces operating in each other's patrolling areas—the Indian Ocean and the South China Sea, respectively—could result in crises.[34] However, even if such clashes involve the sinking of multiple naval or civilian vessels, they are very unlikely to escalate to the nuclear level, unless either side targets a nuclear-delivery submarine, which India and China are unlikely to deploy in vulnerable ocean areas to begin with.

A second concern is that if conventional military crises escalate and China and India are engaged in a limited war, China would likely employ conventional missile strikes against India.[35] In this context, the dual conventional and nuclear status of both sides' short-range missiles, as well as of China's medium-range missiles such as the DF-26 and DF-21, gives rise to the nuclear ambiguity problem noted above, and worsens crisis stability.³⁶ However, both sides' no-first-use policies somewhat reduce these concerns because they convey to the other side that incoming conventional missiles would not be a nuclear strike as long as the other side has not breached the nuclear threshold. Thus, especially if no highly sensitive asset is targeted—such as a nuclear command asset or a nuclear delivery system, which is unlikely to be deployed in forward areas though it could still be struck in rear areas—the risks of either side contemplating even one-off limited nuclear strikes are small. For the above reasons, the risks of a nuclear exchange in Sino-Indian military crises are much less than those in India-Pakistan military crises.

Policy Implications

This chapter has noted that India-Pakistan military crises episodes in 2016 and 2019 were less severe than their crises in 1999–2002. Still, in the late 2010s, both sides ratcheted up their military responses during crises, raising concerns about significant escalation in future cases. Three sets of initiatives could lessen such concerns.

First, Pakistan and India could maintain and expand confidence-building and risk-reduction measures; U.S. diplomatic and nongovernmental dialogues with both sides could reinforce the relevance of such measures. For example, Pakistan and India have annually exchanged lists of nuclear facilities under their 1988 bilateral understanding not to attack these; this could be expanded to cover nuclear command and control systems, early warning systems, and critical computers, and to prohibit cyberattacks.³⁷ As another example, under a 2005 bilateral arrangement, both states notify each other some days ahead of missile tests. Such notification is part of the international Hague Code of Conduct, which India joined in 2016. Pakistan, as well as China, could be encouraged to join the Code, which also requires transparency declarations about their missile forces. In addition, Pakistan and India could enhance hotlines for communication between senior military, intelligence, and political officials. These were used, to varying degrees, in past crises, and they could help prevent miscommunication and misperception that can cause crisis escalation. Another crisis-stability measure would entail the separation of short-range conventional missiles from medium-range nuclear missiles on both sides; this would ensure that no short-range missiles are nuclear-armed and would reduce the destabilizing ambiguity in these systems.

Second, the United States could regularly review and refine its standard operating procedures to defuse India-Pakistan crises.[38] These involve U.S. diplomatic action within hours of crisis initiation, whereby high-level officials from the State Department, Defense Department, and White House send a unified coordinated message to their counterparts in Pakistan and India, urging Pakistan to act against militants or take other steps to de-escalate, and urging India to hold back on military action. To be effective, this also requires consistent engagement and interaction, leading to greater familiarization, between the relevant U.S. officials and their counterparts in Pakistan and India. Still, U.S. diplomatic intervention could be counterproductive if it creates a moral hazard, where one or both sides resort to military escalation with the aim of keeping the United States involved in a crisis.[39]

Third, a broader crisis-prevention strategy could become part of overall U.S. foreign policy for the region. One aspect of this strategy could encourage India to opt for diplomatic and economic sticks and carrots, rather than mostly military options, to induce the Pakistani state to undertake significant and persistent efforts against militants.[40] A second aspect could assist India in counterterrorism, to reduce the chances of a high-impact terrorist strike that could trigger Indian military retaliation. (Here, India could also improve its deterrence by denial capabilities to reduce Pakistan's incentives for allowing terror groups to operate from its territory. It could bolster its situational awareness along the border, and make infiltration more difficult through better intelligence and military deployments. And it could ameliorate the political situation in Kashmir so as to reduce alienation that induces at least some persons to join the militancy.) A third aspect could involve sustained U.S. and international diplomatic and financial-economic pressure on, and corresponding incentives for, Pakistan to act against terrorist groups. To be sure, some of the above aspects were undertaken by Indian governments and by the Bush, Obama, and Trump administrations, but at least through the 2010s did not bring about sustained changes in Pakistan's approach on the issue.[41] In the broadest sense, an optimal crisis-mitigation strategy is the normalization of India-Pakistan relations, where both sides are strongly engaged in peacebuilding, so that spoiler terrorist attacks do not disrupt an ongoing peace process and do not generate military crises.

On China-India crises, analysts note that the United States could assist improving India's ability (across the military, economic, cyber, and intelligence domains) to counter Chinese military moves and to withstand Chinese pressure.[42] Further, U.S. diplomatic messaging could support

India against Chinese pressure, but simultaneously encourage restraint and permit face-saving de-escalation. Washington could also clarify that China-India military confrontations, and Indian political or military policies that exacerbate regional tensions and contribute to such confrontations, jeopardize U.S. goals for its relations with India.

On the issue of nuclear arms buildups, what options could restrain India and Pakistan's nuclear expansion? The first is a fissile material cutoff treaty, but there has been little international movement on such a treaty for decades. Second, diplomatic incentives could be offered to attain a fissile material freeze in the subcontinent. These include a civilian nuclear agreement for Pakistan, support for Pakistan and India's membership into the Nuclear Suppliers Group, and support for India's permanent membership in the UN Security Council, in return for their freezing or even ending fissile material production and restraining certain provocative missile deployments. But India may hesitate on any fissile material freeze that does not significantly cover China, though China could be covered in a separate U.S.-China fissile material initiative on strategic nuclear forces.[43] Third, more modest initiatives could seek Indian and Pakistani restraints short of a fissile material freeze. These could entail supporting Pakistan and India's membership into the Nuclear Suppliers Group in return for their ratifying the Comprehensive Nuclear Test Ban Treaty, India's maintaining its no-first-use policy, and Pakistan scaling back its tactical nuclear arsenal and enhancing its nuclear security.

To summarize, different strategies may have to be adopted to address South Asia's main nuclear challenges. The challenge of crisis stability was, in the 2000s and 2010s, more pressing than that of arms buildups, and concerns in this area may persist in the 2020s. Yet, over the long term, arms buildups cannot be ignored because they could worsen crisis stability and make nuclear security harder.

NOTES

1. Daniel Coates, "Statement for the Record: Worldwide Threat Assessment of the U.S. Intelligence Community," Senate Select Committee on Intelligence, January 29, 2019.

2. Information in this paragraph is taken from Shannon Kile and Hans Kristensen, "Pakistani Nuclear Forces," *SIPRI Yearbook 2020* (Stockholm: Stockholm International Peace Research Institute, 2020), pp. 369–74; Hans Kristensen and Matt Korda, "India's Nuclear Forces 2020," *Bulletin of the Atomic Scientists* 76, no. 4 (July 2020).

3. On 1999, see Peter Lavoy, ed., *Asymmetric Warfare in South Asia: The Causes and Consequences of the Kargil Conflict* (Cambridge University Press, 2009); on 2001–2002, see Zach Davis, ed., *The India-Pakistan Military Standoff: Crisis and Escalation in South Asia* (New York: Palgrave Macmillan, 2011); on both these, see P. R. Chari, Pervaiz Cheema, and Stephen P. Cohen, *Four Crises and a Peace Process* (Brookings, 2016).

4. Moeed Yusuf, *Brokering Peace in Nuclear Environments: U.S. Crisis Management in South Asia* (Stanford University Press, 2018).

5. Raj Chengappa, *Weapons of Peace* (New Delhi: HarperCollins, 2000), p. 437.

6. On June 26, Pakistan's prime minister noted that India would suffer "irreparable losses" if it crossed the Line of Control. For other nuclear signals in statements by Foreign Secretary Shamshad Ahmed and by Pakistani Senate leader Raja Zafarul Haq, see Samina Ahmed, "Nuclear Weapons and the Kargil Crisis," in *South Asia's Security Dilemma*, edited by Lowell Dittmer (New York: M. E. Sharpe, 2004), p. 145.

7. See a book by India's former vice-chief of army staff, V. K. Sood: V. K. Sood and Pravin Sawhney, *Operation Parakram: The War Unfinished* (New Delhi: Sage Publications, 2003).

8. Celia Dugger, "The Kashmir Brink," *New York Times*, June 20, 2002.

9. These were noted in a January 11, 2002, press conference by Army Chief General S. Padmanabhan; in a December 30, 2001 interview in the *Hindustan Times* with Defense Minister George Fernandes; and in a January 3, 2002 speech in Lucknow by Prime Minister Vajpayee.

10. "India, Pakistan: Signs of a Coming War," *Stratfor*, December 24, 2008.

11. Yusuf, *Brokering Peace in Nuclear Environments*, p. 140.

12. Nitin A. Gokhale, *Securing India the Modi Way: Pathankot, Surgical Strikes and More* (New Delhi: Bloomsbury India, 2017).

13. Statement by Indian Ministry of External Affairs, February 27, 2019.

14. Snehesh Philips, "Inside Story of Attack on Balakot—from IAF Officer Who Planned and Executed it," *The Print*, February 26, 2020.

15. Statement by Pakistan Ministry of Foreign Affairs, February 27, 2019.

16. Maria Abi-Habib and Hari Kumar, "Pakistani Military Says It Downed Two Indian Warplanes, Capturing Pilot," *New York Times*, February 27, 2019; John Bolton, *The Room Where It Happened* (New York: Simon and Schuster, 2020).

17. Franz-Stefan Gady, "Pakistan's Navy Spotted, Warned Indian Submarine in Arabian Sea," *The Diplomat*, March 5, 2019.

18. Shyam Saran, "Organizing for Crisis Management: Evaluating India's Experience in Three Cases," in *Investigating Crises: South Asia's Lessons, Evolving Dynamics, and Trajectories*, edited by Hannah Haegeland, Michael Krepon, Samir Lalvani, and Yun Sun (Washington, D.C.: Henry L. Stimson Center, 2018).

19. Henry L. Stimson Center, *From Kargil to Balakot: Southern Asian Crisis Dynamics and Future Trajectories* (Washington, D.C., 2020).

20. Yusuf, *Brokering Peace in Nuclear Environments*, p. 136.

21. Sanjeev Miglani and Drazen Jorgic, "India, Pakistan Threatened to Unleash Missiles at Each Other," Reuters, March 16, 2019.

22. Hamza Azhar Salam and Murtaza Ali Shah, "Lt Gen Kidwai Warns India Not to Take Pakistan's Nuclear Capability as a Bluff," *The News*, February 10, 2020.

23. Adil Sultan, "Pakistan's Emerging Nuclear Posture: Impact of Drivers and Technology on Nuclear Doctrine," *Strategic Studies* 31–32 (Winter 2011/Spring 2012), pp. 147–67; Mansoor Ahmed, "Pakistan's Tactical Nuclear Weapons and Their Impact on Stability," *Regional Insight*, Carnegie Endowment for International Peace, June 30, 2016.

24. Shivshankar Menon, *Choices: Inside the Making of India's Foreign Policy* (Brookings, 2016), p. 33. Also, Balraj Nagal, former chief of the Indian Strategic Forces Command, commented on related issues in a 2015 paper.

25. Vipin Narang and Chris Clary, "India's Counterforce Temptations: Strategic Dilemmas, Doctrine, and Capabilities," *International Security* 43, no. 3 (February 2019), pp. 7–52.

26. See Kile and Kristensen, "Pakistan's Nuclear Forces"; Nuclear Threat Initiative, www.nti.org/learn/countries/pakistan/nuclear/; and David Albright, "Thermal Power Plant at the Khushab Plutonium Complex Is Nearly Complete," Institute for Science and International Security, May 2018. For an estimate that Pakistan could have fissile material for 150–190 highly enriched uranium (HEU)-based and 70 plutonium-based weapons in 2020, see Ashley J. Tellis, *A Troubled Transition: Emerging Nuclear Forces in India and Pakistan* (Palo Alto, CA: Hoover Institution, November 2019).

27. Naeem Salik, *Pakistan's Nuclear Force Structure in 2025* (Washington, D.C.: Carnegie Endowment for International Peace, 2016).

28. Kristensen and Korda, "India's Nuclear Forces 2020."

29. Kile and Kristensen, "Pakistan's Nuclear Forces 2020."

30. Chris Clary and Ankit Panda, "Pakistan's Sea-Based Deterrent," *Washington Quarterly* 40, no. 3 (2017), pp. 149–68.

31. Michael Krepon, *Pakistan's Nuclear Strategy and Deterrence Stability* (Washington, D.C.: Henry L. Stimson Center, December 2012).

32. "India, China Came Close to War Last Year, Says Lt-Gen," *Times of India*, February 18, 2021.

33. Johan Englund, "China's Nuclear Policy and Sino–Indian Relations in the Nuclear Realm," in *Nuclear Threshold Lowered?* edited by Hideya Kurata and Jerker Hellström (Yokosuka, Japan: Center for Global Security, National Defense Academy, 2021).

34. Toby Dalton and Tong Zhao, *At a Crossroads? China-India Nuclear Relations after the Border Clash* (Washington, D.C.: Carnegie Endowment for International Peace, August 2020); and Rajesh Basrur, "India and China: A Gathering Storm," *ORF Issue Brief* 248 (July 2018).

35. Frank O'Donnell, "Stabilizing Sino-Indian Security Relations: Man-

aging Strategic Rivalry after Doklam," Carnegie-Tsinghua Center for Global Policy, June 2018, https://carnegieendowment.org/files/CP335_ODonnell_final.pdf.

36. Hans Kristensen and Matt Korda, "Chinese Nuclear Forces 2019," *Bulletin of the Atomic Scientists* 75, no. 4 (2019).

37. Tanvi Kulkarni, "India-Pakistan Nuclear CBMs: A New Approach," *South Asian Voices*, Stimson Center, May 19, 2016.

38. Joshua White, "The Other Nuclear Threat," *The Atlantic*, March 5, 2019.

39. Dinshaw Mistry, "Tempering Optimism about Nuclear Deterrence in South Asia," *Security Studies* 18, no. 1 (2009).

40. Toby Dalton and George Perkovich, *Not War, Not Peace: Motivating Pakistan to Prevent Cross-Border Terrorism* (Washington, D.C.: Carnegie Endowment for International Peace, 2016).

41. Husain Haqqani, "Gentle on Jihadis, Harsh on Dissidents: Ehsanullah's Escape Exposes Pakistan's Intentions," Hudson Institute, February 12, 2020.

42. Daniel Markey, "Preparing for Heightened Tensions between China and India," Council on Foreign Relations, April 19, 2021.

43. James Acton, *Revamping Nuclear Arms Control: Five Near-Term Proposals* (Washington, D.C.: Carnegie Endowment for International Peace, 2020).

SEVEN

Building Up the Indian Air Force

AMIT GUPTA

In 2020, Sino-Indian tensions led to calls for improving the capabilities of the Indian Air Force (IAF), since that service would play an important role in deterring China along the inhospitable and difficult terrain of the Himalayas. Yet, efforts to improve the IAF structure continue to be hindered by the complexities and at times self-defeating arms acquisition policies that India has pursued. This chapter discusses the weapons acquisitions and arms production strategies of India's Air Force as it seeks to develop a compelling force structure to achieve its regional and extraregional goals. The chapter begins by examining IAF capabilities versus those of China and Pakistan, and then examines India's weapons procurement strategies and options for modernizing the IAF fleet.

Conventional Deterrence

Despite the talk about India engaging in extraregional power projection, the primary mission of the IAF continues to be to deter conventional attacks by the Chinese and Pakistani Air Forces and to provide close air support to the Indian Army. In the case of Pakistan, this would entail maintaining air superiority and carrying out interdiction efforts against

Pakistani assets. In the case of China, the IAF would seek to stop a Chinese breakout in the Himalayan regions since, realistically, it cannot strike China's eastern seaboard, which is that country's strategic heartland.

To deal with this two-front threat, the IAF would like to have forty-two to forty-five squadrons of frontline fighters. In the near to medium future, this will consist mainly of about 270 Sukhoi Su-30MKIs. Supporting the Sukhois will be a mixed force of aging Jaguars, the Mirage 2000, the new Rafale, and according to current plans, 123 Tejas light combat aircraft (LCA) (forty in service in the early 2020s, with eighty more by the mid and late 2020s). While much of the force is aging, the Rafale, along with the Su-30, will be the primary strike aircraft; and the IAF believes the Rafale's beyond visual range Meteor missile will provide it with a significant advantage over its regional rivals because the missile has a range of 150 kilometers (km) and would give the Rafale a standoff capability from within Indian territory.[1]

China

The IAF mission versus China involves fighting a conventional air war in Ladakh and in the central and northeastern sectors. Here, China has significant capabilities because its military modernization has an emphasis on advanced fighter aircraft and high-performance beyond visual range missiles. Further, China's People's Liberation Army (PLA) has successfully developed a series of rocket launchers, artillery such as the PHL-03 with ranges of 150 km, and mobile land-based missiles with ranges of 650 km and 1,800 km.[2] Based in Tibet, such weaponry, linked to both satellites and drones for accurate targeting, would be able to deliver ordnance quite accurately against Indian forward positions without being degraded by the payload restrictions that aircraft face while taking off at high altitudes.

In the realm of air power, Arjun Subramaniam has warned about the changed nature of the Chinese threat, arguing that the Chinese not only have more fourth-generation fighters, but also a set of standoff weapons like the DH-10 cruise missile. This missile could carry out "debilitating surface-to-surface missile strikes on IAF combat capability that could severely hamper sortie generation rates, [and] the PLAAF's [People's Liberation Army Air Force's] distinctly superior network paralysing capabilities could seriously impact the IAF's command and control systems."[3] Subramaniam's analysis makes the important point that China is moving quite rapidly toward achieving a twenty-first-century air warfare capability. To counter the Chinese missile and aircraft threat, India asked Russia to accelerate its supply of the S-400 air defense system.

Having said that, Indian air power does give New Delhi the ability to inflict damage on the Chinese forces along the border because, as Frank O'Donnell and Alex Bollfrass argue, India's force structure and numerical strength, as well as the high-altitude terrain on the Chinese side, work to India's advantage.[4] O'Donnell and Bollfrass point to the superiority of the Sukhoi Su-30MKI over the Chinese J-10 (China's better, supposed fifth-generation fighters, the J-20 and J-31, are still in the developmental stage). Further, because they would operate from high-altitude airfields, Chinese aircraft would carry half their specified payload and would require midair refueling—although China only has fifteen tankers, which are also vulnerable to an attack by Indian fighters.[5] Moreover, the number of combat aircraft seems to favor India since the IAF could put up about 250 fighters to China's 170.[6] Such an advantage in aircraft and payload should allow the IAF to provide sufficient air support to the Indian Army as it seeks to deter a major Chinese incursion along the border.

India would still face difficulties in any sustained war with China. While India has conducted an anti-satellite weapons test and has a hypersonic cruise missile, the Brahmos, it lags behind China in building a technologically advanced fighting force that would prevail in a twenty-first-century battlefield environment.[7] As China makes advances in fighter aircraft, hypersonic missiles, anti-satellite weaponry, precision guided munitions, and battlefield management networks, India may find itself at a disadvantage in the coming decade. India would also have to invest substantially in such systems, but with a GDP that is roughly a fifth of China's, sustaining an expensive modernization effort may prove daunting.

A war between India and China would likely be a set of skirmishes along the border, where both sides trade a few ridges, but the Chinese use their surface-based artillery, missiles, and rockets to inflict damage on Indian forward positions.[8] India could fight China to a stalemate along the border, but the situation could change if Chinese military capabilities grow exponentially, thereby putting the Indian Armed Forces at a disadvantage. Even without a growth in Chinese capabilities, the possibility of a two-front war with both China and Pakistan would stretch thin the IAF's resources. And if the goal is to have the ability to fight a two-front war, then the IAF will have to acquire a larger squadron strength of more modern combat aircraft with better missiles and a capable air battle management system. These requirements were apparent in the aftermath of the 2019 IAF strike on Balakot in Pakistan.

Pakistan

Since the 1999 Kargil War, the IAF has been confident about its ability to prevail over the Pakistan Air Force (PAF). As one analyst has written, "The PAF today is no match for the IAF, as it is beset by both technological and numerical inferiority. The PAF today has very limited stand-off Precision Guided Munitions (PGM) delivery capability. Strategically and tactically, PAF is biased primarily toward Air Defence and limited Battlefield Air Strike (BAS) support to the Pakistan Army. Thus, today's PAF does not pose a major challenge to the IAF."[9] The IAF believes it could maintain air superiority and also provide the air support needed to pursue the Cold Start doctrine, which the Indian Army developed to deliver a rapid response to aggressive acts (including state-sponsored terrorism) by Pakistan.[10] The IAF may have painted an overly optimistic picture of its advantage, because the February 2019 confrontation between the IAF and the PAF exposed some shortcomings in the IAF's capabilities.

In response to the February 12, 2019 terrorist strike by a Jaish-e-Mohammed group suicide bomber, killing forty Indian paramilitary officers, the IAF, on February 26, crossed the Line of Control and bombed a Jaish facility near Balakot in Pakistan. Pakistan questioned the success of the strike, claiming that the bombs had missed the target and that the IAF, in fact, bombed a forest. Conversely, the IAF argued that it had used penetration bombs against the target, and, consequently, there was little damage to the exterior of the structures.

The next day, February 27, the PAF launched an attack with twenty-four aircraft that was countered by the IAF; in the engagement, the IAF lost a MiG-21 while claiming to have shot down a Pakistani F-16, though the kill could not be confirmed since the plane fell on the Pakistani side of the border.[11] With such conflicting claims, it is difficult to judge the effectiveness of either the IAF or the PAF, but some lessons can be learned from the air battle. First, the IAF was able to go about 60 kilometers into Pakistan and carry out a strike, thus giving some credence to its claim that it could penetrate Pakistani airspace to inflict damage. Moreover, it showed that the Indian political and military leadership was no longer going to be deterred by the threat of Pakistani nuclear retaliation.

On the other hand, the IAF was surprised by the quick reaction time of the PAF, and due to various factors had not kept enough airplanes at forward bases to meet the Pakistani attack.[12] India was to respond with a mix of Sukhois, MiG-21s, and Mirage 2000s to an attack by twenty-four Pakistani planes. The Sukhois had to take defensive measures to avoid Pakistani beyond-visual-range missiles launched by F-16s, and they could not get a lock on the PAF planes with their own air-to-air missiles.[13] The Sukhoi Su-30 Russian missiles lacked the range to shoot down Pakistani F-16s, which were launching advanced medium-range air-to-air missiles (AMRAAMs) from within Pakistani territory. This has led the IAF to seek the more capable Israeli Derby missile as well as to try to buy longer-range Russian missiles.[14] The Indian aircraft reportedly also had problems with their operational data links, and the PAF was perceived as having better jamming systems; this has resulted in the IAF seeking Software Defined Radios and better and more secure data links.[15] Further, the lack of a coordinated defense on the Indian side may have led to the friendly-fire shooting down of an Indian helicopter.

The IAF is also in the process of creating a singular air defense command and inducting more Airborne Early Warning and Control (AEW&C) aircraft along with a variety of high-end air defense systems to counter the PAF's AEW&C platforms, which provided it with a better air picture in the 2019 crisis.[16] It is apparent that the IAF did not have the technological advantage it thought, and it is seeking to regain the technology edge over the PAF. As mentioned below, this will require timely purchases, something that the Indian acquisitions system is not good at, and the purchase of appropriate technologies.

Nuclear Mission

The third important mission of the IAF is to deliver nuclear weapons, and this role is vital given India's stated nuclear doctrine and the concerns of its political leadership. India's nuclear doctrine stresses no first use, and its leadership is particularly concerned with preventing unauthorized and accidental launches. An IAF role helps reinforce civilian control over the military in nuclear decisionmaking. This is important, as the former head of the Indian National Security Advisory Board stated, because "the very nature of nuclear deterrence as practiced by a civilian democracy dictates that decisions relating to the nature and scope of the arsenal, its deployment and use, be anchored in the larger architecture of democratic governance."¹⁷ IAF nuclear weapons delivery missions would be under tight civilian control. Also, given their rapid deployment ability and mobility of transfer between air bases, the nuclear delivery aircraft would not have to be located in forward areas where the threat of being overrun exists.

Understanding Indian Weapons Acquisition and Production Policies

It has long been understood that while the demand for weapons in India came from the threat environment and the bureaucratic politics of the Indian military services and the national leadership, the ability to acquire these weapons came from either the availability of financial resources or external suppliers who were willing to provide such systems. The other possibility was to develop and build these weapons domestically.[18] There was an inherent tension in the bureaucratic agendas of the armed services and the national leadership, since the latter sought to build weapons domestically as this would lead to autonomy in foreign policy and help build up the industrial and technological base of the country.

Thus, the Nehru government gave the go-ahead to build the HF-24 Marut combat aircraft (along with a group of trainer aircraft) so that it could serve as the basis for creating a modern aircraft industry in the country that would go on to build passenger planes. Yet, at that time, India lacked the necessary industrial infrastructure and trained scientific personnel to build an aircraft from the ground up, and so the German designer Kurt Tank was enlisted along with a German design team to design and develop the aircraft. The plane depended heavily on imported components, could not achieve its goal of supersonic flight, and was obsolescent by the time it entered service with the IAF.[19] The desire of the political leadership and the defense science industry to produce weaponry indigenously did not go away with the failure of the Marut program. Both the MiG-21 and the Gnat were license produced in the country, although in neither case was the production of the aircraft fully indigenized, as critical components continued to be imported.

Despite these initial setbacks, both the political leadership and the defense science industry sought to continue the indigenous development of weaponry as India's defense production base grew in the 1960s and 1970s. By the 1980s, Prime Minister Indira Gandhi was to agree to the indigenous production of a light combat aircraft (later named Tejas) as well as an Indigenous Guided Missile Development Programme (IGMDP), which was to produce a series of air-launched, ground-launched, sea-launched, and ballistic missiles. The original idea for the Tejas was a lightweight fighter that replaced the MiG-21, which by the early 1980s was starting to show its age (though the MiG remains in service in smaller numbers). Additionally, following the Falklands War, the Indian political leadership recognized the need for both an indigenous defense production capability—Argentina, despite being an American ally was subjected to sanctions—and missiles like the French Exocet that had performed well in the conflict. This influenced the creation of the IGMDP in 1983.

Further, the armed services preferred to buy weapons abroad and, when given the option of buying domestically produced systems, demanded that indigenous weaponry be comparable to the best that was available abroad. The latter demand led to repeated changes in the requirements from the manufacturer, and this resulted in lengthy delays to the point that weaponry became obsolescent when it entered service. As a consequence, domestically produced systems were never fully integrated into the Indian fighting forces. India remained dependent on Western suppliers of conventional weapons but, in the case of weapons of mass destruction and their associated delivery systems, where India was unable to get an external supplier, domestic programs not only reached fruition but were integrated into the Indian Armed Forces—nuclear weapons and ballistic missiles being a case in point. The acquisition patterns of the IAF continue to follow these determinants.

The Acquisition Dilemma

Stephen Cohen once made the argument that the Indians believed that if they held out long enough in a negotiation for weapons purchases, they would get a good deal. Instead, what happened was that the requirements of the armed forces were delayed to the point that it adversely affected the country's force structure. Thus, the negotiations to buy the British Aerospace Hawk trainer took twenty years, while the Rafale acquisition took close to fifteen years from negotiations to the first delivery. In the former case, the lengthy time for acquisition led the IAF to complain that it had a severe shortage of trainer aircraft to instruct new pilots. In the latter case, the delayed acquisition of the Rafale, in much reduced numbers, led to the number of active combat squadrons slipping from a desired forty-two to thirty-one, and caused concern about the IAF's ability to maintain air superiority over Pakistan and to wage a two-front war against China and Pakistan. The government response to this declining squadron strength has been ad hoc: strong-arming the IAF to buy eighty-three additional Tejas planes from Hindustan Aeronautics Limited (HAL) for about $7 billion, with delivery in the mid and late 2020s; and, in 2020, falling back on Russia by ordering twelve more Sukhoi Su-30s and twenty-one mothballed MiG-29s reportedly in mint condition.

The IAF was reluctant about the Tejas because HAL was slow in production—it built only eight Tejas aircraft every year, taking two years to put one squadron into place—and because the Tejas Mark 1 was seen as not meeting required standards. The IAF had to agree to reduce standards to accept the aircraft. As India's comptroller general noted, "LCA Mark-I, which achieved Initial Operational Clearance (December 2013) has significant shortfalls (53 permanent waivers/concessions) in meeting the ASR [Air Staff Requirements] as a result of which, it will have reduced operational capabilities and reduced survivability, thereby limiting its operational employability when inducted into IAF squadrons."[20]

The IAF eventually gave Final Operation Clearance and accepted the plane, although it is not clear whether all of its requirements were met or whether compromises were made.[21] Financial pressures created by the softening of the Indian economy—both through a policy of demonetization, which hurt small businesses, and the crippling effect of COVID-19—seem to have influenced the IAF to buy eighty-three more Tejas Mark 1As and later, possibly, purchase the Tejas Mark 2 and an indigenously developed Advanced Medium Combat Aircraft (AMCA).[22] Yet it is unrealistic to expect that the AMCA will be designed and developed in a timely manner; it would likely not enter squadron service soon enough to make a favorable impact on India's military capabilities.

The government was also not clear on whether it would import 114 aircraft or opt for indigenous aircraft to fill the expected gap in India's fighter capabilities. As is the case in India, contradictory statements often emerge on weapons purchases. After the chief of defense staff (CDS), General Bipin Rawat, stated that India would not pursue the 114 fighter aircraft deal involving a foreign buyer, the chief of the IAF said that the competition to buy a new fighter for the IAF was still on. General Rawat said, "The Indian Air Force is switching that [order for foreign fighters] to the [Indian-built] LCA. The IAF is saying, I would rather take the indigenous fighter, it is good."[23] The IAF chief then contradicted the CDS, saying that the IAF was still going ahead with the import competition, with a component made in India: "This project (114 jets) is in the middle-weight and is in the Rafale class, in this issue, we will deal with it in the Make in India region, with an increase in [foreign direct investment] FDI, with support to the private sector. I think in future this will bring in technology which is required to support the aviation sector. I think it is important to have another generation of aircraft in terms of capability, technology as we go along [sic]."[24] India's arms acquisition pathologies appeared, once again, to be putting the IAF in a situation where it could end up with the worst of all worlds: the Tejas will likely not come in time to beef up the squadron levels that the IAF would like to maintain; and because the Tejas is to be delivered, the IAF may not get the funds to find a suitable imported aircraft.

In part, the desire to go with the Tejas and to scrap the indigenous production of the Rafale is based on the financial inability to undertake costly imports. In the past, India canceled or delayed deals when faced with financial constraints. A similar situation arose in the 2010s, when India kept its defense expenditure near 2 percent of GDP and, instead, funded social welfare programs.[25] In this context, defense spending becomes a casualty as the government asks the armed forces to continue using obsolescent weaponry and rely on what can be produced domestically.

Thus, the IAF needs to rectify the problem of stagnating defense budgets, declining squadron strength, a diminished technological advantage over Pakistan, the need to match a significantly advanced technological challenge from China, a lengthy and complex acquisition process that delays the induction of imported aircraft into squadron service, and a domestic supplier in HAL that has had trouble meeting the quantity and quality requirements of the IAF. In this context, the United States may be able to not only build up the capability of the IAF but also help grow the broader India-U.S. relationship into a more genuine security partnership.

The U.S.-India Partnership and the Role of Air Power

Over the past decade, one of the areas where U.S.-India cooperation has significantly increased is in the realm of arms sales, and the IAF has been the major beneficiary of such transactions. It obtained C-130J Hercules and C-17 heavy-lift aircraft to substantially increase its transport capabilities as well as its extraregional reach. Yet the United States tried unsuccessfully to sell fighter aircraft to India in the early 2010s, with the IAF then selecting the French Rafale over American F-16s and F-18s. From an Indian perspective, the use of air power to boost the Indo-U.S. relationship can be achieved through three methods: first, to use military sales to help attain the "Make in India" program of the Indian government; second, to help enhance the military capabilities of the IAF; third, to make arms sales and technology transfers so enticing that they would make India feel like a valued strategic partner.

One of the cornerstones for the Indian government's plan for economic development is to increase the manufacturing base in the country by getting foreign corporations to make products in India. The "Make in India" initiative focuses on twenty-five sectors where the government welcomes foreign investment; from an aerospace perspective the three key sectors are aviation, defense manufacturing, and space.[26] The Indian government should be focusing on the other twenty-two sectors in the Make in India initiative, since many of them require far less investment and do not require the same levels of technical and scientific competencies that are needed for the indigenous manufacture of modern weaponry.[27] The pitfalls of this obsession became apparent when the Indian government had to give up plans to indigenously manufacture the Rafale because HAL's labor costs were three times higher than those of Dassault, and it became cheaper to import the plane rather than to indigenously produce it.[28] More importantly, the IAF wanted Dassault to assume liability for the jets produced by HAL, but Dassault obviously refused because it did not have control over the production process.[29]

Similarly, a number of political, military, and financial problems would arise if Lockheed were to secure a contract for the F-21 (the new name for the F-16 given to soothe Indian sensitivities about Pakistan using the aircraft). Ashley Tellis made a compelling case for the plane, pointing out that the F-16 variant would be high-performance and cost-effective, and serve as a bridge to the eventual purchase of the F-35—the latter aircraft, it was felt, would give the IAF a major qualitative advantage over both Pakistan and China.[30] The IAF, however, is not keen to acquire the F-21 because it believes that the PAF is familiar with the performance parameters of the plane, and, after the 2019 Balakot strikes, there is a degree of resentment in air force circles that the plane was used against India.[31] Moreover, there are questions about who the end user would be for aircraft or spares produced in India, and some analysts are concerned about Indian-produced aircraft and spares going to less friendly nations.[32] It makes no sense, therefore, to keep trying to persuade the Indian government to buy a plane that, while extremely capable, comes with a lot of political and military baggage.

While the F-21 may not be the plane for India, the United States has to acknowledge that there is a consensus in India to engage in techno-nationalism and develop weapons systems indigenously, and that is why successive Indian governments have not killed the Tejas fighter program. Washington, therefore, has to think in terms of programs that are appropriate for India's defense manufacturing base and can fit into India's Make in India agenda. Three such projects could be transferring the C-17 production line to India, helping with the redesign of the Tejas Mark 2 and weaponizing the Hawk trainer, and building up India's unmanned aerial vehicles (UAV) force.

First, India has acquired the C-130J and the C-17 medium- and heavy-lift transport aircraft—to the extent that the IAF now has eleven C-17s, giving it the world's second-largest C-17 fleet. The C-17 production line is closed, but before it was, several countries expressed an interest in acquiring the aircraft since it gave allies and coalition partners an easy way to "plug and play" with the United States. Offering India the C-17 production line, if the machine tools and other infrastructure are available, would give HAL a guaranteed production line and the plane itself would not be as technologically complex or subject to obsolescence as a modern fighter aircraft would.

Second, the IAF has committed to an additional eighty-three Tejas Mark 1A fighters, and eventually by 2025–2026, HAL could be building prototypes and test versions of the Tejas Mark 2 fighter. The Tejas Mark 2 will have an American F414 engine, an Israeli Active Electronically Scanned Array (AESA) radar, as well as improvements in the configuration of the cockpit.[33] Still, the plane will have to undergo major redesign. As Ashley Tellis argued, the problems on the Tejas can be mitigated, and it can be made into a satisfactory standoff fighter if it can successfully integrate the AESA radar and a lethal beyond visual range missile like the AIM-120 AMRAAM or the Israeli Derby[34] (the AIM-120 has been offered to India as part of an Integrated Air Defense Weapons System package).[35] One way to bring the Tejas Mark 2 program to timely fruition is for the United States to offer India technological and managerial assistance in successfully completing the program, especially since critical American technology is being integrated into the plane.

A related solution may lie in weaponizing the IAF's eighty odd training aircraft, the Hawk, which has been used by the United States to train its pilots. A weaponized Hawk, with a decent radar, can carry the AIM-120 missile and air-to-ground ordnance, thus offering a relatively cheaper solution to the shortfall in squadron numbers. While there is talk in India of weaponizing the Hawk through indigenous efforts, American assistance would lead to the rapid development of a cheaper but lethal aircraft for the IAF.[36]

Third, the United States can also work with the Indian government to both transfer technology and create a manufacturing base in India by coproducing UAVs to meet India's requirements for intelligence, surveillance, and reconnaissance (ISR), border security, and for using firepower in less demanding combat situations. In 2020, the IAF decided not to purchase armed UAVs because, after Iran shot down a Global Hawk, the thinking in New Delhi was that the aircraft was expensive and vulnerable to a hostile surface-to-air defense environment (in 2021, however, India revisited the issue and was considering the purchase of thirty armed Predator/Sky Guardian drones).[37] Yet, UAVs would fulfill multiple requirements for the IAF and its sister services, especially in the ISR and border security missions. The 2008 Mumbai terror attack occurred because Mumbai harbor was not properly monitored. In 2020, an Indian colonel lost his life at Galwan river valley in Ladakh in a situation where Indian forces in the area did not have tactical drones to fly over the contested territory, and therefore had to send a reconnaissance patrol with tragic results. Building a series of drones in India—from tactical to high-altitude long-endurance ones—would give the Indian Armed Forces real-time intelligence and, where the air space is not contested, allow for promoting border security because such UAVs would help in detecting incursions by terrorist groups.

A domestic UAV production line would fit into the Indian government's demand to Make in India but, unlike more complex systems like fourth- and fifth-generation fighter aircraft, building a range of drones would be within the technological capabilities of India's defense industry. Manufacturing such aircraft in India would also allow for their export to other countries.

The cash-strapped armed services are proposing partnering with Israel Aircraft Industries, under Project Cheetah, to modernize India's ninety Heron drones (operational across all three branches of the military) with satellite navigation, air-to-ground missiles, and precision weapons. Separately, in 2020, the Indian Navy leased two Sky Guardians to monitor the Indian Ocean region and the Strait of Malacca. There still exists, therefore, the opportunity to set up a U.S. drone coproduction agreement with India since American drones offer a more advanced technological capability than their Israeli counterparts. The question for the Indian government is whether the United States will facilitate offsets and the transfer of technology, and, in fact, this was one of the major reasons the Sky Guardian deal fell through in 2020.[38]

The jewel in the crown, however, would be for the United States to think in terms of selling India the F-35 Lightning fighter. Apart from the desire to maintain a qualitative edge over its neighbors, the Indian government has also viewed arms transfers as a way to obtain transfers of technology and to leverage political gains from the arms relationship. While, for reasons discussed above, technology transfers, especially in the case of the F-35 (which is a fifth-generation fighter, and, therefore, the manufacture of which would require a costly investment by India in infrastructure, machine tools, and trained scientific personnel) would not be achieved; however, the other two objectives of such an arms transfer would be met. Transfer of the F-35 would ensure that India maintained a qualitative advantage over Chinese fourth- and fifth-generation fighters—the J16, J-20, and J-31. It would also be another game changer in the U.S.-India relationship much in the way of the nuclear deal of the mid-2000s. And it would prove to the skeptics in New Delhi policy circles that the United States is serious about building a strategic relationship with India.

Lastly, for the two countries and two air forces to come together, the IAF should be able to communicate with other potential coalition partners in the Indo-Pacific region, which would entail buying a common data link system. If the IAF is to work with American partners in Southwest and Southeast Asia, then its aircraft need to be able to communicate and share data with them. It would also, if the strategic partnership becomes stronger, permit India to access U.S. electronic and space assets in a future conflict.

In conclusion, the IAF has to work around a set of pathologies that have plagued Indian weapons acquisition and force development since independence. In such circumstances, what the United States can do for the IAF is constrained by domestic pressures in India, most notably the desire to indigenously design and produce weaponry. The other problem is the one faced by many democracies, which is the choice between using governmental resources for social welfare projects or for defense modernization. Given such constraints, the United States can work to incrementally build Indian capabilities, but to bring about a major shift in military capability would require a change in the attitude of the Indian government and a fundamental reorientation of the country's political economy to encourage a techno-global as opposed to a techno-national approach to weapons acquisition and arms production.

NOTES

1. Ajit K. Dubey, "Meteor Missile Deal Set to Win Back India's Aerial Supremacy against Rivals," *Daily Mail* (U.K.), December 18, 2017.

2. CSIS Missile Defense Project, "Missiles of China," Center for Strategic and International Studies, Washington, D.C., July 16, 2020; *Military and Security Developments Involving the People's Republic of China 2019,* Annual Report to Congress, Office of the Secretary of Defense, 2019, p. 48.

3. Arjun Subramaniam, "Closing the Gap: A Doctrinal & Capability Appraisal of the IAF & the PLAAF," Observer Research Foundation online paper, May 2, 2018.

4. Frank O'Donnell and Alex Ballfross, *The Strategic Postures of China and India: A Visual Guide* Harvard Kennedy School, Belfer Center Science in International Affairs Report, 2020, pp. 8–9.

5. Ibid., p. 9.

6. Ibid. p. 22.

7. For India's development of hypersonic weapons, see Amit Gupta, "The Missile Age: Is India Ready?" *Geopolitics*, June 2018, pp. 8–11.

8. For a future India-China war in the Himalayas, see Amit Gupta, "4 Reasons Why India Couldn't Win a War with China," *The National Interest*, July 17, 2020.

9. Vivek Kapur, "Challenges for the Indian Air Force 2032," *Journal of Defence Studies* 7, no. 1 (2013), p. 83.

10. See Jaganath Sankaran, "The Enduring Power of Bad Ideas: 'Cold Start' and Battlefield Nuclear Weapons in South Asia," *Arms Control Today*, November 2014.

11. "Pakistan Denies Indian Claims It Used U.S. F-16 Jets to Down Warplane," *The Guardian*, March 3, 2019.

12. Interview with a senior Indian military officer, New Delhi, March 8, 2019.

13. Vishal Thapar, "The Sukhoi Vulnerability and Other Post-Balakot Lessons," *SP's Aviation* 9, 2019.

14. "India Is Turning to Israel after Its Russian Made Missiles Turned into Duds," *Indian Defence News*, March 3, 2020.

15. Sanjiv Varma, "IAF Lacked ODLs during Balakot Strike, Fighters Went Incommunicado," *Times of India*, December 15, 2019.

16. Joy Mitra, "Taking Stock a Year after Balakot: India's Crisis Response and Takeaways," *South Asian Voices*, March 9, 2020.

17. Shyam Saran, Public Lecture at India Habitat Center, New Delhi, April 24, 2013.

18. Amit Gupta, *Building an Arsenal: The Evolution of Regional Power Force Structures* (London and Westport, CT: Praeger, 1997), pp. 14–16.

19. Thomas W. Graham, "India," in *Arms Production in Developing Countries: An Analysis of Decision Making,* edited by James Everett Katz (Lexington, MA: Lexington Books, 1984), p. 170.

20. Report of the Comptroller and Auditor General of India, *Design, Development, Manufacture and Induction of Light Combat Aircraft*, Union Government Defence Services (Air Force) Performance Audit 17 of 2015 (New Delhi, 2015), p. vi.

21. Wilson Thomas, "IAF Operationalises Second LCA Squadron, Inducts First LCA Tejas in FOC Standard," *The Hindu*, May 27, 2020.

22. Dinakar Peri, "83 LCA Mk1A Deal High Priority: Air Chief," *The Hindu*, May 18, 2020.

23. "Tejas to Beat Rafale, F-21? IAF Switching to LCA Says Bipin Rawat," *The Week*, May 15, 2020.

24. Snehesh Alex Phillip, "IAF Chief Contradicts CDS Rawat, Says Plans to Buy 114 Foreign Fighters besides LCA Tejas," *The Print*, May 18, 2020.

25. Mohinder Pal Singh, "India's Defence Budget in a Ten Trillion Economy," *Financial Express*, February 5, 2019. In 2010–2011, defense expenditure was 2.5 percent of GDP and 16.3 percent of central government expenditure; it decreased to 2.1 percent of GDP and 15.5 percent of government expenditure in 2020–2021. See "Demand for Grants 2020–21 Analysis: Defence," PRS (Parliamentary Research Service) Legislative Research, New Delhi, www.prsindia.org/parliamenttrack/budgets/demand-grants-2020-21-analysis-defence#:~:text=The%20expenditure%20on%20defence%20constitutes,estimated%20GDP%20for%202020%2D21.

26. For a list of sectors, see the website www.makeinindia.com/sectors.

27. Amit Gupta, "Grand Strategy for Modi 2.0," *Geopolitics*, July 2019, p. 30.

28. Sudhi Ranjan Sen, "HAL's Jets Costlier Than Foreign Ones, Says Defense Ministry Audit," *Hindustan Times*, October 19, 2018.

29. Gautam Datt, "HAL's Poor Track Record Overshadows IAF Plans to Buy 126 Dassault Rafale Jets," *India Today*, April 5, 2013.

30. Ashley J. Tellis, *Dogfight, India's Medium Multi-Role Combat Aircraft Decision* (Washington, D.C.: Carnegie Endowment for International Peace, 2011), p. 129.

31. Ambika Gupta, "Challenges of F-21 through 'Make in India,'" *Geopolitics*, November 2019, p. 16.

32. Ibid., pp. 16–17.

33. Sudhi Ranjan Sen, "Metal-Cutting for Single-Engine Tejas Fighter Planes to Begin in February," *Hindustan Times*, December 9, 2019.

34. Ashley J. Tellis, *Troubles, They Come in Battalions: The Manifold Travails of the Indian Air Force* (Washington, D.C.: Carnegie Endowment for International Peace, 2016), pp. 30–32.

35. Lalit K. Jha, "US Approves Sale of Integrated Air Defence Weapon System to India," *Mint*, February 11, 2020.

36. Shiv Aroor, "SAAW SOON: HAL's Souped-Up Hawk Trainer All Set to Fire Indian Anti-Airfield Weapon," *Livefist*, February 23, 2019, www.livefistdefence.com/saaw-soon-hals-souped-up-hawk-all-set-to-fire-indian-anti-airfield-weapon/.

37. Shishir Gupta, "India Rethinks Buying US Armed Drones," *Hindustan Times*, June 5, 2020.

38. Sandeep Unnithan, "Why the Indo-US Drone Deal Did Not Go Through," *India Today*, November 3, 2020.

EIGHT

Pakistan's Political Culture and Its Implications for Democracy

MARVIN G. WEINBAUM

Any understanding of Pakistan's difficulties with governance, especially its struggle to achieve sustainable democracy, is incomplete without taking into account the contribution of the country's political culture. The assimilated values and predispositions that together form Pakistan's political culture help explain the behavior of its political institutions and state actors, and broad public attitudes. Embedded political values rooted in the country's founding motifs have been shaped by its seventy-five-year history as well as by ascendant ideologies and societal norms. An understanding of Pakistan's political culture allows a fuller appreciation of the country's aspirations as well as its insecurities and obsessions. Political culture serves as the internalized filter through which many public policy decisions pass, and an examination of political culture enables an understanding of the obstacles to governance reform. While cultural norms can promote national unity and comity, they also contribute to civic intolerance and violence. Their negative influences are clearly visible in the country's widespread distrust of authority and ambivalence toward domestic extremism, and help create the, at times, distorted lens through which Pakistanis look at the external world.

Few commentaries on Pakistan have explicitly identified those behaviors that are traceable to the country's deep cultural wells. Little thought has been given to probing the predisposing factors that guide and constrain political decisionmakers and set much of the tone and direction of public discourse. Nor has enough attention been devoted to the socialization processes by which political values are imbibed. Pakistan's educational system, its widely respected military, and family and peer pressures are among factors that play a critical part in the process. Islamic ideals and prescriptions serve as well as powerful influences. The media, through their ability to shape mass opinion, regularly reinforces many of the society's core political values.

By most estimates Pakistan ranks low among countries in good governance and high as a conflict-ridden and often violent society. It is generally acknowledged to have a poor record in providing basic public services such as education and health. It is also plagued by widespread corruption and other ethical shortcomings and is dominated by narrow interests. Notable as well has been the absence of political will and political instruments necessary to bring reform. Only in recent years has Pakistan begun to come to grips with the challenges to its domestic security posed by militant, extremist groups. At least some of these deficits seem traceable to normative influences. While some elements of the political culture can be a source of national unity and strength, contributing to the stability and predictability on which society and the state depend, much of what constitutes the prevailing political culture in Pakistan is dysfunctional, even for many of the goals to which most Pakistanis aspire. As such, significant reforms of Pakistan's governance, including efforts to reinforce democratic ideals and deal with political radicalism, would seem to hinge on the building of supportive beliefs and values.

Cultural explanations do not, of course, exclude the influence of other factors in accounting for the weakness of governance and fears for basic security in Pakistan. "Objective conditions," such as poverty and income inequality, offer concrete ways of understanding the drivers of public attitudes and policies, as well as of civil conflict. Some observers stress constitutional and electoral provisions among structural factors that are said to undermine responsible and responsive government. The deficit of able leadership through most of the country's history is frequently cited, as is the belief that the country has been let down by corrupt political figures motivated by raw ambition and material gain. Governance is described as encumbered by politicians and bureaucrats who are intent on keeping the political system as a fiefdom of power and privilege. Military asymmetries with India can rationalize security concerns and the army's domestic defensiveness.

A normative approach adds a deeper understanding to Pakistan's experiences with the intimate connections between governance and security. Anatol Lieven has cogently argued that the stability and security that come through those values sustaining kinship ties in much of Pakistani society also impede the country's ability to undertake needed political reforms.[1] In general, an examination of the underlying factors in weak governance can help to better understand Pakistan's frequent incapacity to protect its people and institutions against injustice and violence. Poor local law enforcement is one outcome of the predispositions of government actors in viewing their roles and responsibilities. More clearly, indifferent security adversely affects the capability of governing institutions to deliver services and also influences how citizens evaluate and form expectations about their public servants.

Gabriel Almond and Sidney Verba in their book *Civic Culture: Political Attitudes and Democracy in Five Nations* have described political culture as based on the cognitions, evaluations, and feelings that individuals have toward the political world.[2] As base values and unwritten societal norms, they predispose individuals and groups to political attitudes and motivate political behavior. Unlike ephemeral attitudes occasioned by singular events and personalities, the norms of political culture ordinarily are slow to change and tend to endure. They must also be distinguished from national character, a now largely discredited concept. National character is an overly simplified generalization about a nation and its people. Its features are depicted as so deep-rooted that they seem immune to change. Political culture can evolve, however, and change can be accelerated by transformative, traumatic events.

Cultural explanations must be used judiciously. They ordinarily lack the definitional clarity of other explanatory variables and do not lend themselves to empirical study. (In countries like Pakistan, political opinion surveys are prohibited from asking sensitive questions or are banned entirely.) There is always a danger that the culture variable may be used as a residual category, resorted to when other explanations seem incomplete or unsatisfactory. It is also sometimes difficult to distinguish political culture as a phenomenon from the political behavior with which it is interacting.[3]

This chapter is mainly focused on those cultural values having the greatest impact on the country's governing practices, particularly as they relate to promoting democratic governance and undermining law and order. An examination of the popular culture should help account for how most citizens perceive their institutions and leaders, and for the expectations they have about governance. For all its homage to Pakistan's foundational ideals, this popular culture is subject to a normative climate several of whose features undermine the trust in government necessary to sustain democracy in Pakistan.

But Pakistan's political culture is also segmented. There exist beyond popular culture distinctive subcultures with their own cognitive maps. This chapter describes three subcultures: the country's more politically conscious educated, urban middle class; its federal bureaucracy; and its military. An urban educated culture best expresses the aspirations for an open society. It provides the country's opinion leaders and forms the civil society so vital to carrying forward reform. But this diverse group also values stability and tends to avoid confrontation. Easily disillusioned with politics, it generally lacks the necessary sustained commitment to effect political transformation. The bureaucratic culture, conservative and self-perpetuating, acts as a principal impediment to change. It feels privileged and seeks to avoid responsibility, and its embedded corruption contributes to a closed political system. The military holds an even stronger sense of entitlement. Its subculture stresses its role as the nation's guardian, its ultimate protector. Holding the country's political leadership in disdain, the military believes it has a duty to intervene when civilian rule falters. The three subcultures together, as this chapter reveals, are well positioned to set the pace of political change and determine the prospects for Pakistan's democratic growth.

A fuller picture of the country's political culture landscape than the one presented here would also need to include descriptions of Pakistan's tribal and feudal subcultures, and a fuller recognition of national- and provincial-level differences. It would further have to take account of the mores of the country's Islamic establishment, and especially those elements engaged politically. Even then, a complete picture is impossible without an appreciation of the variations and divisions within the several subcultures. The way the several subcultures interact, both to reinforce some values and to put others in contention, would also contribute to an understanding of their overall impact on political and social outcomes in Pakistan. In concluding, this chapter finds that despite an otherwise largely critical assessment of Pakistan's political culture, some redeeming political and social features leave open the promise of improved governance.

The Popular Culture

As in most societies, citizens in Pakistan have deeply internalized values about family and religion and are preoccupied by the daily economic struggles they face. The political world only occasionally, if at all, impinges on their consciousness and then forms only the most generalized impressions and valuations. These nevertheless shape generalized tendencies that, taken together, help define Pakistan's popular political culture.

Though Pakistan's popular political culture is not without positive qualities, several of its most distinguishable features, namely distrust, detachment, distortion, and denial, work strongly against the achieving of effective governance and state-building. Distrust is responsible for a breakdown in the level of respect for the authority that is necessary to sustain an orderly body politic, particularly a democratic one. Detachment often stems from the feelings of powerlessness among the citizenry that account for passivity and allow for unaccountability and manipulation. Distortion is the tendency to see the political world in an alternate universe of conspiratorial thinking, where nothing is what it seems to be, and the offered authoritative narratives are untrue. Denial often takes the form of blaming others for what plagues the polity and society, and for allowing those who can bring about change to elude responsibility. While some political figures in Pakistan have brought promise of an overhaul of political values and a reshaped narrative of the role of government and public service, their subsequent failures to live up to high expectations have only succeeded in reinforcing the normal skepticism about politics.

Distrust and Detachment

An easily recognized feature of Pakistan's popular political culture is the lack of trust and the cynicism directed toward public institutions. Over Pakistan's history, constitutional crises, breakdowns in law and order, and constant intrigues and corruption have denied opportunities for elected governments wanting to build public confidence and trust. Those in political life are viewed as greedy and manipulative, using their office to protect and enhance their wealth and assure that they remain in power. Most Pakistanis are appalled by the corruption that permeates government, especially in areas where it affects them personally. Authorities are seen as being unable to provide security and as tolerating injustice. Those in public office are held as being unconcerned with the basic social welfare. Much of the system is felt to be closed and conspiratorial, with the business of government largely irrelevant to the real issues. The cynical popular feelings that can serve as a defense against disappointment with government can also make more difficult efforts to mobilize popular support for needed reforms.

In a World Values survey, only 37.0 percent of Pakistanis indicated they were either "very" or "somewhat" interested in politics (by contrast, 89.5 percent of those interviewed labeled religion as "very important" in their lives).[4] The public's low interest is reflected in its ordinarily dismal turnout for national and provincial elections. Only rarely do elections at the national and provincial levels reveal the full indignation of the public over their governance. Large numbers of Pakistanis continue to believe that elections are exercises in intimidation and outright fraud, largely irrelevant to their lives. The public is accustomed to having candidates try to belittle and humiliate opponents. Elections are not expected to offer constructive political dialogue with clear policy alternatives of the kind needed to hold leaders accountable and instill a deep sense of civic virtue and pride in the system. Most national elections have ordinarily seen roughly 40 percent of eligible voters participating. Not until the 2013 and 2018 elections, when turnouts were nearly 60 percent, was there evidence of more active public engagement with the electoral process. Despite some complaints that the 2018 election lacked fairness and transparency, a survey found that 84 percent of the public was willing to accept the results.[5]

A great number of Pakistanis are ignorant of and uninvolved with the state. The public's experience with governance in Pakistan over the years has led most to avoid, if not dread, contacts with state institutions. There is no better illustration of how the public is disposed toward the bureaucracy and the political system more generally than the government's glaring inability to collect taxes. Pakistan's low tax extraction reflects the power of entrenched elite interests to block reform. Most taxpayers justify their resistance to paying what is due by citing the poor delivery of government services and the questionable uses to which taxes are put. More deeply, tax avoidance is an expression of deep-seated beliefs about unfairness in the system.

Further reflecting distrust is the fact that only those who are better off in the society are perceived as able to make claims against the system. The average citizen sees the protection of the laws as applying to only a privileged few. As V. S. Naipaul wrote, there are public lies and private truths.[6] Private truths hold that the systems of political and economic justice have little to offer the common man. Naipaul observed that in Pakistan everybody—civil servants, politicians, the military, etc.—tries to fool everybody else, but in fact nobody is really fooled.

Overall, Pakistan's citizens exhibit a low sense of political efficacy—believing that ordinary people can do little to influence the course of events. Although this has shown some signs of changing, a great number of Pakistanis have accepted the idea that they are spectators to the political process, onlookers to a privileged higher-level contestation for power. Though given opportunities to participate, their choices seem controlled and predetermined. As much as citizens may be appalled at unethical behavior among their politicians, law officers, judges, and even clerics, they seem much of the time reconciled. This leads to passivity and to resignation in the face of corruption and nepotism. Only recently have many in the public begun to question the ascent of political party leaders chosen along dynastic lines. Yet there is still no popular clamor for intraparty democracy.

Some trace public submissiveness to a Pakistan that has failed to throw off those semifeudal qualities that stand in the way of holding the state accountable to its citizenry and that profit from keeping people ignorant. Others find the cynical views of government as possibly deriving from Pakistan being popularized as an idealized Islamic state. By this reckoning, having established a homeland for Muslims and laid the groundwork for an ethical regime, the subsequent behavior of those holding power in Pakistan has cast doubt on the ability of secular institutions to measure up to expectations. Measured against Islamic authority, Pakistan's leadership seems especially unworthy in its inability to provide the expected qualities of dedication, piety, and achievement. This provides, of course, an opening for Islamic extremist claims that only rule by Sharia provides salvation for the state.

Despite the low esteem in which Pakistan's citizens view their leaders, the broad public periodically shows a willingness to place its faith in individuals perceived as larger-than-life. These figures are somehow expected to transcend politics, rectify injustices, and alleviate people's hardships. But given these high expectations, all the nation's putative heroes are bound to disappoint their followers and are ultimately pulled down from their pedestals and discredited. Only the iconic Mohammad Ali Jinnah, or Quaid-i-Azam ("Great Leader"), the nation's founding father, has been spared, likely saved by the ambiguity of his public utterances and his tragically short tenure as the nation's leader. Others who rose initially to high public esteem were destined to disappoint and had ignominious ends.

Most Pakistanis would agree that their country's democratic future is clouded, and most feel insecure about their own prospects. In an opinion survey done for the International Republican Institute in 2018, 60 percent of Pakistanis, disturbed mainly by inflation and unemployment, believed their country was headed in the wrong direction.[7] Many in Pakistan regret what they consider to be the deterioration of what was once more effective public administration. Some even look back longingly at what they believe was the greater efficiency and legal ethics of the country's colonial legacy. They resent leaders' autocratic behavior and the endemic corruption. Much pent-up anger at government is directed at the absence of a social safety net and delivery of essential services. Overall, the alienation from Pakistan's authority figures and institutions, born of distrust and detachment in the public sphere, helps to form, along with socioeconomic factors, the soil in which political radicalism takes root.

Distortion and Denial

Notwithstanding the pride that most of Pakistan's citizens take in their religious heritage, they appear to lack psychological armor, the confidence and self-assuredness that are normally found in countries with longer and stronger national identities. One manifestation is the paranoid thinking that seems to account for much of Pakistan's fears of nefarious outside forces working against the state and its people.

Collective political paranoia easily gives rise to conspiracy theories. Writing about Pakistan, Emma Duncan once observed, it often seems that "everybody is an amateur conspiracy theorist, nothing is taken at face value."[8] Intrigue and deception are seen as the rule, not the exception. The result is a popular willingness to embrace wild conjectures that rest on a thin reed of plausibility.

Political paranoia has its roots in an absence of government transparency in making available full, creditable information. It is fed by a general distrust of official explanations, the feeling that the full truth must lie elsewhere. Conspiracy theories put a face on the public's belief that confounding and manipulating forces shape their lives and the country's fate. Formal allocations of power prescribed by the constitution or laws are viewed as masking the actions of the real power brokers, whose hands reach into every corridor of government. Stories transmitted by rumors discrediting political actors acquire credibility for their familiarity through repetition, and because they originate from multiple sources. As a means of constructing reality, this is either an invitation to apathy in politics or an inducement to move toward more violent means of political expression. It leaves mass publics susceptible to those who offer quick and simplistic solutions.

There arises from the same cultural climate an inclination to blame others for most of Pakistan's deepest problems. Rather than Pakistan's own domestic policies, the United States, India, and the International Monetary Fund are often held accountable as predatory external actors for the country's economic woes. A "foreign hand" is often cited in explaining dangers facing the country. Once identified almost exclusively with the British, this has been used in alleging conspiratorial behavior on the part of Americans, Indians, Afghans, or Israelis. Together, in the public's eye, Pakistan's enemies are seen as plotting to neutralize, if not seize, Pakistan's nuclear assets and discredit Islam. In a spirit of denial, for years policy elites and the public downplayed responsibility for the threats posed by domestic extremism. To some degree the growth of radical militancy and sectarian violence is still explained as the targeted efforts of Pakistan's enemies to create national discord and disunity. Insurgency in the tribal areas and in Baluchistan is widely seen as occurring at the instigation and with the quiet backing of external powers.

A popular view among Pakistanis that has faded little over the years, including among the political elites, is that 9/11 was an American conspiracy. In 2011 when an American military operation killed Osama bin Laden, many claimed that bin Laden was never at the attack site, or if he had been, the CIA had placed him there. A Pew poll found that 63 percent of Pakistanis disapproved of the American operation and a further 55 percent regretted bin Laden was dead.[9] A widely expressed belief that bin Laden had died as a martyr was revived in June 2020 by Prime Minister Imran Khan in public remarks critical of the United States.[10] Any sense of Pakistan's responsibility for bin Laden's presence in Abbottabad or its military's defensive failings has been deflected by allegations of the immoral or sinister behavior of others.

Despite the great number of media outlets in the country, the public seems uncomfortable and frequently intolerant of views that challenge the popular narrative. There has been no wide public demand for serious debate about how to engage the Americans or the West or how to address domestic terrorism. The country's military and civilian leaders refrain from taking issue with even the most bizarre conspiracy tales and frequently amplify them. For elected officials to speak up is politically risky. Only a few intrepid media commentators have dared to air unpopular views. Even they know to steer clear of certain sensitive issues, especially those touching on the military's prerogatives and the exercise of Islamic doctrine. Truly investigative journalism is rare, and those few who have ventured have had to fear for their careers and sometimes their lives.

Educated, Urban Middle-Class Subculture

Within the popular culture are several distinguishable subcultures, one of the more prominent is associated with Pakistan's middle class. Actually, the country can be described as having several middle classes. Disaggregated, there are at least four broad groups: better-educated, Western-oriented individuals, many in professional and technical occupations; middle- and most upper-level government employees; smaller merchants; and clerics. These groups differ to some degree in their educational backgrounds, income levels, political affiliations, and policy preferences. The urban better-educated are most clearly distinguishable from a lower-middle class of shopkeepers and clerics, who are generally more politically, religiously, and socially conservative; less tolerant of civil and human rights, especially women's rights; and less enamored with things Western.[11] The better-educated urban middle class is often distinctive in many normative attributes, including its expectations about government institutions and leaders. This subculture is more likely than any other to be disillusioned and deeply cynical about the state and a political leadership seen as incompetent and self-serving. It is from this body of the population that cricketer-turned-politician Imran Khan initially attracted followers and with which he built an electoral base broad enough to propel him to the office of prime minister in 2018.

Members of this segment of the middle class largely reside in Pakistan's urban centers and are comparatively well-off and educated. Because they have a major presence in the media, higher education, and the professions, their voices in national affairs are heard disproportionately. Activists within the expanding civil society are mainly drawn from this educated middle class. Their more liberal predispositions are not free of many of the suspicions, doubts, and distortions that characterize the popular culture, and the class has found ways to coexist with the countryry's feudals, who still dominate much of the country's politics. In an increasingly urbanizing society and globalizing economy, the urban educated form a critical mass of people whose futures are dependent on a modern economy and a more open society. They are also that element of society best positioned to present counternarratives to those proffered by the country's extremist groups.

Maleeha Lodhi has argued that an emerging middle class can bring about a "shift in the centers and instruments of power and influence," and allow for the transformation of Pakistan's politics. She saw indications that with continuing economic growth and consumerism as well as a freed media, this class may be able to pose a threat to a narrow oligarchy drawn from landowning and mercantile elites and civilian and military bureaucracies.[12] Democratic theory has regularly stressed that middle-class values play an influential role in creating and sustaining a responsible, representative system of government. The interests and values of an educated middle class have historically been instrumental in promoting institutions that widen participation and expand political freedoms. Middle-class material gains are often portrayed as paving the way for wider segments of the society to acquire a voice in choosing their rulers and influencing policy.

The politically aware urban middle class in Pakistan makes up a decidedly minor proportion of the population and of the middle class as a whole. Estimates of the total size of the urban middle class among Pakistan's roughly 205 million people vary widely. Writing in 2013, Lodhi believed it numbers some 30 million.[13] A 2017 study has placed the number in this urban, educated middle class at 50 million.[14] Lodhi included among this group educated professionals, technically trained individuals, and the middle-income employees of the state and of business enterprises. Economist Shahid Javed Burki has depicted them as an upwardly mobile, educated class with democratic instincts and a stake in a growing modern economy and civil society.[15]

The idea that a better-educated segment of the middle class could spearhead democratic and constitutional reforms received a great boost with the organization of the lawyers' movement in 2007. It emerged following President Pervez Musharraf's ouster of Pakistan's chief justice, which ultimately led to Musharraf's removal. Together with an amendment to the constitution intended to strengthen government checks and balances, it was widely viewed at the time as a victory by a middle class seeking long overdue reforms. It was said to show that when properly organized, civil society organizations are able to mobilize public opinion against elites accustomed to dictating policy.

But subsequent events illustrated the diversity among civil society groups and the difficulty of generalizing about so broad a modern urban middle class. Even though the lawyers claimed to be championing constitutional governance and democratic change, subsequent actions revealed a socially conservative set of beliefs. The cohesion in the lawyers' movement, which was so impressive through 2008, slowly dissolved once the single issue of reinstating the ousted chief justice was resolved. But just three years later, the country's lawyers voiced broad vocal sympathy for the assassin of the pro-reform Punjab governor Salman Taseer. And in 2018, the lawyers, as a group, drew attention for their vigorous defense of the badly abused blasphemy law in the highly publicized Asia Bibi case.

There have been serious obstacles to an educated middle class providing the new leadership. Access to the top positions of power is often blocked by elite nepotism and corruption. Because Pakistan's major political party organizations are not internally democratic, opportunities for upper mobility within their ranks is limited. Promotion of the progressive agenda is also difficult because an indigenous liberal intellectual tradition is underdeveloped. Many of the core values of liberal political thinking have been imported without much adaption to Pakistan's political landscape. Interestingly, considerable intellectual energy that might have gone into evolving more compatible institutional forms has been absorbed in debate over the country's historical legacy.

The great number of those sharing the better-educated middle-class subculture identify with the Jinnah legacy, which they seek to interpret as having prescribed for Pakistan a tolerant, inclusive liberal society. Mohammad Ali Jinnah is seen as having championed a state with moderate, progressive, and democratic norms, where a person's class, creed, and religion would not be the business of government. There has been profound disappointment with what has been judged a discarding of Jinnah's vision by Pakistan's leadership. The program of Islamization born in the last days of Zulfikar Ali Bhutto's regime and brought to maturity under the direction of General Zia-ul-Haq advanced an alternate, illiberal interpretation of Jinnah's prescriptive ideas.

The better-educated, more politically aware sectors of society give voice to disappointments with successive governments' intolerance and seemingly insincere efforts to curb the most violent of these groups. This urban middle-class subculture is, at the same time, largely disposed to addressing Pakistan's struggles with militancy through peaceful, political means, and is usually reluctant to license the use of military force. The military is seen as having overstepped its writ with its extrajudicial behavior toward dissidents and repressive measures against liberal voices in the print and electronic media. While preferring elected government over military rule, members of this middle class also strongly value societal stability and have shown their willingness to approve military intervention when framed as necessary to restore order and cleanse corrupt government. Ordinarily, however, any honeymoon with the military is short-lived.

Many of those in the better-educated middle class, potentially best-positioned to fashion governance reforms and rally the public, have in their frustration with politics turned elsewhere over the years. Opportunities afforded by an invigorated private sector economy draw off the most ambitious and skilled among an increasingly self-absorbed educated class. The upwardly mobile middle-class professional sector has also encountered difficulty in gaining entry into what is, like the political system, a largely closed economic system.[16] Pamela Constable observes that there is not enough modern economic opportunity to absorb those who want to enter. There are also too many bureaucratic barriers, too few opportunities for the right kind of education, and other obstacles posed by a network of political connections.[17]

The urban educated subculture gives priority to a national identity over more parochial attachments in a trend away from regionalism. Its members also tend to normatively evaluate Pakistan's politics through the lens of external standards. Most have values visibly fashioned through contacts with Europe and the United States. Some also find their points of reference in Arab or Muslim countries. Despite being culturally inclined toward the West, those subscribing to the subculture can be highly critical of its policies. Most have grown increasingly distrustful of the United States and resentful of what they perceive as its preference for military-led Pakistani governments and its double standards. Large numbers of this class are ready to accept the idea that the West and the United States in particular have in the guise of fighting global terrorism targeted Islam.

There is reason for concern that disappointment with a Khan government, on which so many of the better-educated of the middle class had placed high hopes, may have shaken their faith in government and a democratic political system. It may increase the numbers of those seeking to relocate to the West. Others may withdraw emotionally, thereby giving greater ground to authoritarian influences, and a small number from among the more educated ranks may be attracted to radical causes. Without these individuals, a major constituency for the promotion of progressive values will be lost to Pakistan. At least for the time being, however, there remain in the country those, largely from this middle class, who continue to believe that with the right leadership and policies, the country's myriad problems can be best addressed through democratic institutions.

The Bureaucratic Subculture

Over the course of Pakistan's history, the civil service has carried the burden of governance. Even the strongest political actors have needed to enlist bureaucratic cooperation to realize their policy objectives. Pakistan's powerful military cannot exercise its domestic sway without allying with the bureaucracy. The source of much of the bureaucracy's outsized influence in governance is its institutionalized norms. Civil servants are inculcated with their professional values through the formal training and socialization processes that occur in Islamabad's Civil Service Academy and for senior bureaucrats in Lahore's National School of Public Policy. However, most of these norms are inherited from previous generations of bureaucrats and honed by the day-to-day work environment.

As a subculture, Pakistan's civil bureaucracy leans toward conservatism and the protection of privilege. Perceiving themselves to be members of an "elite governmental club," officials strive for respect.[18] They have been depicted as a "self-generating and self-perpetuating class," authoritarian and aloof.[19] Bureaucrats have also been described as "benevolent despots," clearly separated from those ruled by a "Brahmanism" inherited from their colonial forebears. Although many in the bureaucracy feel a commitment to public service and may want to believe they can uphold the administrative neutrality of the kind idealized by the Western rationalist Weberian model, it is their sense of privilege and low estimation of the public that is more visible. Members of the bureaucracy consider themselves responsible to their own professional norms and not subject to public scrutiny. Though sensitive to the demands of the governing party, they usually see no obligation to be representative or responsive to a broad public. The professionalization to which bureaucrats may proudly subscribe encourages impudence and arrogance rather than accountability and transparency. Operating within Pakistan's patronage-based political system, bureaucrats are able to enjoy considerable power and prestige. They often demonstrate their power by the very arbitrariness of their decisions. Any efforts to achieve efficiency and effectiveness are likely to be undermined by a hierarchic system of management in which civil servants are usually able to elude individual responsibility for decisions.

There is a noticeable absence of an ethical dimension in government service. The bureaucratic culture finds little fault in manipulating information for what is considered to be the greater good. Obfuscation and feigned ignorance are justified when used in the furtherance of what is rationalized as the national interest. There is ample license for officials to enrich themselves at the public's expense. Once entrapped in a web of corruption, civil servants cannot think of exposing wrongdoing without also implicating themselves. These norms are so deeply engrained that it is doubtful that the bureaucracy has either the means or the will to cleanse itself.

Many have accused the bureaucracy of having political biases that can override objective judgments. It has a reputation for being instinctively suspicious of India, bearing responsibility over the years, along with the military, for blocking possible avenues of compromise with India over Kashmir. The bureaucratic style in negotiations has been described as putting as little on the table as possible in order to have as much as possible to trade later. As a result, the negotiating process usually fails to develop much momentum.[20] Members of the bureaucracy as well as the political leadership are often seen as using the festering Kashmir issue to avoid dealing with the country's social and economic problems.

When in power, Pakistan's democratic governments have regularly had to fulfill promises to party faithful, coalition partners, and others by promising employment in the public sector. Understandably, members of the bureaucracy are resentful when their career ladders are shortened or distorted. Yet, for all their arrogance toward the public, bureaucrats have avoided openly defying strong political leaders. When they have offered some resistance, it has usually been subtle and indirect rather than confrontational.

For all its recognizable attributes, the bureaucracy's discretionary powers have varied under different regimes. Zulfikar Ali Bhutto's nationalization policies gave the bureaucracy considerable influence. At the same time, the government's emphasis on lateral entry—introduced to ensure that the prime minister's policies were implemented—reduced merit in recruitment in favor of loyalty to the party and the selection of personnel endorsed by politicians. Under Zia, military personnel were planted in the civil service as well as civil society organizations—a practice that persists. The 1990s saw recruitment to the civil service widen to include some members of the lower-middle class. This decade also witnessed political parties under alternating democratic regimes competing to place loyal officials in positions in the bureaucracy, leaving "the civil services polarized, inefficient and interest-driven."[21]

During the 1990s, Nawaz Sharif's "reforms" of the bureaucracy to better implement government policies, in effect, further politicized it. As had Z. A. Bhutto two decades earlier, Sharif sought to dominate the bureaucracy to enhance his own personal control over the national levers of power. During the Musharraf years, the military, through manipulation of the civil administration along with the legislature and courts, took full control of economic and foreign policymaking. Serving and retired army officers were also appointed to head many civil institutions and private organizations, where they were expected to inject the military's values. With the return of democratic governments beginning in 2008, the military withdrew from many of its civilian activities but retained its exclusive control over defense and foreign policy,[22] as well as its ability to veto domestic policies it found objectionable. This continued into the Khan administration. As prime minister, Imran Khan has demonstrated his debt to the military with the placement of retired officers in high positions in the bureaucracy and has deferred to the military's actions, curtailing civil liberties.

The bureaucracy has traditional links to the military through interests and values that are often overlapping. They have similar understandings and interpretations of Pakistan's security issues.[23] Both the military and bureaucracy are similar in that they rely on a set of perks and privileges from which they derive some of their power.

The military depends on the bureaucracy to implement its vision of society and safeguard it against interference from political elites perceived as both incompetent and venal. The bureaucracy counts on the military to help stave off heavy interference by the politicians. Yet the usually cozy relationship between the bureaucracy and military is not infrequently strained. The military has no illusions about the civil bureaucracy. It views its own administrative capacity as superior in being more competent and less corruptible. Meanwhile, the civil bureaucracy resents the military's overriding influence in several areas of domestic policymaking. At times there are institutional rivalries between civilian and military intelligence agencies. Administrators are also envious that a commissioned officer's net worth at the end of his career is far greater than that of a civil bureaucrat.

Military Subculture

Cultural values particularly distinctive to the military are instrumental to understanding how it interprets its place in Pakistan's society. These values provide insight into what the military sees as its responsibilities in providing for the country's security against perceived enemies, external and internal. Popular attitudes and public policy toward India, the United States, and domestic extremist groups bear the imprint of powerfully held convictions within the military. The military's normative feelings about the country's political class are crucial in understanding the way the Pakistani public views its elected civilian officials. This in turn visibly influences Pakistan's ability to achieve a democratic polity built on popular accountability and transparency.

The military's norms, rooted in Mughal and British occupations—and driven, soon after the birth of Pakistan, by feelings of threat from without and within—led Pakistan to become a "national security state." The military sees itself as Pakistan's ultimate protector, its "security shield,"[24] the "primary defender of the national sovereignty, and ultimately the guarantor of domestic stability."[25] Obsessed with India as the permanent enemy and Kashmir as the permanent wound, the culture portrays the military as not only protecting the nation from its enemies but as preserving Pakistan's unity. Aqil Shah points out, when the national interest is involved, the army views itself as the final arbiter, with a duty to intervene even through irregular means and outside the constitution.[26]

Subtly, the military perpetuates the outdated notion that Muslims of the subcontinent constitute a martial race. In more contemporary terms, the military's officers are socialized to believe they hold membership in the nation's paramount national institution. The military, argues Stephen Cohen, is "an intensely bureaucratized total institution that makes an explicit effort to mold and shape the beliefs of its members according to a formal ideology."[27] Subject to groupthink, army leaders value "consensus, and cohesion and decision-making unity."[28] The armed forces have a distinctive organizational and institutional ethos that stresses professionalism in the form of discipline, competence, and incorruptibility. Its promotion system assures loyalty and conformity with these and other norms and also the continuity of military culture over time. Adherence to the interests and integrity of the army takes precedence over other loyalties including, arguably, the state itself. Religious convictions are no barrier to advancement so long as individuals remain moderately Islamic. Potential dissidents are identified and weeded out.

Contrasting itself against civilian institutions, the military considers itself a meritocracy. Its self-image as the country's most honest and competent institution underlies its paternalistic belief that it best understands the national interest and should own the country's foreign and security policies.[29] Elected officials are generally thought incapable of dealing with those issues directly linked to the survival of the Pakistani state. Contempt for the politicians and much of civil society runs deep. Perceiving civilian rule as mostly corrupt and inefficient, the military feels justified in adopting a guardianship role that calls for monitoring the government's performance, even if it may hesitate to assume power to clean up the politicians' mess. This aspect of military culture has been entrenched by recent army chiefs.

As Nasim Zehra suggests, the army has acquired "special status in society that would give it immunity from criticism and civilian-managed accountability."[30] The military has operated under the assumption that its actions were not subject to the country's legal system. A sense of entitlement justifies the enormous sums spent to further the well-being of those retired personnel who have loyally served in the military's higher ranks. The military sees its benefits and advantages as repayment for the heavy burden of responsibility it feels it has assumed in defending the nation. Repayment takes the form of land grants and various forms of welfare funded by military foundations with investments in corporate ventures in the economy, notably in agricultural and industrial interests.[31]

As the budget of the armed services is not subjected to close parliamentary scrutiny, the military holds a virtual veto over any policies that it feels threaten its institutional perks. With these privileges and prerogatives protected, the army is usually content to remain in the barracks. But if the past is any guide, toleration of civilian governments is likely to run out either when politicians are thought to have acted in ways that seriously weaken the state or when they make a bid to gain the upper hand over the military. As prime minister, Sharif learned this when he sought to influence the composition of the army's commander corps in 1999 and was ousted. President Asif Zardari had a stark reminder of the limits of his office early in his tenure when he sought civilian oversight over the Inter-Services Intelligence (ISI) division. Sharif's unwelcomed foreign policy initiatives with India and Afghanistan, and his often feckless stewardship of domestic affairs are believed to have provoked the generals into encouraging political movements seeking to depose the prime minister in 2014. While Sharif finished out his term in office, he continued to irritate the military. It exacted its vengeance by exposing wide corruption in his government and succeeded in having Sharif barred by the Supreme Court from holding office. Imran Khan received valuable backing from the military in the 2018 elections but only at the price of having to cede to the military important areas of civil authority.

The military chooses to believe that it remains close to the Pakistani people. As such, it fears popular humiliation. It has shown a willingness to take strong measures to avoid having its reputation tarnished. How the military sees itself portrayed in the electronic and print media has always been of critical importance. Sensitivity to criticism was clearly on view in the aftermath of the 2011 bin Laden raid, which threatened to smear the military's image. U.S. unilateralism reinforced a long-held disposition within the military to suspect American motives and see the intervention as evincing an absence of respect for Pakistan and its military. Much like the rest of the country, the army is conspiratorially minded. Also like the rest of the country, it distorts reality to hide failure. Going on the defense, the military enlisted, as it has often done, the Pakistani media to influence popular discourse. After the raid in Abbottabad, the military succeeded in turning public criticism over its inability to intercept the American operation to anger directed against the United States for its violation of the country's sovereignty.[32] The military's muzzling of any media comment casting it in a bad light and its sensitivity to ethnic nationalism was especially in evidence with the appearance of the Pashtun Tahafuz Movement (PTM) in early 2018. Expressing a wide range of Pashtun grievances, the PTM's massive rallies, criticizing the army's counterterrorist operations in the tribal regions, drew the ire of the military and resulted in repressive measures.

Deeply embedded biases underlie how the military's officer corps views the United States. There exists a deep-seated contempt in the army and its intelligence services for their American counterparts even while offering selective cooperation. Feelings have remained remarkably resistant to change and, in the anti-American narrative, similar to Pakistan's broader political culture. Washington's policies are viewed skeptically. U.S. motives are highly suspect, and its commitments felt to be unreliable. It is generally assumed that Washington is heavily inclined toward India. Persistent U.S. pressures are resented and resisted, and taken as evidence of American policymakers' overall disrespect for Pakistan.

Pakistan's military culture clearly incorporates strategic thinking derived mainly from perceived threats from India. Christine Fair observes that the strategic culture of Pakistan's Army leads it to portray itself as the institution "best suited to protect Pakistan's ideological as well as territorial frontiers."[33] Fair cites the army's ingrained views of India as having made it difficult for Pakistan for so long to acknowledge the threats imposed by domestic extremists. While Pakistan now concedes it has serious internal cleavages to address, India is held responsible for their very existence or at least for exploiting the country's ethnic and sectarian differences. The military has also cultivated popular views of the United States and China that exaggerate American untrustworthiness and excuse disappointments concerning China by painting it as an always faithful ally.[34]

The determination that led Pakistan to develop nuclear weapons, often explained in realist terms, cannot be understood without reference to the military's strategic culture.[35] It holds beliefs that India is bent on turning Pakistan into a vassal state and would, if it could, undo Partition. With its disadvantage in conventional forces, Pakistan can only be assured of survival through nuclear parity with India. This mindset also accounts for some of Pakistan's strategic blunders in its several conventional conflicts with its neighbor. Belief in its fighting prowess and moral superiority figure in the army's overconfidence in its own capabilities. The Pakistan Army has repeatedly undertaken military actions that, while promising to bring some near-term success, have ignored or misinterpreted the longer-term consequences. All of Pakistan's wars with India from 1947 to the 1999 Kargil conflict offer examples.

Because the military promotes the idea that it is always acting according to the best interest of the public,[36] it avoids appearing to be openly disrespectful of democratic prescriptions and, when possible, would prefer to justify its actions as lawful and legitimate. The military's guardian-cum-savior complex, essentially a paternalistic attitude to the people and organs of government, is, however, difficult to reconcile with the democratic norms embedded in Pakistan's largely liberal constitution. Moreover, many believe that the recurring military rule and the threat of military intervention have impeded the maturation of a modern, democratically oriented political system and civil society. Those who welcomed a military government in the hope that it might sweep away patronage-based politics and implement badly needed reforms in governance or end domestic violence have met with disappointment. Instead, the military in power has proven not very different than the politicians—fearful that change could upend their privileged claims.

Polling on Pakistan's military and civilian governments is very restricted, but available evidence suggests that a substantial portion of the public remains disposed to believe that civilian rule should be the norm for governance and the constitution the touchstone for those exercising authority. At the same time, the military remains clearly the most popular national institution; 75 percent of those surveyed in 2018 strongly approved of the job performed by of the military.[37] Confidence in the military does not necessarily translate into support for military rule. While the general public has at times welcomed military rule, the military's writ has ordinarily been thought of as less legitimate. And with the last military government still within memory, the country does not seem easily disposed to having another army general wrest the reins of government.

Conclusion

For Pakistan to realize more responsible, transparent, and capable governance will require sufficient political will, a legal framework, and effective enforcement mechanisms. Pakistan has not produced the kind of national leadership willing to take political risks and champion a legislative agenda that addresses needed structural economic reforms. And while Imran Khan broke new ground in 2019 in proposing a far-reaching program of social reform, his agenda languished for lack of dedicated follow-through. As this chapter has sought to show, many of the values and predispositions associated with Pakistan's popular culture and distinctive subcultures militate against change. They stand in the way of government accountability and effectiveness in meeting public needs. Deeply embedded, these norms will not easily yield. Only positively reinforcing events, education, and determined leadership are likely to modify over time the values that now account for public and elite attitudes and behavior.

There exists little evidence that Pakistan is likely to experience the popular uprisings on the scale experienced across the Arab world and elsewhere. Even the most reform-minded members of Pakistan's civil society are committed to change that comes incrementally. The underlying discontent in the country notwithstanding, no movement has emerged nationally to mobilize citizens to engage in a thorough cleansing of Pakistan's entrenched political and economic elites. Whether out of distrust, cynicism, or indifference, the public, despite its attractions to charismatic and populist figures like Z. A. Bhutto and Imran Khan, has also never fallen for a demagogic leader.

All things considered, there remains in Pakistan the normative foundation on which to build a modern, progressive Islamic state. Pakistan's Islamic traditions need not preclude accommodation with liberal democratic practice, nor are they inimical to good governance. Most Pakistanis find no moral predicament in believing that they can remain true to an authentic Islam and also realize the liberties, material benefits, and level of security identified with the West. Even though Pakistanis often express disapproval of the societal values of secularism, materialism, individualism, and morality they associate with the West, most liberal political values win approval. Despite growing Islamic politicization and radicalization in Pakistan, voters continue overwhelmingly to draw the line against entrusting Islamic leadership with political office.

The deficits of Pakistan's political culture notwithstanding, as a people most Pakistanis aspire to have a political system that allows for fairness and equality, freedom of expression, the ability to vote and hold officials accountable, and the rule of law. Unlike citizens of many other countries that share Pakistan's socioeconomic profile, large numbers of Pakistanis have a clear sense of what it means to have responsible assemblies, independent courts, and clean elections. They have not given up on the belief that better governance and a more just and secure society are possible. Despite everything it has endured, Touqir Hussain insists that the nation seems to have retained "a great resilience, a strong will to survive, and a faith-based sense of optimism and exceptionalism."[38]

NOTES

1. Anatol Lieven, *Pakistan: A Hard Country* (New York: Public Affairs Books, 2011); see, especially, chapter 1.

2. Gabriel A. Almond and Sidney Verba, *Civic Culture: Political Attitudes and Democracy in Five Nations* (Boston and Toronto: Little, Brown and Company, 1965).

3. C. Christine Fair, *Fighting to the End: The Pakistan Army's Way of War* (Oxford University Press, 2014), p. 281.

4. Gallup Pakistan, World Values Survey, May 2014, pp. 7, 10, www.worldvaluessurvey.org/WVSContents.jsp.

5. International Republican Institute, National Survey of Public Opinion,

conducted by the Center for Insights in Survey Research in Pakistan, March 14, 2019, www.iri.org/resource/new-pakistan-poll-strong-approval-new-govern ment-economic-concerns.

6. V. S. Naipaul, *Among the Believers: An Islamic Journey* (New York: Vintage Books, 1982), pp. 123–24.

7. International Republican Institute, National Survey, conducted November 1–22, 2018, pp. 4–9.

8. Emma Duncan, *Breaking the Curfew: A Political Journey through Pakistan* (London: Arrow Books Limited, 1989), p. 33.

9. Pew Research Center, poll conducted on June 21, 2011, www.pewresearch.org/global/2011/06/21/u-s-image-in-pakistan-falls-no-further-following-bin-laden-killing/.

10. Salman Masood, "Pakistan's Prime Minister Suggests Osama bin Laden Was a Martyr," *New York Times*, June 26, 2020, www.nytimes.com/2020/06/26/world/asia/pakistan-imran-khan-bin-laden-martyr.html.

11. See Lieven, *Pakistan: A Hard Country*, p. 240 for a discussion of the lower-middle class' cultural conservatism.

12. Maleeha Lodhi, ed., *Pakistan: Beyond the Crisis State* (Columbia University Press, 2011), p. 71.

13. Ibid.

14. Umair Javed, "Pakistan's Middle Class," *Dawn*, November 20, 2017, www.dawn.com/news/1371675.

15. Shahid Javed Burki, quoted in Pamela Constable, *Playing with Fire* (New York: Random House, 2011), p. 47.

16. Constable, *Playing with Fire*, p. 31.

17. Ibid., p. 46.

18. Sumrin Kalia, "Bureaucratic Policy Making in Pakistan," *The Dialogue* 8, no. 2 (2013), p. 160.

19. Shuja Nawaz, *Crossed Swords: Pakistan, Its Army, and the Wars Within* (Oxford University Press, 2008), p. 122.

20. See Howard B. Schaffer and Teresita C. Schaffer, *How Pakistan Negotiates with the United States: Riding the Roller Coaster* (Washington, D.C.: The United States Institute of Peace, 2011).

21. Kalia, "Bureaucratic Policy Making in Pakistan," pp. 158–59, 163.

22. Ibid., pp. 163–65.

23. Hassan Askari Rizvi, "Pakistan's Strategic Culture," in *South Asia in 2020, Future Strategic Balances and Alliances*, edited by Michael Chambers (Carlisle, PA: Strategic Studies Institute, U.S. Army War College, 2002).

24. Hasan-Askari Rizvi, *Military, State and Society in Pakistan* (New York: Palgrave MacMillan, 2000), p. 34.

25. John R. Schmidt, *The Unraveling: Pakistan in the Age of Jihad* (New York: Farrar Straus Giroux, 2011), p. 47. See also Fair, *Fighting to the End*, p. 281.

26. Aqil Shah, *The Army and Democracy; Military Politics in Pakistan* (Harvard University Press, 2014), p. 24.

27. Stephen P. Cohen, *The Pakistani Army* (University of California Press, 1984), p. 54.

28. T. V. Paul, *The Warrior State: Pakistan in the Contemporary World* (Oxford University Press, 2014), p. 29.

29. Stephen P. Cohen, *The Idea of Pakistan* (Brookings, 2004), pp. 126–28.

30. Nasim Zehra, "Civil-Military Distrust," *The News* (Islamabad), November 5, 2006.

31. Schmidt, *The Unraveling*, p. 50. For the most thorough study of the Pakistan military's penetration of the economy, see Ayesha Siddia, *Military, Inc.: Inside Pakistan's Military Economy* (London: Pluto Press, 2007).

32. Mosharraf Zaidi, "The Lies They Tell Us: Can the Pakistani Government's Web of Deceit Survive the Death of Osama bin Laden," *Foreign Policy*, May 2, 2011; Luv Puri, "The bin Laden Aftermath: Pakistan's Urdu Media Reacts," *Foreign Policy*, May 16, 2011.

33. Fair, *Fighting to the End*, pp. 279–80.

34. Ibid.

35. Feroz Hassan Khan, *Eating Grass: The Making of the Pakistani Bomb* (Stanford University Press, 2012), p. 4.

36. Husain Haqqani, *Pakistan: Between Mosque and Military* (Washington, D.C.: Carnegie Endowment for International Peace, 2005), p. 129.

37. International Republican Institute, National Survey, November 1–22, 2018, p. 21.

38. Touqir Hussain, "Democracy and Governance," *Dawn* (Karachi), July 12, 2004, www.dawn.com/news/1066199.

NINE

Baloch Nationalism and the Garrison State in Pakistan

KAVITA R. KHORY

The province of Balochistan, according to Asad Durrani, the former head of Pakistan's Inter-Services Intelligence (ISI), "may be a ruler's nightmare but a geo-strategists dream."[1] Durrani's perspective is widely shared by civilian and military elites who have long exploited Balochistan's resources and, more recently, its geographic location. The largest of Pakistan's four provinces, Balochistan has the smallest population and ranks the lowest in human development.[2] The site of recurring violence and insurgencies since 1948, it remains locked in a low-intensity conflict waged between a subset of Baloch nationalists and government forces.

This chapter focuses on three issues: one, the emergence and evolution of the Baloch nationalist movement in relation to the government's nation- and state-building endeavors, which have suppressed local and regional identities and denied the legitimate claims of ethnic and religious minorities for political rights and economic justice. Two, the grievances that have fueled the nationalist movement and an armed insurgency, and the motivations of Baloch leaders who have a history of cooperating with the government in Islamabad but also resisting central power and authority. Three, the role of the state in the conflict and policies aimed at addressing ethno-nationalist demands in Balochistan and other provinces. The sources of conflict, though domestic in origin, cannot be studied in isolation from the growing involvement of external forces, state and nonstate actors, that further threaten the security and welfare of Balochistan and its people. Armed violence is not limited to Baloch nationalists and security forces, as both domestic and foreign militants operate with impunity in the province, and often with the connivance of state authorities. What are the implications of the long-running conflict for Pakistan's security and foreign policy? While taking the history of the conflict into account, the chapter examines recent trends in nationalist politics and state policies.

Ethnic Identity and Political Mobilization

The assertion of a distinctive ethnic identity and the framing of political claims along ethno-nationalist lines is a familiar story in Pakistan's politics. Examples include the Bengali nationalist movement culminating in the creation of Bangladesh in 1971, the mobilization of Sindhi nationalism in opposition to General Zia ul-Haq's regime in the 1980s, the assertion of a Muhajir "ethnic" identity in the 1980s and 1990s, and a resurgent Pashtun nationalist movement that so far remains peaceful. Although these nationalist movements have their own distinctive characteristics and motivations, they hold three things in common: first, the colonial antecedents of these movements have shaped their interactions with the Pakistani state; second, they have challenged the singular and exclusionary Pakistani national identity defined by Islam and the Urdu language; and third, they have protested discriminatory state policies and engaged in armed resistance at one time or another. In spite of shared grievances, ethno-nationalist movements in Pakistan have rarely forged a common front against the state.

Despite its ethnic claims, the Baloch nationalist movement is not about ethnicity per se. Rather, ethnic identity is politically salient because the state codifies and institutionalizes public policy in ways that privilege some groups while discriminating against others.[3] This creates a powerful incentive for asserting political claims using ethnic categories. Military and state elites, drawn heavily from the province of Punjab, are viewed by the Baloch and others as the principal beneficiaries of federal allocations and a national quota system that perpetuates unequal power relations.

Baloch mobilization in the early 1930s was part of a broader anti-colonial movement. Faced with the imminent departure of the British from India, the Kalat National Party, formed in 1935, advocated for an independent Balochistan that would include the princely state of Kalat, Baloch territory under British control, and Baloch-populated areas in Iran as well as parts of Sindh and Punjab.[4] The idea of an independent Balochistan, however, was in direct conflict with Mohammad Ali Jinnah and the Muslim League's territorial vision for Pakistan. In 1948, the new Muslim League government merged—and formally annexed—the Baloch princely states, Kalat, Kharan, Makran, Lasbella, and British Balochistan.

For nationalists, resistance to the forced annexation of Balochistan, though short-lived, marks the beginning of their struggle against the Pakistani state and its exploitation of Baloch land and natural resources. Observed annually as a "Black Day" by Balochis at home and abroad, the date of annexation, March 27, 1948, has become a central point of reference for a younger generation of activists fighting against the Pakistan Army's "occupation" of Balochistan.

Baloch identity is grounded in distinctive linguistic and cultural traditions, shared histories, and a strong territorial attachment to the "Baloch homeland," extending across Pakistan's borders with Iran and Afghanistan. Baloch nationalists stress the cultural and symbolic value of language, and have lobbied for the Baloch language to be taught in schools and colleges in the province. The Baloch movement is notable for its linguistic heterogeneity, as both Balochi- and Brahui-speakers are considered to be Baloch.[5] Language, however, seems less important for the Baloch cause than in other cases where it is central to the nationalist project.

Like other nationalist movements, land and territory are powerful signifiers of Baloch identity and the movement for political authority and autonomy. Although calls for an independent Balochistan have grown louder in the face of sustained military operations, self-determination for most nationalists means having the power and authority to govern Balochistan in a genuinely democratic, federal, and equitable Pakistan. The idea of a "Greater Balochistan," carved out of Pakistan, Iran, and Afghanistan, has not gained much traction, even among the most ardent nationalists.[6] Balochistan's heterogeneous population (Baloch, Brahui, and Pashtuns self-identify as "indigenous" people) complicates nationalist territorial claims and heightens demographic anxieties among Balochis.

The Baloch nationalist movement is riven by socioeconomic divisions, political ideologies, and internecine conflicts. The coterie of tribal chiefs whose rivalries and interests had long defined the nationalist movement is being slowly replaced by more diverse, often urban-based civil society activists, community organizations, and political parties. In particular, the 2006 killing of Nawab Akbar Khan Bugti by security forces galvanized educated, middle-class Balochis outside of the traditional tribal leadership and social hierarchies.[7]

Frustrated by both the government and nationalist leaders, a younger generation of politically active Balochis, including a growing number of women, is setting its own priorities and goals. Some have chosen to work with the state and participate in electoral politics. Others have looked to civil society organizations and social movements for achieving political change. Still others have turned to armed resistance against a recalcitrant state with a history of failed policies, broken promises, and brutal violence. Despite generational and class differences, Baloch nationalists share a profound sense of deprivation and injustice that has become even more acute in the last two decades.

Sources of Conflict

Sanaullah Baloch, a member of the Balochistan Provincial Assembly, believes the "issue" of Balochistan is "simultaneously political, psychological, cultural, and geographical. It is either the good luck or the bad luck of Balochistan that its geographical location is of extreme strategic and economic importance."[8] This pithy observation conveys the breadth of Baloch grievances and suggests why it is considered one of South Asia's most intractable conflicts—a product of political and economic grievances, cultural and demographic anxieties, and state repression.

The quest for political autonomy in a federal system and demands for robust democratic institutions with effective power-sharing mechanisms have been central to the Baloch nationalist cause since its inception, and remain so today. Consolidating state power was a key objective of Pakistan's leaders following Partition. The government in 1955 merged all of West Pakistan into a single administrative unit in an effort to suppress competing ethnic and provincial identities and curb the power of regional elites. Because of the one-unit scheme, Balochistan did not receive full provincial status until 1970—a major demand of nationalists at the time.

A new constitution, drafted after the creation of Bangladesh in 1971, restored the federal system of government and its provincial administrative units. In reality, the state remained highly centralized regardless of who controlled the government. Prime Minister Zulfiqar Ali Bhutto's dismissal in 1973 of the National Awami Party's popularly elected governments in Khyber Pakhtunkhwa and Balochistan, which included prominent Baloch leaders like Attaullah Mengal, Akbar Khan Bugti, Nawab Khair Baksh Marri, and Mir Hazar Khan Bizenjo, triggered mass protests and intensified nationalist and separatist sentiments, leading to an insurgency that lasted from 1973 to 1977.[9]

From 1988 to 1999, the governments of Benazir Bhutto and Nawaz Sharif did a somewhat better job of addressing the demands of Baloch nationalists through competitive elections, inducements, and co-optation. Still, neither leader could mitigate the sense of relative deprivation, rooted in structural inequities and chronic underdevelopment, with few, if any, institutional means available for achieving redistributive justice. Any hope of a political solution faded with the army's return to power under General Pervez Musharraf in 1999. Musharraf's regime further escalated tensions, setting off another insurgency, which shows few signs of abating despite protracted counterinsurgency operations and a massive military presence in the province.

Balochistan's changing demographics and urbanization have deepened ethnic cleavages. Pakistan's urban growth rate is rising faster than India, Nepal, or Sri Lanka's, and the rate of rural to urban migration in Balochistan is among the highest in Pakistan. Migration is driven by a combination of factors, from the destruction of fragile rural economies by environmental stressors and counterinsurgency operations and "tribal wars" to the promise of jobs and educational opportunities in larger towns and cities.[10] But crumbling infrastructure, inadequate housing and health care, and dwindling supplies of water and power make it hard for cities, even big ones like Quetta and Turbat, to accommodate large numbers of migrants from rural areas of Balochistan and other parts of Pakistan, not to mention refugees from neighboring Afghanistan, many of whom have been living in Balochistan since the late 1970s. Overcrowding in urban localities and competition for scarce resources worsen tensions and hostility toward ethnic and religious minorities, which sometimes escalate into outright conflict and even violence.

Demographic fears are fueling an exclusionary, even xenophobic, turn in the nationalist movement. The perception of being "outnumbered" is common to many ethno-nationalist movements. Demographic anxieties in Pakistan, and Balochistan specifically, have been amplified by controversies over census data and their significance for electoral politics and resource allocation.[11] In Baloch nationalist circles, Punjabi "settlers,"

Urdu-speakers, Afghan refugees, and Chinese workers are considered to be interlopers of one sort or another. The online campaign against "fake" domicile certificates, for example, is aimed at exposing "outsiders" who are seen as taking advantage of Balochistan's quotas for educational institutions and civil service jobs by falsely claiming residency in the province.[12]

Baloch leaders have long sought control over the province's gas and oil reserves and minerals. The struggle for Balochistan's resources became even more urgent in the early 1990s, when Pakistan began to adopt a neoliberal model of development as part of a structural adjustment program. State control of the economy gave way to free market principles, privatization of industry and public utilities, and foreign direct investment. In embracing the neo liberal model as a solution to Pakistan's low growth rates and debt crisis, the military regime under Musharraf opened up the economy—and Balochistan's untapped resource wealth—to foreign investment. It was also during Musharraf's regime that the military developed its own commercial interests to an unprecedented level and entrenched itself even more firmly in Pakistan's political economy.[13]

Balochistan presents a South Asian version of the so-called resource curse.[14] For decades, Balochis have complained that the province, though resource-rich, neither profits from nor controls the earnings from its minerals and oil and gas reserves. Instead of investing Balochistan's resource wealth in critical infrastructure, industry, education, and employment opportunities in the province, the central government siphons off oil and gas royalties and disburses the funds according to its own priorities. Local and provincial leaders are often excluded from the planning process for "megadevelopment" projects like the Gwadar Port.[15]

The conflict over resources involves three principal issues: energy, minerals, and the port city of Gwadar. Pakistan's first gas field was discovered in 1952 in the Sui district located in Dera Bugti. By 1953 gas from Sui had already reached the major urban areas of Punjab and Sindh, but towns and cities in Balochistan did not receive direct gas supplies from Sui until 1986. Even now, only fourteen towns among thirty-four districts in Balochistan have access to natural gas.[16] Balochistan is the second-largest producer of natural gas in Pakistan, yet its consumption level is the lowest in the country. The fact that Punjab and Sindh have benefited enormously from Balochistan's natural gas reserves while its own towns and villages still depend heavily on coal and wood adds to the perception of exploitation by the state, and creates more resentment toward Punjabis and Sindhis, who are seen as prospering at the expense of Balochis.[17]

The Pakistan government's development in 2002 of the Saindak Copper Gold Project in Chagai, 670 kilometers (km) west of Quetta, and a second copper-gold mining project in Rekodiq reinforces the sense of exploitation and injustice. Under the authority of the Federal Ministry of Petroleum and Natural Resources, the projects involve investors from Australia, Chile, Canada, and China. In 2002, the Musharraf government signed a ten-year lease with the Chinese Metallurgical Construction Company for developing the Saindak mines, which was renewed in 2017 for another five years.[18] Prime Minister Imran Khan's government renewed the agreement in July 2020 for an additional fifteen years. Licenses for these projects, like others in Balochistan, were issued to foreign companies without consulting local officials, and are believed to be largely benefiting the Pakistani government and its foreign partners, with Balochistan receiving only a small amount of royalties.[19] Disputes over the revenues generated by Balochistan's energy and mineral resources demonstrate the long-standing tensions between the development priorities of the Pakistani government, on the one hand, and Baloch nationalists, on the other hand, who see massive state-led projects as further evidence of a greedy regime amassing wealth for itself.

The Gwadar Port is the most controversial project to date. Gwadar's proximity to the Persian Gulf and the Strait of Hormuz makes it a prime location for a deep-sea port linking major maritime and overland trade routes in a twenty-first- century version of the Silk Road. Often referred to as the "linchpin" of the China-Pakistan Economic Corridor (CPEC) connecting Gwadar with China's Xinjiang region, the Gwadar Port and its massive industrial and commercial complex is the largest project so far in China's Belt and Road Initiative (BRI).

An ambitious, multipurpose endeavor with an estimated price tag of over $62 billion, CPEC includes plans for a wide range of energy and infrastructure projects to be built in Pakistan. In 2015, China and Pakistan signed a series of agreements totaling $42 billion in loans and grants to finance CPEC projects through 2030.[20] Part of a series of high-profile development initiatives, the first phase of the Gwadar Port was completed in 2005 at a cost of $248 million.[21] Pakistan has signed a forty-year lease with the China Overseas Port Holding Company for developing the port—an agreement that is seen as another move by the Pakistan government to deny Balochis control over their own territory while leaving most of the profits in Chinese hands.[22]

The Pakistan-China venture, nationalists argue, is a severe "violation of the ownership and proprietary rights of the people of Balochistan over their land, sea and natural resources."²³ Dr. Allah Nazar Baloch, the leader of the Baloch Liberation Front (BLF), believes the port is another example of the Pakistani state "doing what it had always done; using development as an excuse to exploit Balochistan's natural resources."²⁴ In addition to land erosion and pollution, the port and the East Bay Expressway, linking Gwadar with the coastal highway, have restricted access to the sea for communities that depend on fishing for their livelihood. Despite Prime Minister Imran Khan's promises of "inclusive development," the people of Gwadar lack even the most basic amenities like clean drinking water, power, and health care,²⁵ and many of the jobs in Gwadar that pay a decent wage have gone to skilled workers and laborers from other provinces.²⁶

The Gwadar project's ramifications extend far beyond the port city and its immediate problems. First, it has intensified resentment and hostility toward the government and security forces. Rather than offer practical solutions to impacted communities, the government is deploying security forces around Gwadar, suppressing anti-CPEC protests and harassing displaced residents. In addition to a new Special Security Division set up in 2016, a combination of regular armed forces, paramilitary forces, and private security companies provide security for Chinese companies and workers in Gwadar. Indeed, the plight of Gwadar and its disenfranchised people is driving nationalist recruitment and political action throughout Balochistan.²⁷

Second, the security crackdown to protect Chinese investments in Gwadar has turned CPEC and China into legitimate targets for Baloch insurgents for whom China, an "oppressor" and "occupier" of their land, is now altering the province's demography by bringing in thousands of Chinese workers. Between November 2018 and June 2019, Baloch insurgents attacked three high-profile targets connected to China and CPEC. On November 23, 2018, the Baloch Liberation Army (BLA) attacked the Chinese consulate in Karachi; in April 2019, militants from the Baloch Raaji Aajoi Sangar (BRAS), a "coalition" of separatist groups, executed fourteen members of Pakistan's Armed Forces after stopping their bus on a coastal highway connecting Gwadar and Karachi; and less than a month later, the BLA attacked the five-star Zaver Pearl Continental Hotel in Gwadar.²⁸

Third, the unprecedented militarization of Gwadar is replicated in other parts of Balochistan as well. Garrisons built in the early 2000s in Kohlu, Dera Bugti, and Gwadar and checkpoints scattered throughout the province have become an inescapable part of the everyday lives of ordinary citizens, regardless of their politics. These sorts of "routine" encounters with security forces heighten perceptions of an unjust state, radicalize populations, and increase the likelihood of violent reprisals against government officials and military personnel.[29]

Human rights violations by state agencies and security forces, more so than anything else, have deepened Baloch alienation in recent years and generated greater sympathy and support for armed separatists. Baloch activists complain of constant surveillance and intimidation, in particular the abduction and "disappearance" of students, journalists, doctors, lawyers, and civil society activists who dare to call into question government policies and military conduct. Cases of "enforced disappearances," however, are not limited to Balochistan, as torture and extrajudicial killings have been documented in other parts of Pakistan too.[30]

It is nearly impossible to find accurate information on the number and identities of people who have been kidnapped, killed, or simply "disappeared." Families are afraid to report these incidents, the government denies any wrongdoing, and the army and paramilitary forces are mostly silent. According to the Baloch Human Rights Council, based in Europe, at least 20,000 Baloch activists have been missing since 2000.[31] The Voice of Baloch Missing Persons, a non governmental organization (NGO) representing the families of missing persons, claims that approximately 47,000 Baloch remain unaccounted for, while the government's Commission of Enquiry on Enforced Disappearances maintains that Balochistan in 2019 had the lowest number of missing persons in Pakistan. Lately, women activists from Dera Bugti, Awaran, and elsewhere in Balochistan have joined the ranks of "missing" persons" and exiles who have fled Pakistan, among them Karima Baloch, the first woman to have led the Baloch Student Organization (BSO-Azad).[32]

Given the extraordinary power of security forces in Balochistan, it is unlikely that the cases of missing persons will be solved in the near future and that those responsible for mass atrocities will be brought to justice. The governor of Balochistan, Amanullah Khan, went so far as to advise members of the Human Rights Commission of Pakistan to keep "their focus on those missing persons who have returned home, as the circumstances were not suitable for prosecuting those responsible for perpetrating these acts."[33]

Armed Resistance: What Is Different?

Prior to the onset of the latest insurgency in 2005, there were four previous uprisings. The first, led by Abdul Karim, the brother of the Khan of Kalat, was precipitated by the annexure of Kalat in 1948. The decision to merge the provinces of West Pakistan into one unit, followed by the military coup in 1958, sparked the second rebellion. The third took place in 1962–1963, when Baloch leaders Khair Buksh Marri and Ataullah Mengal were dismissed from office by General Ayub Khan, following nonparty-based elections in which they had won seats. Armed conflict in the first three instances was brought under control fairly quickly without posing a serious threat to the state. Though the insurgency from 1973 to 1977 lasted longer, it was limited to the Marri and Mengal tribes and confined to a small number of districts in Balochistan.

Whereas the first four insurgencies crystalized around threats to the political power of tribal leaders, the origins and scope of the insurgency that began in 2005 are very different. This time the catalyst was the rape of Dr. Shazia Khalid by an army officer in the Pakistan petroleum company enclave in Sui. For angry Balochis, the "violation of a Baloch woman's honor," and efforts to cover it up, were yet another example of the military's disrespect and blatant disregard for the law.

By the time Nawab Akbar Khan Bugti, the chief of the Bugti tribe and the former governor and chief minister of Balochistan, was killed in a military operation in August 2006, armed resistance, many Balochis believed, was the only option left: "Nationalist leaders tried political negotiation . . . committees and subcommittees, peaceful protests and parliamentary speeches, but it doesn't work. The center is not willing to listen. We throw one rocket launcher and immediately get attention . . . the struggle is being waged by educated people who have lost hope."[34]

The post-2005 insurgency is distinctive in three respects. First, it is led by a new generation of fighters with firsthand experience of military brutality. Many are middle-class students radicalized on college and university campuses, where student unions are banned and security forces patrol the hallways.[35] In the meantime, younger tribal leaders (Hyrbyair Marri, Brahumdagh Bugti, and the Khan of Kalat, Mir Suleman Ahmedzai) remain in exile. It is not clear to what extent, if at all, the fighters on the ground are coordinating with each other, or with leaders abroad who no longer seem to exercise the same degree of control or authority as their fathers and grandfathers.[36]

Second, the insurgency covers a much larger geographic area, with a broader range of targets and more pervasive violence. The scope of the insurgency has shifted from Dera Bugti and Kohlu in the north, toward Quetta and central Balochistan and further south to Awaran, Turbat, and Gwadar. Targeted attacks have moved from small towns to major urban areas in Balochistan and beyond, for example, the June 2020 attack on the Pakistan Stock Exchange (PSE) in Karachi. The Baloch Liberation Army (BLA) claimed responsibility for the PSE attack as well as an earlier operation targeting the Chinese Consulate.

Third, militant organizations have alternated between high-profile attacks that receive global media attention and intermittent strikes on military vehicles and personnel that rarely make the headlines, even in Pakistan, where information about the insurgency is tightly controlled. Initially, they conducted small-scale operations in southern Balochistan, targeting energy infrastructure and transportation (gas fields, power lines, and railway tracks) and military convoys and soldiers at checkpoints.[37] Lately, militants have gone after high-impact targets such as government installations, diplomatic missions, and national symbols like Jinnah's house in Ziarat. In a first for Baloch separatists, the BLA has used suicide bombers for missions targeting Chinese operations and workers in Pakistan. Militants have also been accused of attacking Punjabis living in Balochistan and of killing fellow Balochis on suspicions of colluding with the government.[38]

Even as the organization, targets, and tactics of the insurgency have shifted, the broader strategy beyond wearing down the state and security forces is not entirely clear. Sources of funding for the insurgency remain nebulous as well. One reputed source is the Baloch diaspora in the Gulf countries, Europe, and the United States. Diaspora organizations and exiled leaders also play an important role in communicating with foreign audiences. They can bypass government censorship when drawing public and media attention to the nationalist cause and human rights violations in Balochistan.[39] Another source of revenue appears to be drug trafficking. According to some estimates, one-third of the drugs from Afghanistan are smuggled through Balochistan's coastal areas. There is also a lucrative market for weapons and human trafficking, facilitated by government and security agencies.[40]

Political Autonomy and Power-Sharing Post-2008

Following the return to democratic politics in 2008, the Pakistan People's Party (PPP) government introduced two major initiatives aimed at addressing the unequal power relations between the center and the provinces. The first was the Eighteenth Amendment to Pakistan's Constitution, passed unanimously by parliament in April 2010. In addition to placing limits on presidential power and strengthening parliamentary authority, the amendment calls for substantial devolution of power to the provinces and for transfer of legislative and regulatory authority to provincial assemblies, particularly for economic and fiscal policy.

The second was to change the National Finance Commission (NFC) formula for allocating resources by the federal government to provincial administrations, including the distribution of tax revenues. Constituted at five-year intervals, the NFC awards until 2010 were based solely on the population of each province, which left Balochistan with just 5–6 percent of Pakistan's population (12.34 million as per the 2017 census) at a distinct disadvantage. Although population remained the chief measure for allocations, beginning in 2010 the federal government expanded the criteria to include poverty levels, revenue generation, and inverse population density.[41] Under the NFC award in 2010, for example, Balochistan's share of federal revenues increased from 5.11 percent to 9.09 percent.[42]

In the absence of political solutions, instituting new criteria for resource allocations has neither mitigated Baloch grievances nor produced favorable developments. There are three major obstacles to implementing power-sharing arrangements in Balochistan. The first is unresolved grievances, which diminishes trust and good will while strengthening hardliners on all sides. The second is the lack of will and capacity of the federal government to follow through on its agreements. The third, and most serious impediment, is rampant human rights abuses and the tight control of public and political space, information, and the media by security forces in Balochistan.

A combination of these three factors led to the collapse in June 2020 of a two-year coalition between the ruling Pakistan Tehreek-e-Insaaf (PTI) government and the Balochistan National Party (BNP-Mengal). Sardar Akhtar Mengal, the former chief minister of Balochistan and president of the BNP, cited the government's failure to address fundamental issues —the recovery of missing persons, repatriating Afghan refugees, implementing the 6 percent jobs quota reserved for the province, and addressing the severe water crisis in Balochistan—as the reason for his withdrawal from the coalition.[43] While announcing some development projects for Gwadar, Prime Minister Imran Khan said in July 2021 that he was considering talking with Baloch insurgents in an effort to address the grievances of the people of Balochistan. However, it was not clear how or when the federal government would follow through on these intentions, or under what conditions and with whom it would be willing to negotiate.

Tackling the problems of Balochistan in short order would be difficult for any government, but particularly when the military's power far exceeds that of civilian authorities. As Mohammed Aslam Bhootani, Gwadar's elected representative in the National Assembly, put it: "The PTI has little control over Balochistan since the military calls the shots on matters pertaining to the province, which it treats as a high-security zone."[44] In fact, the Pakistan Army is even more firmly in control of Balochistan—and Pakistan's—political economy since the establishment in 2019 of the China-Pakistan Economic Corridor Authority, charged with overseeing a vast network of lucrative infrastructure and energy projects and the ongoing development of the Gwadar Port. In November 2019, Asim Bajwa, a retired army officer, was appointed as the chairman of the CPEC Authority. Shortly before assuming his new position, Bajwa headed the army's Southern Command, which is in charge of Balochistan.[45]

International Dimensions

The conflict in Balochistan is complicated by the presence and involvement of a number of state and non-state actors with competing interests that extend beyond Pakistan. In addition to China, the list includes Iran, Afghanistan, India, the United States, and the Taliban. Though anti-CPEC protests and a volatile security situation, among other factors, have delayed some phases of the Gwadar project and limited its operations, China's vast investments and geopolitical ambitions, despite dire predictions, have not been diminished by the insurgency or even a global pandemic.[46]

Iran fears that the insurgency in Balochistan will spill over into its own Sistan-Balochistan province, where militants are fighting for the rights of Iran's Sunni Muslims. In the 1970s, the Shah of Iran dispatched Iranian fighter jets to aid the Pakistani military against Baloch insurgents. Today the situation is somewhat different in that Pakistan and Iran have accused each other of providing cross-border support for Baloch insurgents fighting their respective governments—claims that both countries have denied. Families of some Baloch insurgent leaders have sought refuge in Iran, but there is no evidence to suggest that Iran is actively supporting the insurgency.

Another complicating factor for Pakistan is the Iran-Saudi rivalry. In 2019, Saudi Arabia signed an agreement with Pakistan to invest in CPEC, including building a $10 billion oil refinery in Gwadar, which sits about 172 km from Iran's Chabahar Port. Although Iran is concerned that Pakistan will allow Saudi Arabia to use Balochistan as a base for destabilizing the government in Tehran, the status of the Saudi project remains uncertain in light of recent reports that the refinery would more likely be built in Hub, on the outskirts of Karachi, instead of in Gwadar, which does not have any other oil or gas facilities. In a further twist in the geopolitical tangle, Gwadar's electricity since 1999 has been supplied by Iran.[47]

Afghanistan's irredentist claims on Pakistan's territory and support for Pashtun nationalists have long colored Pakistan's relationship with its neighbor. Aside from offering sanctuary and tacit support to Baloch insurgents in the 1970s, and more recently to Brahamdagh Bugti, who fled to Kabul after the military operation that killed his grandfather Nawab Akbar Khan Bugti, Afghanistan is not a significant player in the insurgency itself.

Pakistan's most strident allegations of foreign interference in Balochistan are directed at India. Among other things, it accuses India of funding and arming insurgents through its consulates in Mazar-i-Sharif, Jalalabad, and Kandahar, providing refuge for exiled nationalists and supporting insurgent groups like the BLA. Although some Baloch have called on India to provide moral and material support to the nationalist cause, it has refrained from doing so with some notable exceptions. The first was Prime Minister Narendra Modi's reference to Balochistan on the occasion of India's Independence Day in 2016, which at the time gave some fodder to Pakistan's claims of Indian collusion with Baloch nationalists. India has also raised the issue of Balochistan at the UN to counter Pakistan's criticism of India's appalling human rights record in Kashmir.

During the war in Afghanistan, the Taliban were given refuge by Pakistan and allowed to regroup in Quetta. The formation of the Taliban leadership's "Quetta Shura" inevitably brought the U.S. war on terror into Balochistan, leading to more violence—independent of the insurgency—and an even larger military presence in and around Quetta. Some Balochis believe that the Taliban were deliberately brought into the province to counter the largely secular Baloch nationalist movement.[48] Additionally, U.S. forces used the Shamsi Airbase in Balochistan from 2004 to 2011 to conduct intelligence operations and launch drone strikes against Taliban targets in Afghanistan.[49] Supported by the military, Sunni extremist groups like Lashkar-e-Jhangvi (LeJ) have also set up operations in Balochistan and been implicated in attacks against Hazaras and other minority communities.

Conclusion

The "ruler's nightmare" in Balochistan will likely persist for a number of reasons. First, prospects for a political solution are dim. Hailed as "groundbreaking" at the time, neither the Eighteenth Amendment nor a revised NFC formula has addressed long-standing grievances or successfully promoted Balochistan's development goals, as civilian governments for one reason or another have proved reluctant or incapable of genuinely sharing power between the federal government and provinces.

Second, the long drawn-out insurgency, though weak and diffuse, may not quickly dissipate. Angry and alienated, ordinary Baloch may express greater support for insurgents and even for independence, but moral support alone is insufficient. Moreover, there is no country at present that is likely to extend critical material support or offer sanctuary and training for Baloch insurgents. Yet massive military deployments and paramilitary forces have not been able to defeat the movement. Instead, indiscriminate military attacks on civilian populations and brutal reprisals against critics of the government, without any justice for victims or their families, have turned even moderate nationalists against the state and put more pressure on Baloch leaders and political parties to stop cooperating with the government.

Third, from the beginning, the nationalist movement and conflicts in Balochistan have been viewed almost entirely through a security lens. As a result, military force and counterinsurgency have taken precedence over political mechanisms for resolving outstanding conflicts. Efforts to win the "hearts and minds" of young Balochis by setting up schools and cadet colleges in Dera Bugti and Kohlu and lowering the requirements for entrance into the military cannot placate a population that considers the military itself to be the main problem. Most of all, the military's deep entrenchment in Pakistan's politics and economy cannot be separated from its actions in Balochistan. As long as Pakistan's domestic and foreign policies are driven by the strategic and commercial interests of the garrison state, the conflict in Balochistan will likely remain intractable.

NOTES

1. Asad Durrani, *Pakistan Adrift: Navigating Troubled Waters* (London: Hurst & Company, 2018), p. 149.

2. Between Pakistan's fifth national census in 1998 and its sixth in 2017, Balochistan's population nearly doubled from 6.566 million to 12.350 million. Pakistan's total population over the same period grew from 134.8 million to 207.9 million.

3. Andreas Wimmer, *Ethnic Boundary Making: Institutions, Power, Networks* (Oxford University Press, 2013), pp. 4–5.

4. Adeel Khan, *Politics of Identity: Ethnic Nationalism and the State in Pakistan* (Thousand Oaks, CA: Sage, 2005), p. 114.

5. Salman Rafi Sheikh, *The Genesis of Baloch Nationalism: Politics and Ethnicity in Pakistan, 1947–1977* (New York: Routledge, 2018), p. 21.

6. On the notion of "Greater Balochistan," see Manzoor Ahmed, "The Dynamics of (Ethno) Nationalism and Federalism in Postcolonial Balochistan, Pakistan," *Journal of Asian and African Studies* 55, no. 7 (November 2020), p. 985.

7. Shah Meer Baloch, "Akbar Bugti's Death and the Revival of the Baloch Insurgency," *Herald Magazine*, September 16, 2017.

8. Ibid., p. 30.

9. Rizwan Zeb, "Pakistan's Political Chess Board: Bhutto, Bugti and the National Awami Party Government in Balochistan (1972–1977)," *Journal of South Asian and Middle Eastern Studies* 42, no. 1 (Fall 2018), p. 68.

10. Saeed Shafqat and Saba Shahid, "Migration, Urbanization and Security: Challenges of Governance and Development in Balochistan" (Lahore, Pakistan: Centre for Public Policy and Governance, Forman Christian College, 2017), pp. 3–6.

11. According to the 2017 census (the official results were not ratified until December 2020), about 55 percent of the province's population identifies as Baloch or Baloch-speakers. Pashtu-speakers, the second-largest group in Balochistan, are about 26 percent of the population. Mubarak Zeb Khan, "Number of Baloch-Speaking People in Balochistan Falls," *Dawn*, September 11, 2017.

12. Mariyam Suleman and Rahim Khetran, "Balochistan Protests against Fake Domicile and Local Certificates," *The Diplomat*, July 7, 2020.

13. For an analysis of the Pakistan military's commercial operations, see Ayesha Siddiqa-Agha, *Military Inc.: Inside Pakistan's Military Economy* (London: Pluto Press, 2007).

14. Shakoor Ahmad Wani, "The Changing Dynamics of the Baloch Nationalist Movement in Pakistan: From Autonomy toward Secession," *Asian Survey* 56, no. 5 (2016), p. 817.

15. Robert G. Wirsing, *Baloch Nationalism and the Geopolitics of Energy Resources: The Changing Context of Separatism in Pakistan* (Carlisle, PA: Strategic Studies Institute, U.S. Army War College, 2008), p. 4.

16. Sher Jan Shohaz, "Balochistan Gas," *Dawn*, January 16, 2019.

17. Wani, "The Changing Dynamics of the Baloch Nationalist Movement in Pakistan," p. 817.

18. Yunas Samad, "Understanding the Insurgency in Balochistan," in *State and Nation-Building in Pakistan: Beyond Islam and Security*, edited by Robert D. Long, Yunas Samad, Gurharpal Singh, and Ian Talbot (New York: Routledge, 2016), p. 127.

19. Mir Mohammed Ali Talpur, "The Saindak Saga," *Daily Times*, December 5, 2009.

20. Arif Rafiq, *The China-Pakistan Economic Corridor: Barriers and Impact* (Washington, D.C.: United States Institute of Peace, 2017), p. 9.

21. Arif Rafiq, "China's $62 Billion Bet on Pakistan: Letter from Gwadar," *Foreign Affairs*, October 24, 2017.

22. Michael Kovrig, "National Ambitions Meet Local Opposition along the China-Pakistan Economic Corridor," *The Diplomat*, July 23, 2018.

23. Rahim Baloch, "Baloch Nationalism against Chinese Hegemony," *Daily Pioneer*, February 3, 2019.

24. Mahvish Ahmad, "Home Front: The Changing Face of Balochistan's Separatist Insurgency," *The Caravan*, June 30, 2014, p. 53.

25. Mariyam Suleman, "Will China's Plans for Gwadar Destroy Fishermen's Livelihood?" *The Diplomat*, April 3, 2019.

26. Mahvish Ahmad, "Balochistan Betrayed," in *Dispatches from Pakistan*, edited by Madiha R. Tahir, Qalandar Bux Menon, and Vijay Prashad (University of Minnesota Press, 2014), p. 159.

27. Kovrig, "National Ambitions Meet Local Opposition."

28. Adnan Amir, "How Baloch Separatists Are Trying to Derail China's Investments in Pakistan," *World Politics Review*, May 20, 2019.

29. Donatella della Porta, *Clandestine Violence* (Cambridge University Press, 2013), p. 68.

30. "Pakistan: Enduring Enforced Disappearances," Amnesty International, March 27, 2019.

31. M. Ilyas Khan, "The Middle-Class Pakistani Students Fighting for a Homeland Dream," BBC News, July 31, 2020.

32. Human Rights Commission of Pakistan, *Balochistan Neglected Still: An HRCP Fact-Finding Report* (Lahore, Pakistan, 2019), pp. 6–7.

33. Ibid., p. 22.

34. Gulmina Bilal, "Interview with a BLA Member," *Newsline*, January 2007, p. 3.

35. Zahid Hussain, "Student Awakening," *Dawn*, December 4, 2019.

36. Francesca Marino, "Baloch Movement Stilled by Lack of Leadership, Strategy," *Firstpost*, January 26, 2019.

37. Mahvish Ahmad, "Home Front," p. 55.

38. Frederic Grare, *Balochistan: The State Versus the Nation* (Washington, D.C.: The Carnegie Endowment for International Peace, 2012), p. 14.

39. Samad, "Understanding the Insurgency in Balochistan," pp. 131–32.

40. Ali Dayan Hasan, *Balochistan: Caught in the Fragility Trap* (Washington, D.C.: U.S. Institute of Peace, 2016), p. 3.

41. Ahmed, "The Dynamics of (Ethno) Nationalism and Federalism," p. 1001.

42. Adnan Amir, "NFC Award: Balochistan's Wish List," *The Friday Times*, March 15, 2019.

43. Javaid-ur-Rahman, "BNP-Mengal Quits PTI Ruling Alliance," *The Nation* (Pakistan), June 22, 2020.

44. Malik Siraj Akbar, "Eight Months In, How Is Balochistan Fairing?" *Dawn*, April 5, 2009.

45. Arif Rafiq, "The Pakistan Army's Belt and Road Putsch," *Foreign Policy*, August 26, 2020.

46. Adnan Amir, "How Baloch Separatists Are Trying to Derail China's Investments in Pakistan," *World Politics Review*, May 20, 2019.

47. Isaac B. Kardon, Connor M. Kennedy, and Peter A. Dutton, "China's Potential Strategic Strongpoint in Pakistan," *China Maritime Report, No. 7* (Newport, RI: U.S. Naval War College, August 2020), p. 34.

48. Haseeb Arif, "In Conversation with Brahamdagh Bugti," *Dawn*, December 19, 2015.

49. Michael Kugelman, "Why Did Washington Wait So Long to Take Its Drone War to Balochistan," *War on the Rocks*, June 7, 2016.

TEN

Internal Security Threats in Nepal, Bangladesh, Maldives, and Other Cases: Learning from Comparative Responses

CHETAN KUMAR

Internal security threats in South Asia have included classic insurgencies centered on issues of marginalization and identity; violent extremism; and insurgencies that lurch between the classic and the "violent extremist" format, such as the erstwhile Liberation Tigers of Tamil Eelam (LTTE) insurgency in Sri Lanka. States have had varying degrees of success in addressing these threats. This chapter examines insurgencies in Nepal and Myanmar, and the issue of Preventing and Countering Violent Extremism (PCVE) in Bangladesh and Maldives.[1]

Nepal was a successful case of a nationally led peace process, with the 2006 peace agreement culminating in a new constitution ten years later, and with the main insurgent group integrating into the political system and the army. Myanmar, in contrast, has seen a stalled peace process, with the national cease-fire agreement involving fourteen armed groups implemented intermittently, and with a permanent peace accord not attained.

Maldives itself has not faced any high-fatality extremist attacks, but Maldivians have been radicalized, and traveled abroad in larger numbers to join extremist groups. The growing political influence of deeply conservative groups has limited the government's options. The focus has been on providing youth with socioeconomic alternatives, but in a middle-income country where resources are less of an issue, these have not had a large impact. Bangladesh has seen significant acts of violence committed by extremist groups, and moderate voices in society have been targeted. The government has deployed an array of measures against extremist groups, and attacks have lessened significantly since 2018. However, a comprehensive national strategy to increase resilience to violent radicalization needs to be developed and implemented based on convergence among all key political and civic actors.

Finally, while not a South Asian case, the Philippines provides a strong reference point in that identity-based conflicts have characterized much of its modern history and have also provided a breeding ground for contemporary violent extremism. After initial attempts to suppress insurgencies by force, the Philippines adopted in the 1990s a systematic framework for addressing internal conflicts through peace processes. A new government entity was created for this purpose as a part of the executive, the Office of the Presidential Adviser to the Peace Process (OPAPP). The Philippines has also been the first country in the wider Asia-Pacific region to adopt a National Action Plan (NAP) on PCVE, albeit others such as Indonesia, Bangladesh, Malaysia, Thailand, and Sri Lanka were, in 2018–2020, working on such plans and could adopt them for implementation in subsequent years.

This chapter does not examine other cases in South Asia, such as India, Afghanistan, Pakistan, and Sri Lanka, though they offer material for further study and comparison.[2]

Nepal

A Summary of the Insurgency

Under its historic monarchy, Nepal was a deeply divided society where political and economic power was held by a small elite in Kathmandu, and residents of the surrounding hills, rural areas, and Madhes/Terai, the region bordering India, were excluded. India nudged Nepal toward the establishment of a liberal political order in 1990, with a constitutional form of government. The country's many political parties came together for this moment, but thereafter were deadlocked in terms of delivering significant change—a pattern that repeated itself over the next two decades. In 1996, the radical Communist Party of Nepal (Maoist) broke ranks from other political actors and declared an armed struggle against the established order. It gathered support from a disenchanted population and was able to weaken government control in Kathmandu and its suburbs by 2004. Entire communities were decimated in the violent struggle.[3]

King Birendra attempted to find accommodation, but for unrelated reasons was assassinated alongside much of the royal family in 2001. King Gyanendra deployed greater force against the insurgency and suspended the constitutional monarchy in 2005. This move united the fractious political parties and led them to find common cause with the Maoists in restoring Nepal's freedoms. The political convergence was backed by a popular uprising against authoritarianism supported by both the Maoists and the conventional political parties, as well as discreet support from India. Faced with national unity among contentious civilian groups, the military did not suppress the popular movement on behalf of the unpopular Gyanendra. Over the next year, sufficient agreement was reached between different segments of the political leadership for a Comprehensive Peace Agreement to be signed in 2006. India's commitment to ensure that insurgent groups did not find refuge across the India-Nepal border also helped.

The agreement mandated a new republic (Gyanendra departed in 2008, once the monarchy was abolished under the interim constitution), provided for the integration of the Maoist combatants into the Nepali Army, instituted a truth and reconciliation process (never fully realized), and provided for the development of a new constitution to form a federal political system.

Analyzing the Peace Process and Peace Agreement

Two points are critical to note regarding the process leading to the peace agreement. First, it was underpinned by a genuine national awakening and consensus facilitated by senior national intermediaries (Padma Ratna Tuladhar and Dhaman Nath Dhungana played critical roles) who were viewed as neutral in their political affiliations and had the trust of both traditional political parties as well as the Maoists. Second, international interlocutors were playing supportive roles rather than trying to dominate the process. India and China found consensus on the importance of peace. The United Nations and Western donors assisted the parties when needed without taking the center stage.

The operational side of the agreement—the disarming of Maoist combatants and their integration into the national army or rehabilitation into civilian lives—was completed by 2013. A UN mission was deployed from 2007 to 2011 and assisted this process, but with a more limited mandate than other post-peace accord "nation-building" operations. It was mandated primarily to assist with elections in 2008, monitoring arms and decommissioning and reintegrating Maoist combatants. At its height in 2008, it numbered close to 1,000 technical staff, including a hundred military experts. Postelections, it was downsized to 300. Observers and support staff from the mission were deployed in areas where the insurgency had been active.

Far more challenging was the political side of the agreement. The Maoists won the first post-peace agreement elections. However, Nepal soon reverted to political deadlock and rivalry between the Maoists and the traditional parties. By 2012, Nepal's first Constituent Assembly had failed to find consensus on a new constitution. A new one was elected in 2013, and was able to agree on a draft charter in 2015 largely because of the shock of a natural disaster—a massive earthquake that caused much destruction in Kathmandu, and the resulting calls for national unity and for the political class to come together amidst a moment of crisis helped agreement on the constitution.

Beginning in 2009, two groups of senior intermediaries, supported by the United Nations Development Programme (UNDP) via its role as a resident agency rather than an external UN political mission, played various roles in sustaining political dialogue. These were the Steering Committee on Collaborative Leadership (comprising approximately ten senior advisers to the major political parties) and the Senior Facilitators' Group (comprising the two facilitators from the 2006 peace process, plus four others identified with their assistance). They served as intermediaries among the major parties, and helped address political deadlocks as well as differences over policy in the Constituent Assembly. They also helped prevent more widespread violence by sponsoring capacity-development and training for a group of younger mediators, who were deployed in the countryside to help resolve (at times identity-based) disputes over land and resources. At the community level, "local peace committees" formed under the auspices of the Ministry for Peace and Reconstruction prevented or resolved violent conflicts in some instances, although on many occasions their memberships mirrored the political deadlocks at the national level. A U.S.-supported dialogue platform, the National Transition to Peace

Program, also played an important role in keeping dialogue open. This program was able to convene different configurations of political actors around critical policy questions and played an important role in keeping the new legislators well-equipped to perform their responsibilities.

The net result of these initiatives was that intermittent deadlock, political upheaval, and local violence did not coalesce again into an armed conflagration as had happened in 1996, and at critical moments enough consensus was found to keep the political transformation plodding along.

The primary deadlocks during constitution-making had been over boundary delineation, that is, how the borders of the new federal states would be formed. Political actors and Constituent Assembly members remained split largely down the middle on whether this should be done based on language and ethnicity (as is the case with India) or economic and resource considerations. A complex formula accommodating both sets of concerns was eventually developed with the assistance of senior intermediaries referred to above, and seven federal provinces were defined for Nepal. The formula essentially aggregated Nepal's existing seventy-five districts into these new provinces, with some changes to accommodate both ethnic and economic concerns. After the new political map and a federal constitution were adopted by Nepal's major political parties in 2015, some representatives of the Madhes/Terai region continued to object—sometimes violently and allegedly with backing from interests across the Indian border—against this dispensation. An additional district was proposed to be added to the Terai province, but unrest persisted.

In addition to the critical role of intermediaries, two further lessons can be drawn from the Nepal process. First, wholesale transformations envisaged in comprehensive peace agreements require significant time, and, therefore, there is a need for a continued investment in local capacities for dialogue and "insider mediation," as new conflicts and disputes emerge due to the realignment of resources and power. Nepal's further progress toward the Sustainable Development Goals (SDGs) will require the application of these capabilities as tensions continue to simmer over the application of the new federal system. Second, cataclysmic events can make or break peace processes or agreements, even if they unfold over a period of time, as they reset attitudes and behaviors. The Indian Ocean/Pacific tsunami of 2004 and the Nepal earthquake of 2015 both provided an impetus to the Aceh and the Nepali peace processes. Conversely, the tsunami did not have any positive impact in the Sri Lankan conflict or in the peace process in southern Thailand. One difference is that both the

Maoists in Nepal as well as the Gerakan Aceh Merdeka in Indonesia enjoyed significant support among the larger public and among the country's intelligentsia and were therefore already poised to play a wider unifying role. The natural cataclysms provided further clarity and impetus.

Myanmar
Trends in Internal Conflict

Myanmar is not, technically, in South Asia, but it shares borders with South Asian states, and, more importantly, has internal conflicts comparable to South Asian cases. Myanmar's civil conflict consists of a series of armed insurgencies by ethnic groups considering themselves marginalized by a state dominated by the Burmese. Many insurgencies (as many as twenty) started when the military took over then Burma in 1960. The Shan, Kachin, Kayah, Rakhine, and Kayin States have been the epicenter of these insurgencies. For many insurgent leaders, their cause emanates from the perceived betrayal by the military government of the promises of federalism made by the country's founding father Aung San. Insurgents at various times received cross-border support from Myanmar's neighbors.

After the 1990 electoral victory of Aung San Suu Kyi's National League for Democracy (NLD), when the military government did not hand over power and instead imprisoned members of the opposition, the Myanmar military sought to create a stronger foundation for its rule by negotiating cease-fires with individual insurgent groups. Led by its intelligence wing, these negotiations yielded stable cease-fires that, surprisingly, required little monitoring on the ground. They tactically benefited all sides, given the stalemates on the ground; the military did not require the armed groups to disarm; and promises of significant economic investments were made by the government. However, slow follow-up to various commitments eventually led to the collapse of the cease-fires.

In 2011, the military government allowed a carefully managed transition to civilian rule. A new constitution divided power between the military and civilian components of the government. General Thein Sein took over as president of this new hybrid system. He continued the overall transition to a more open system and revived sustained negotiations with all major armed groups, but with the new objective of obtaining a national cease-fire agreement. Eventually, ten of the groups (eight armed, two civilian)—All Burma Students' Democratic Forum; Arakan Liberation Army; Chin National Front; Democratic Karen Buddhist Army, Brigade

5; Karen National Union; KNU/KNLA Peace Council; Lahu Democratic Union; New Mon State Party; Pa-O National Liberation Army; and Restoration Council of Shan State—signed the Nationwide Ceasefire Agreement (NCA) in 2015. The new approach marked an important recognition of the systemic issues—related to the division of political and economic power between the center and the regions—that have driven Myanmar's many insurgencies and therefore underlined the need for a national effort. It also recognized an important precept of peace processes, that comprehensive and lasting settlements cannot be reached with fragmented parties. At the same time, the continued mistrust between several major groups and the military led to these groups staying out of the agreement—most prominent being the United Wa State Army, the Kachin Independence Army, and the Shan State Army-North. The government pursued separate peace agreements with these groups while simultaneously urging them to join the NCA. These processes were intended to eventually lead to a final peace agreement that would also correspond to additional governance reforms and potentially a new national charter.

Analyzing the Peace Agreement and Its Limitations

The NCA does not offer a comprehensive peace agreement, but an agreed-upon roadmap. Further negotiations and agreement were to be sought on fundamental reforms, and once these were agreed to, a final peace agreement leading to conclusive disarmament could be achieved.[4]

First, the NCA provides for a Joint Ceasefire Monitoring Committee, which was constituted at the national, state, and local levels to implement the cease-fire, with each level of the committee chaired by an army officer, and a representative of an armed group as deputy chair.

Second, a National Peace and Reconciliation Office was also formed in the Presidency to anchor this architecture. A Union Peace Commission brought together the key government and political leaders, while armed groups participating in the NCA constituted their own Steering Committee.

Third, a key feature of the agreement was that peace dividends would be brought to the insurgency-afflicted areas in an inclusive manner, thus allowing for socioeconomic benefits and improved service delivery for previously marginalized populations.

The process received a further boost when the National League for Democracy won national elections in March 2016, and an NLD member became the country's first civilian president since 1960. Aung San Suu Kyi assumed the role of state counselor, effectively holding authority over the government and its policies. One of her first policy initiatives was to convene a national dialogue forum (referred to as "Panglong" after a similar consultation convened by her father in 1947–1948) to create a wider basis for the NCA and to chart a route toward an eventual national agreement. However, the forum, while yielding some wider points of convergence, did not lead to a specific way forward.

Despite its being comprehensive in nature, the process had stalled by 2020 due to the factors discussed below, which were often recognized by the parties themselves. It should be noted that China also sought to play an intermediary role between the national government and the ethnic armed groups via a special envoy; China's concern stems primarily from the spillover of Myanmar's conflicts into its Yunnan region.

First, the Joint Ceasefire Monitoring Committee system needed to act as an effective conflict resolution mechanism for the process. Composed as it was primarily of the military and the armed groups that it was fighting, it often tended to reflect their differences rather than resolve them.

Second, as a part of the Presidency, the National Peace and Reconciliation Office played a largely bureaucratic and procedural role. While administering the process, it needed also to address its deadlocks or tensions. Again, comprising the parties to the peace process plus civil servants, it tended to reflect differences among the parties rather than to resolve them.

Third, while several experts and independent groups were involved in advising the peace process, the architecture needed the types of resources—in the form of track-two initiatives and informal groups of senior intermediaries—available to the parties in Nepal and in the Philippines. By 2020, increased support from development partners and by the parties themselves for such initiatives held out some promise for the future.

Fourth, while international development partners played roles that involved technical support, observation, advice, and resource mobilization for the government's peace architecture, they were not mandated to facilitate convergence on ways forward, however informally.

Fifth, most proceedings of the peace process, including meetings of its many committees and the national dialogue forum convened in 2016 by Aung San Suu Kyi, were conducted in formal settings, with highly restricted and stylized settings and formats. Informal consultations or track-two diplomacy was also needed to find convergence on critical issues but was often not carried out. This was because, for many officials, the government was not just a party to the process; rather, the peace process itself was a part of the system of government. While laudable, this way of thinking might have also constrained the process.

Sixth, and despite the availability of national and international resources as well as goodwill, both peace and "peace dividends" remained absent at the local level. With factions of the major armed groups as well as sundry local militias challenging them on the ground, and invested in illicit local political economies, horizontal violence continued. Significant differences of approach among leaders of armed groups and the government on the methods to develop and implement effective programs also halted progress in this area.

Seventh, decisionmaking within the peace process may have also been made more complex by the large number of committees, subcommittees, thematic working groups, and commissions, all formal and each requiring its own precise governmental process.

Eighth, progress toward a final peace accord may have been hampered by the fact that the insurgencies were expected by the military to be fully resolved before any fundamental changes were made in governance or to the constitution; however, some of these changes would actually be necessary to achieving a final peace agreement, thus leaving Myanmar with a "chicken-and-egg" dilemma. The NLD administration tried to address this by pushing for decentralization initiatives that did not involve constitutional changes, but implementation posed a challenge.

Ninth, the fallout from the military actions in Rakhine State set back relations with international partners and increasingly distracted the efforts of the government.

The overall challenges of implementation widened the gaps between the signatories to the NCA and the government, and by 2018, trust had been sufficiently eroded for two of the major signatories representing the Shan and Karen groups to temporarily pull out. Renewed clashes on the ground between the military and major armed groups also undermined trust. However, the state counselor's informal diplomacy, and the convincing win of Aung San Suu Kyi's NLD Party in the national elections in November 2020, brought these groups to a reengagement with the peace process. Subsequently, the process was affected by the 2021 military takeover in Myanmar, which resulted in the NCA being considered frozen or dead by several of its signatories. Some armed ethnic groups maintained lines of communication with the military government while also supporting anti-military protestors and the deposed civilian government.

Bangladesh
Background to Domestic Terrorism

Bangladesh has faced a challenge that is also found in other moderate or nominally moderate Muslim-majority states in the South and Southeast Asian region: balancing the beliefs and sensibilities of the majority with a modern polity and economy and the protection of minorities. Four sets of circumstances allowed extremists to make inroads into these countries. First, existing political processes and institutions failed to deliver public services effectively or appeared tainted by corruption and factionalism, and extremists offered religiously based alternatives involving the violent creation of "purer" Islamic systems. Second, the abuse of religion and identity in politics opened gateways to violent extremism. Third, the onset of social media and the internet rapidly accelerated the manipulation of identity and grievances to advance alienation and violent radicalization. Fourth, development provided openings for violent extremism because the rapid advancement of previously marginalized groups (including women), sociocultural change, and the onset of new patterns of resource allocation and economic priorities all threatened previously secure hierarchies and identities.

Bangladesh has been impacted by all four factors.[5] During the Afghan civil war, thousands of Bangladeshis fought against Soviet forces, influenced by an ideology of a purifying struggle against evil. Returning to their homeland, and not finding an outlet to protest what they perceived as corruption and ineffective politics, they increasingly turned toward organizing for armed struggle. This phase culminated in 450 bomb attacks on August 17, 2005, in sixty-four of Bangladesh's sixty-five districts, by Jamaatul Mujahidden Bangladesh (JMB), though causing only two fatalities. By 2007, most JMB leaders had been arrested and executed, including its national leader. A narrative was quickly created by militants that JMB had struggled against a corrupt state and been martyred. While many of JMB's adherents came from rural or semi-urban areas, the new narrative accelerated recruitment on college campuses, especially as the internet became more freely available. The state was not able to mount a sufficiently strong counternarrative. The major political parties that were the only mainstream vehicles for mobilization did not appear to offer a sufficiently strong alternative to those attracted to the emerging extremist refrain. Despite its initial decimation, the JMB survived in both rural and urban areas, and its remaining elements appeared to have teamed up with ISIS by 2016.

Thereafter, as the influence of al Qaeda in South Asia (AQIS) grew in Bangladesh, advocates of secular ideas, members of religious minorities, and bloggers were targeted for selected killings over the next decade, with the most concerted attacks taking place in 2013. The government attributed the problem to domestic politics instead of transnational terrorism, but it did establish, in 2009, a National Committee on Militancy Resistance and Prevention (NCMRP) comprising seventeen government departments and security agencies. The NCMRP carried out a sustained security offensive against extremism and initially appeared to have reduced the numbers of attacks.

This changed with the attack on the Holey Artisan Bakery and Café on July 1, 2016. ISIS-affiliated militants killed twenty foreign nationals and two police officers. The incident brought international attention to Bangladesh's problem of violent extremism. The incident was especially significant because the government had targeted and arrested at least 11,000 individuals suspected of belonging to extremist groups earlier that year.

Responses and Future Directions

With assistance from international development partners and UN agencies, after the 2016 attacks, Bangladesh launched a multipronged effort to counter violent extremism. A "peace observatory" was established with assistance from UNDP. A significantly greater effort was put into "soft" initiatives that reached out to alienated youth on campuses, involved women and communities in peacebuilding at the local level, and sought ideas and initiatives from faith-based leaders to develop counternarratives to those of violent radicalization. Efforts by youth groups have focused on engaging their peers in online and radio forums to encourage peaceful activism. For example, the Bangladesh NGO Network for Radio and Communication (BNNRC) supported, with European Union (EU) assistance, a network of young producers working with community radio outlets. Similarly, five women's community action groups in six districts (Dinajpur, Joypurhat, Moulobhi Bazar, Cox's Bazar, Jessore, and Satkhira), with Japanese support, assisted women in countering violent extremism through greater empowerment and participation in local economies and decisionmaking.

Simultaneously, the Bangladesh government upgraded its security response and targeted particularly a range of training facilities, bomb-making labs, and hideouts of suspected militants.

At the time of writing, there has not been another attack on the scale of the Holey Artisan Bakery, although sporadic attacks have taken place primarily on security agencies and facilities. With the collapse of the "caliphate" in the Middle East, Bangladesh faces the problem of returning "foreign terrorist fighters," and at least two plots by these individuals have been preempted. Extremist narratives also continue to circulate on social media and to draw recruits, especially on campuses. Bangladesh's rapid economic growth and diversifying middle class do help prevent extremism, since they provide opportunities for what would otherwise be an even larger number of alienated individuals. However, a significant number of persons are still alienated by what is perceived to be perennial deadlock and dysfunction in the political system, and its inability to deliver equality and inclusion for all citizens. Many individuals also do not consider traditional political parties to be offering appropriate venues for struggles for social justice.

A number of measures would help Bangladesh address terrorism and extremism over the long term. First, it could work with its youth, women, and faith-based leaders to engage and suggest peaceful alternatives for those seeking social justice or transformative change. Peers, female family members, and teachers and preachers in local religious establishments are often the first line of engagement with those who are on the verge of being alienated or violently radicalized; while efforts are being made to engage them, these still need to reach a critical mass of the population to have a large impact.

Second, Bangladesh could ensure that both the security or "kinetic" as well as "soft" PCVE efforts reach more of the population; this will require a much larger mobilization of national effort.

Third, Bangladesh could promote a joint effort by the country's fractious political class against violent extremism, including an agreement on core principles and parameters when dealing with extremists, and a firm mutual commitment to eschew the use of violent groups in politics.

Fourth, it could develop and implement a National Action Plan (NAP) on PCVE, approved in parliament, with a budget, clear outputs, and timelines. By 2020, Bangladesh had begun the development of a NAP-PCVE with UN assistance.

Maldives

The Growth of Violent Extremism

The number of terror or suspected terror attacks in Maldives is no more than a handful, and these have involved virtually no fatalities.[6] The number of potential Maldivian extremists per capita is high. In December 2019, the Maldives commissioner of police suggested that there could be a few hundred, perhaps a thousand, extremists in Maldives who adhere to ISIS ideology, and revealed that 423 Maldivians had attempted to travel to Syria and 170 had succeeded.[7] Much earlier, in the 2000s, Maldivian youth went to Pakistan for training under the Lashkar-e-Taibah (LeT) terror group. An estimated twelve died in terrorist attacks in Pakistan in 2008–2009, and some were caught trying to enter Afghanistan. Two Maldivians died fighting in Kashmir in early 2007.[8]

Two factors contributed to making Maldives, with a population just over 500,000, susceptible to violent extremism: the influence of financing by Middle East–based entities in the country's religious and educational institutions (with the important caveat that Wahhabi ideology does not equate to violent extremism); and its geography.[9]

For nearly thirty years, from 1978–2008, the authoritarian Maumoon Gayoom presidency kept extremism in check through careful management of the islands' religious institutions, and of external influence on them. The period after independence in 1965 saw an influx of conservative ideas, especially from Saudi Arabia. Academic research shows that conservative Wahhabism provides a passive framework for extremism but is not in and of itself a cause for violent radicalization. President Gayoom's management of religion through state prowess ended when he lost the 2008 elections. Succeeding governments were less adept at managing extreme manifestations of religious ideology. Over the next ten years, Maldives became the largest per capita exporter of religious fighters to the Middle East, with close to 200—which is 4 of every 10,000—Maldivians becoming foreign fighters in the Middle East. Simultaneously, Wahhabi influence increased; conservative religious parties were formed and exercised significant political influence; and the practice of Islam in the country became more dogmatic.

Geography added to the problem. Malé, the country's capital, has 100,000 residents on an island just one square mile in area (the luxurious tourist resorts are on other islands). In this environment, unemployment, crime, gangs, and radicalization in prisons induce youth toward violence and extremism. A combination of gang violence and extremist ideology creates conditions for terrorism, which could grow further if radicalized fighters returning from the Middle East (estimated at 170 in the mid- and late 2010s) turn to domestic terrorism. A failed bomb plot by such individuals was reportedly covered up in 2017 by the Yameen administration, possibly to avoid attracting public attention to the problem.

The Way Forward

In 2018, in part because of recognition of the above issues, newly elected president Ibrahim Solih launched a new approach toward PCVE. First, a National Reintegration Center was completed and launched in 2020, on an island some distance from Malé, to provide for the comprehensive rehabilitation of Maldivians returning from foreign battlefields. Second, an anti-terror law from 1990 was revised and upgraded to better target and prosecute those engaged in financing or actively supporting violent extremist groups. The government also worked to establish a National Counter Terrorism Centre to better coordinate the work of all relevant agencies and departments. Third, the government worked toward a National Action Plan on PCVE, and exchanged best practices in this regard with Bangladesh, Indonesia, and the Philippines with assistance from UNDP. Fourth, the government made some concerted efforts to engage conservative religious parties that had become an integral part of the political system to provide an alternative faith-based narrative to violent extremism. Fifth, and while treated previously as a group to be shaped rather than consulted, youth began playing a more active role in voicing their concerns and shaping a national agenda through both social and conventional media. Major parties have youth platforms. These opportunities offer peaceful avenues for positive change and become alternatives to violent extremism.

Beyond the above measures by the Solih administration, additional policies may be necessary to more fully address violent extremism. Given the growing centrality of conservative Islam to Maldivian religion and politics, the government will have to find a way to foster dialogue between all Islamic beliefs and practices in the country. A common narrative will have to be developed against violent extremism, and scriptural guidance established for the nonviolent practice of faith, including in pursuit of various types of social or ideological change. To be sure, unlike other countries in the region, Maldives, at the time of writing (early 2021), had not experienced major domestic terrorist attacks at home—it was still in the "preventing" part of "PCVE" rather than the "countering" part of the issue. With comprehensive and inclusive approaches, it could stay that way.

The Philippines

The Philippines provides an interesting point of reference for the cases summarized above. While there are differences with South Asian cases in terms of its history and politics, the Philippines has comprehensively attempted both peacebuilding and PCVE with varying (mostly high) levels of success and has lessons to offer South Asia.

The Mindanao Peace Process

Insurgency in Mindanao, involving its Muslim inhabitants, the Moros, had prevailed in one form or another for decades, until the 2014 Comprehensive Agreement on the Bangsamoro (CAB) between the Philippines government and the Moro Islamic Liberation Front (MILF).[10] As background, since the 1960s, various Moro armed groups coalesced into the Moro National Liberation Front (MNLF). Appreciating the widespread popularity of the insurgency, and the tactical impossibility of fully vanquishing it, the government signed two peace agreements with the rebels in 1976 and 1996. These led to the establishment of the Autonomous Region in Muslim Mindanao (ARMM) with Nur Misuari, the MNLF leader, as its governor, and with the Moros having accepted substantial autonomy instead of independence.

However, two groups broke away from the MNLF—the Abu Sayyaf Group (ASG) and the MILF, which, notwithstanding its name, had the same secular cause as the MNLF, but claimed that the promised autonomy was never delivered. The ASG later morphed into a full-scale extremist operation, claiming allegiance to al Qaeda and ISIS and practicing many of their methods.

In terms of bureaucratic organizational structure, in 1994, the Philippines government launched the Office of the Presidential Adviser of the Peace Process (OPAPP) to support negotiations with the country's several insurgencies (Moros, Cordilleran separatists, Communists, and others). OPAPP still serves as the primary governmental focal point for the Mindanao peace process, and for all international development partners supporting the process.

By 2009, the revived Moro conflict had led to additional violence and influenced the government and the MILF to revive negotiations. The peace process was nationally led (much of the heavy lifting being done by OPAPP), but gently facilitated by Malaysia and observed by an international contact group that included development partners and several international nongovernmental organizations. From 2013 onward, critical technical assistance for the process (and especially for building the MILF's capabilities) was provided by a joint UNDP-World Bank Facility for Advisory Support for Transition Capacities, or FASTRAC, which also provided an occasional venue for track-two discussions at a technical level, when needed. Both the Nepal and Myanmar processes had lacked this dimension. FASTRAC was also welcomed by the Philippines government as an important contribution to equalizing the capabilities of the negotiators from both sides.

In 2014, the government of the Philippines and the MILF signed the CAB. The joint Government-MILF Bangsamoro Transition Commission established under the CAB pursued the task of drafting the legislation—the Bangsamoro Basic Law (BBL)—which would establish the autonomous entity of Bangsamoro with significantly greater powers than enjoyed by the ARMM. The 2014 agreement had a political track, whereby the ex-rebels would form an interim government in Bangsamoro from 2019 to 2022, after which elections would be held. It also had a normalization track to support the Bangsamoro region shift from war to peace. This included disarming 40,000 MILF guerrillas before the planned 2022 elections; assisting economic development in the region; building trust in conflict-affected areas; dissolving other militias; and developing transitional justice arrangements.[11]

Neither the processes of the negotiation of the CAB nor the drafting of the BBL involved the Moro National Liberation Front. And the BBL remained stalled in the Congress until the Duterte presidency commenced in 2016. That year, President Rodrigo Duterte formed a new, more inclusive, Bangsamoro Transition Commission (BTC) including both the MILF as well as the dominant factions of the MNLF. The Misuari wing of the MNLF refused to join the new commission.

While the BTC was able to produce a consensus draft, it could not obtain the larger convergence sought by the president and segments of the Moro leadership. During this period, three critical intermediary efforts came into play with international (specifically UNDP) assistance. One involved the Friends of Peace group, led by the Christian cardinal of Cotabato City, Orlando Quevedo, which comprised a senior group of influencers at the national level. It helped keep the peace process alive following the Mamasapano incident (a 2015 cease-fire violation that left forty-four police and sixteen insurgents dead) through public advocacy, especially in Congress, and also once Duterte assumed the presidency.

Another was the Insider Mediators' Group, comprising senior advisers to the key players in the peace process (including MILF, Misuari, and the dominant MNLF factions) and independent intermediaries linked informally through professional and family associations. It was formed with the support of UNDP and the Netherlands Clingendael Institute. It met frequently, but informally, and managed to converge Moro leaderships around supporting the new Bangsamoro legislation, now called the Bangsamoro Organic Law (BOL), in Congress. Misuari did not agree to actively support the BOL, but did not publicly oppose it either (having been promised a role in a new federal system being developed for the Philippines by the president). When the BOL finally came to the floor of the Congress in August 2018, the Insider Mediators worked closely with key senators and congresspersons to get it passed.

A third was Christians for Peace, an ecumenical group supported by UNDP, which undertook preventive measures on the ground and defused tensions. It was useful when potentially violent tensions arose between minority Christians and other Moro groups, with the former being apprehensive of their continued safety in a Muslim-majority autonomous region.

In February 2019, the Bangsamoro Transitional Authority was sworn in as the interim government of the new Bangsamoro Autonomous Region in Muslim Mindanao (BARMM) with the MILF at the helm. In September 2019, the formal decommissioning and rehabilitation of MILF combatants commenced; by 2020, about 12,000 MILF fighters had laid down their weapons. And while FASTRAC and Friends of Peace had concluded by 2020, the Insider Mediators' Group and Christians for Peace remained actively engaged in keeping Moro groups united behind the objective of a successful transition culminating in elections for a Bangsamoro government in 2022.[12]

Advent of Violent Extremism

In Mindanao, several push and pull factors made youth susceptible to recruitment by groups claiming affiliation to global jihadi networks.[13] A critical "push" factor was the stalling of the Bangsamoro peace process around 2015, and the perception that the Philippines would not end discrimination against the Moros. Conversely, the lure of engaging in heroic violence in defense of an Islamic *ummah* was an important "pull" factor.

In addition to the Bangsamoro Islamic Freedom Fighters (BIFF), which left the MILF's military wing and resumed violent insurgency, and the continued activities of the ASG, this period also saw the emergence of the so-called Maute Group. The Maute brothers converted a clan militia into a separate armed group, with the primary purpose of intimidating local political and economic competition, but with the ideological veneer of global jihad, and sought to break away from the MILF umbrella. They attracted young Moros disillusioned with the mainstream Moro leadership, who were viewed as unable to deliver change, as well as with the slow pace of the implementation of the Comprehensive Agreement on the Bangsamoro.

The Maute Group formed an alliance with the Abu Sayyaf and both pledged allegiance to ISIS. These groups were not linked operationally to al Qaeda or ISIS—their ISIS allegiance was influenced by the desire to acquire local notoriety and intimidate opponents rather than any deep ideological affinity. Still, the global networks—especially ISIS—saw an opportunity to establish a bridgehead in Mindanao through these groups. Through a Malaysian intermediary, ISIS supported a leader of the Abu Sayyaf, Isnilon Hapilon, to organize militant groups in Mindanao to take over a portion of the Bangsamoro territory as their "caliphate" in Southeast Asia. Led by Hapilon, and empowered through resources obtained via ISIS as well as from local criminal groups, members of the Maute Group laid siege to Marawi City in May 2017. The eventual military operations and fighting killed more than 1,000 people, mostly armed fighters, and displaced about 600,000 residents in the city and neighboring towns; Hapilon and the Maute brothers were also killed in these operations.

Governmental Efforts in the Late 2010s

The Marawi episode (and a fatal bombing in Davao City in 2016 organized by a disaffected member of the MNLF) galvanized the Philippines and its development partners into heightened action to counter extremism.

First, with facilitation and technical support from UNDP, a new National Action Plan on PCVE was finalized and adopted in 2019 by the National Security Council and the Anti-Terrorism Council. It began being implemented with assistance from Australia, Japan, the EU, and the United States.

Second, both the national government and the Bangsamoro Transitional Authority encouraged civic groups to step into the breach. A UNDP-supported platform, the Faith-Based Leaders (FBL) Group, brought together religious scholars from the Shia, Sunni, Ahmadiyya, and Sufi groups to define a common alternative narrative based on scripture that was then actively promoted in schools and mosques; when extremist groups attempted to use the COVID-19 crisis to promote misinformation and hate speech, the FBL responded swiftly and preempted these efforts.

Third, the provincial government of Lanao del Sur and the Armed Forces of the Philippines worked with UNDP to establish a comprehensive deradicalization program for those who joined extremist groups.

Fourth, the Bangsamoro government moved toward establishing a systematic early-warning-and-response system for extremist violence; it also sought to establish a youth volunteer program for young persons seeking to bring about meaningful change in their communities.

Conclusion

The five cases examined above offer several policy lessons for dealing with insurgencies and violent extremism in South Asia.

First, both Myanmar and the Philippines have had to deal with multiple insurgencies. Myanmar has taken the route of trying to bring different cease-fires into a national accord. The Philippines has signed consecutive peace deals with different armed groups and then attempted to converge them.

Second, Nepal is the only case to deal with a unified insurgency. In both Nepal and the Philippines, the primary insurgent group formed the postconflict government, in Nepal at the national level and in the Philippines at the regional level.

Third, in Nepal and Myanmar, peace processes have been a part of a wider transition to a more inclusive political system. In the Philippines, the formation of the Bangsamoro Autonomous Region is viewed as merging eventually with a wider transition to a federal system for the entire country.

Fourth, of the three countries countering insurgencies, the Philippines made the most active use of intermediary groups. The International Contact Group, FASTRAC, Friends of Peace, the Insider Mediators' Group, and Christians for Peace all provided Filipino parties with multiple options and roads to peace. Nepal's domestic facilitators provided it an important internal resource, but one that may not have been fully utilized. Myanmar had not developed or used any of these options.

Fifth, and looking more widely at South Asia, and especially from the reference point of the Philippines, peace processes and negotiations with insurgents are more likely to work if they widen the circle of trust and participation, especially through "insider mediation."

Sixth, the Philippines is one of the only two countries in the wider Asia-Pacific region that has a government department specifically dealing with these issues, the other being the Ministry of Peace and Reconstruction in Nepal. Myanmar and Afghanistan had temporary mechanisms related to then ongoing peace processes.

Seventh, and in all three cases of countering insurgencies, UN and international roles have been played quietly and humbly, and without overwhelming domestic capabilities, and with due regard for national processes, ownership, and sovereignty. The UN and its agencies have served as informal intermediaries and facilitators when called on to do so, but primarily as the providers of technical capabilities, relevant lessons learned, and policy and programmatic accompaniment. It is important to note that in the context of South and Southeast Asia, this role may have been more appropriate given high levels of national capacity and awareness. In all cases, it can be argued that the absence of this assistance would have made achieving peace process goals a slower and more complicated task. At the same time, it is challenging to assert that UN roles were absolutely critical to achieving cease-fires or peace agreements, or to their implementation.

These cases also reveal that South Asia has not sought to apply systematic lessons from other peacemaking and peacebuilding cases from around the world, especially on dealing with subnational armed groups. Additionally, many subnational conflicts in South Asia originate from accumulated grievances over perceptions of marginalization, prolonged local violence and internal displacement over land and natural resources, and environmental damage. There is significant regional and international experience that can be drawn upon to address these challenges within the framework of development cooperation, and with an emphasis on building the relevant national and local capacities. On both peacebuilding and PCVE in the Philippines, UN agencies and international partners have acted within this framework and in the context of national leadership, and this provides a good precedent for South Asian countries to avail themselves of experiences and technical support without compromising ownership or sovereignty.

On the issue of PCVE, the Philippines moved rapidly ahead to formulate and implement its National Action Plan. An updating of its Human Security Act into an anti-terror law in 2020 generated significant public controversy, but a dialogue was taking place between the security sector and faith-based leaders to ensure that the law is properly implemented for the Bangsamoro Autonomous Region.

Unlike Maldives and Bangladesh, the Philippines has managed to achieve greater convergence and joint action among different practices of Islam and sustain more systematic intrafaith and interfaith dialogue. Similarly, the involvement of youth and women, especially with deradicalization, has been significant.

Both Maldives and Bangladesh will have to find ways to involve a greater number of civic and faith-based leaders, and also to use them as a part of an effective community warning and response system at the local level. However, this is more a matter of bringing current efforts to scale than of lack of capacity, and both countries have begun to move in the right direction.

Both Bangladesh and Maldives, despite concerted and initially successful responses to short-term risks, are still searching for an effective longer-term strategy for keeping alienated or radicalized individuals from extremist groups. A key step in this regard would be to credibly engage three key groups that have been empirically established as having great success in pulling alienated individuals and groups back from extremism: youth (especially on social media), women (especially within their families and communities), and faith-based leaders.

To conclude, this comparative analysis of select internal security threats in South and Southeast Asia offers useful lessons for South Asian states. International support and partnerships, tailored to the local situation and in coordination with national governments and other stakeholders, can assist these states in countering the challenges of insurgency and violent extremism.

NOTES

1. The views expressed in this chapter are strictly the author's own and not those of the UNDP.

2. For a comparison of several cases, see Shanthie Mariet D'Souza, ed., *Countering Insurgencies and Violent Extremism in South and South East Asia* (New York: Routledge, 2019).

3. For a discussion, see Prakash Adhikari and Steven Samford, "The Nepali

State and the Dynamics of the Maoist Insurgency," *Studies in Comparative International Development* 48, no. 4 (2013), pp. 457–81; and Sebastian von Einsiedel, David M. Malone, and Suman Pradhan, eds., *Nepal in Transition: From People's War to Fragile Peace* (Cambridge University Press, 2012).

4. For a related discussion, see Jacques Bertrand, Alexandre Pelletier, and Ardeth Maung Thawnghmung, "First Movers, Democratization and Unilateral Concessions: Overcoming Commitment Problems and Negotiating a 'Nationwide Cease-Fire' in Myanmar," *Asian Security* 16, no. 1 (2020), pp. 15–34.

5. For a discussion, see Shahab Enam Khan, "Bangladesh: The Changing Dynamics of Violent Extremism and the Response of the State," *Small Wars & Insurgencies* 28, no. 1 (2017), pp. 191–217; and Ali Riaz, "Who Are the Bangladeshi 'Islamist Militants'?" *Perspectives on Terrorism* 10, no. 1 (2016), pp. 2–18.

6. One significant attack was in 2007, when twelve tourists were injured by an Improvised Explosive Device in Malé. Four murders possibly linked to violent extremism involved a government official (2006), a religious scholar (2013), a journalist (2014), and a blogger (2017), while a journalist was stabbed in 2012. In February 2020, three tourists were stabbed by Islamist extremists (but survived), and individuals with suspected ties to ISIS claimed responsibility in a video. These were believed to be revenge attacks after a government crackdown on violent extremism, which intensified after the United States designated a Maldivian national as a terrorist in September 2019, and after a Maldivian presidential commission investigating the above 2013–2017 murders linked them to religious extremists. In May 2021, the Maldives speaker of parliament (who had been president in 2008–2012) was injured in a bomb attack. See Azim Zahir, "Islamic State Terror Arrives in the Maldives," *The Diplomat*, April 18, 2020.

7. See "The Maldives' Foreign Fighter Phenomenon—Theories and Perspectives," European Foundation for South Asian Studies (EFSAS), April 20, 2020.

8. See "The Maldives: Return of Democracy and the Challenges Ahead," European Foundation for South Asian Studies (EFSAS), January 2019.

9. For a discussion of the 2000s, see Mahwish Hafeez, "Growing Islamic Militancy in Maldives," *Strategic Studies* 28, no. 1 (2008), pp. 251–67.

10. Primitivo Cabanes Ragandang III, "Philippines: Factors of Century-Old Conflict and Current Violent Extremism in the South," *Conflict Studies Quarterly* 22 (2018).

11. International Crisis Group, *Southern Philippines: Keeping Normalisation on Track in the Bangsamoro* (Brussels: International Crisis Group, April 2021).

12. Zachary Abuza and Luke Lischin, "The Challenges Facing the Philippines' Bangsamoro Autonomous Region at One Year," USIP Special Report, United States Institute of Peace, June 10, 2020.

13. Peter Chalk, "Militant Islamic Extremism in the Southern Philippines," in *Islam in Asia,* edited by Jason F. Isaacson and Colin Rubenstein (New York: Routledge, 2017), pp. 187–222.

Contributors

KANTI BAJPAI is Professor and Wilmar Chair of Asian Studies and Director, Centre on Asia and Globalisation, Lee Kuan Yew School of Public Policy, National University of Singapore. He specializes in and has written extensively on Indian foreign policy and national security. His most recent book is *India Versus China: Why They Are Not Friends*.

ŠUMIT GANGULY is Distinguished Professor of Political Science and Rabindranath Tagore Chair in Indian Cultures and Civilizations at Indiana University, Bloomington. He is a Senior Fellow at the Foreign Policy Research Institute, a member of the Council on Foreign Relations, and a Fellow of the American Academy of Arts and Sciences. His most recent books are the *Oxford Short Introduction to Indian Foreign Policy*; *Deadly Impasse: Indo-Pakistani Relations at the Dawn of a New Century*; *Ascending India and Its State Capacity*; and *The Oxford Handbook of India's National Security*.

AMIT GUPTA is Associate Professor in the Department of International Security Studies at USAF Air War College, Maxwell Air Force Base, Alabama. His research covers military forces and armed force modernization in regional powers, as well as Indian security policy. His books include *Building an Arsenal: The Evolution of Regional Power Force Structures*; *Global Security Watch—India*; and the edited volume *Air Forces: The Next Generation*.

KAVITA R. KHORY is Ruth Lawson Professor of Politics and Carol Hoffmann Collins Director of the McCulloch Center for Global Initiatives at Mount Holyoke College. Her scholarship and research ranges from analyzing political violence in South Asia to tackling questions of political identity and citizenship in multicultural societies. She has written about nationalism and ethnic conflict in Pakistan, insurgency movements and regional security challenges in South Asia, and the domestic and foreign policy implications for Pakistan of the war in Afghanistan.

EDWARD KOLODZIEJ is Professor Emeritus of Political Science at the University of Illinois at Urbana-Champaign, where he also served as Director of the Office of Global Studies and Director of the Program on Arms Control, Disarmament, and International Security. His books include *From Superpower to Besieged Global Power: Restoring World Order after the Bush Doctrine's Failure*; *Security and International Relations*; and *A Force Profonde: The Power, Politics, and Promise of Human Rights*.

CHETAN KUMAR is Senior Advisor on Peacebuilding to the UN Resident Coordinator and the United Nations Development Program (UNDP) in the Philippines. His work has focused on building national and local capacities for the prevention and resolution of conflicts, the promotion of dialogue, and the constructive management of diversity through the reform of governance.

DINSHAW MISTRY is Professor of International Relations and Asian Studies at the University of Cincinnati. He has also been a Council on Foreign Relations International Affairs Fellow, and a Fellow at the Woodrow Wilson Center, Harvard's Belfer Center for Science and International Affairs, and Stanford's Center for International Security and Cooperation. He specializes in the areas of nuclear and missile proliferation, as well as South Asian security and U.S. foreign policy in the region. He is the author of *Containing Missile Proliferation* and *The US-India Nuclear Agreement*.

MARVIN G. WEINBAUM is Director for Afghanistan and Pakistan Studies at the Middle East Institute. He is Professor Emeritus of Political Science at the University of Illinois at Urbana-Champaign, and served as analyst for Pakistan and Afghanistan in the U.S. Department of State's Bureau of Intelligence and Research from 1999 to 2003. His research, teaching, and consultancies have focused on the issues of national security, state-building, democratization, and political economy in Afghanistan and Pakistan. He is the author or editor of six books and has written more than 100 journal articles and book chapters on these and related issues.

Index

Page numbers followed by t represent tables.

Abbott, Tony, 101
Abe, Shinzo, 60–61
Advani, L. K., 92
Afghanistan: Democracy Index score, 11; drug smuggling, 182; Fragile States Index, 11; Freedom House political freedom score, 11; Haqqani network, 38; Human Development Index score, 10; humanitarian aid from India, 36; human trafficking, 182; immigrant persecution, 77–78; India relations, 35, 36–37; infrastructure project financing from India, 36; interests in Balochistan, 184, 185; internal security threats, 17; Jalalabad, 185; Kandahar, 185; Kandahar–Herat Highway, 36; Mazar-i-Sharif, 185; military arms transfers, 36; National Security Forces, 37; ongoing peace process with Myanmar, 209; Parliament building, 36; per capita GDP, 10; reconstruction efforts, 35; refugees in Balochistan, 176, 177, 183; Salma Hydroelectric Dam, 36; Soviet invasion, 199; Taliban (*see* Taliban); trilateral meetings, 35; Turkmenistan-Afghanistan-Pakistan-India (TAPI) energy pipeline agreement, 99; U.S. economic aid, 10; U.S. infrastructure investment projects, 5; U.S. state-building efforts, 36, 156; war in, 2, 12, 18, 25, 37–39, 42, 185; weapons trafficking, 182
Ahmedzai, Mir Suleman, 181
Almond, Gabriel, 150
al Qaeda, 37, 200, 204, 207
al Zawahari, Ayman, 37
Angola, 59
Antony, A. K., 97
Argentina, 139
ARMM. *See* Philippines, Autonomous Region in Muslim Mindanao
ASEAN. *See* Association of Southeast Asian Nations

ASG. *See* Philippines, Abu Sayyaf Group
Association of Southeast Asian Nations (ASEAN), 30: East Asia Summit, 30; Regional Forum, 30
Aung San, 195
Aung San Suu Kyi, 195, 197, 198
Australia: bilateral defense interaction with India, 28, 29; Blue Dot Network, 4–5; GDP, 26; infrastructure investment projects, 5, 178; Lowry Institute scale of power, 27; Malabar naval exercise, 32; military spending, 26–27; National Action Plan on PCVE implementation in the Philippines, 207; Quadrilateral Security Dialogue, 13, 29–30, 61; trilateral leader summits, 29
Australia Group (chemical and biological controls), 42

Baloch, Allah Nazar, 179
Baloch, Karima, 180
Baloch, Sanaullah, 175
Balochistan province (Pakistan): Afghan refugees, 176, 177, 183; Balochi language, 174; Baloch Liberation Army (BLA), 179, 182; Baloch Liberation Front (BLF), 179; Balochistan National Party (BNP-Mengal), 183; Baloch Raaji Aajoi Sangar (BRAS), 279; Baloch Student Organization (BSO-Azad), 180; Brahui language, 174; British Balochistan state, 174; Chinese Consulate, 182; Chinese workers, 177; drug smuggling, 182; ethnic identity and political mobilization, 173–175, 176; Hazaras minority community, 186; Human Rights Council, 180; human rights issues, 189, 181, 182, 183; insurgency, 16, 98, 156, 172–173, 176, 179, 181–182; international dimensions, 184–186; Kalat National Party, 174; land and territory, 174; missing persons, 180, 183–184; National Awami Party, 176; nationalist movement, 9, 173–175; natural resources curse, 177–178, 183–184; non-state actors, 184–186; Pakistan occupation, 174; Pakistan Tehreek-e-Insaaf (PTI) government, 183; political autonomy and power-sharing, 175, 183–184; provincial status, 175; Shamsi Airbase, 186; sources of conflict, 175–180; Urdu language, 173, 177. *See also* Pakistan
Bangladesh: Cox's Bazar, 200; creation of, 173, 175; debt distress and vulnerability to Chinese, 5; democracy and development, 8, 9; Democracy Index score, 11; Dinajpur, 200; economic and security links to China, 6, 54–55; economic growth, 201; exports, 6; Fragile States Index, 11; Freedom House political freedom score, 11; Human Development Index score, 10; immigrant persecution, 77–78; independence, 78; infrastructure investments in, 6, 55, 58; internal security threats, 17, 18, 191, 199–201, 210; Jamattul Mujahidden Bangladesh (JMB), 199; Jessore, 200; Joypurhat, 200; maritime security, 4; middle class, 201; military arms procurement, 6; Moulobhi Bazar, 200; National Action Plan on PCVE, 201, 203; National Committee on Militancy Resistance and Prevention (NCMRP), 200; "peace observatory," 200; Pekua, 55; per capita GDP, 10; Preventing and Countering Violent Extremism (PCVE), 190, 201; Satkhira, 200; Soviet invasion of Afghanistan, 199; UN peacekeeping contributor, 3–4; U.S. economic aid, 10
Bangladesh NGO Network for Radio and Communication (BNNRC), 200
BARMM. *See* Philippines, Bangsamoro Autonomous Region in Muslim Mindanao
Baru, Sanjaya, 96
Basrur, Rajesh, 88
BBL. *See* Philippines, Bangsamoro Basic Law
Belarus, 68
Belt and Road Initiative (BRI). *See* People's Republic of China, Belt and Road Initiative

Bengali nationalist movement, 173
Bhargava, Rajeev, 76
Bharatiya Janata Party (BJP). *See* India
Bhootani, Aslam, 184
Bhutan, 27, 50, 52
Bhutto, Benazir, 98, 176
Bhutto, Zulfikar Ali, 159, 162, 163, 169, 175–176
Bibi, Asia, 159
Biden, Joseph, 3
BIFF. *See* Philippines, Bangsamoro Islamic Freedom Fighters
bin Laden, Osama, 37, 156, 166
Birendra, King, 192
Bizenjo, Mir Hazar Khan, 176
BJP. *See* India, Bharatiya Janata Party
Blackwill, Robert, 2
Blair, Tony, 112–113
BLA. *See* Baloch Liberation Army
BLF. *See* Baloch Liberation Front
Blue Dot Network, 4–5
BNNRC. *See* Bangladesh NGO Network for Radio and Communication
BNP-Mengal. *See* Balochistan National Party
BOL. *See* Philippines, Bangsamoro Organic Law
Bollfrass, Alex, 135
Bo Xilai, 72
BRAS. *See* Baloch Raaji Aajoi Sangar
Brazil, 30, 44
Brazil, Russia, India, China, South Africa (BRICS) group, 44
BRI. *See* China, Belt and Road Initiative
BRICS group. *See* Brazil, Russia, India, China, South Africa group
Brunei, 10
BSO-Azad. *See* Baloch Student Organization
BTC. *See* Philippines, Bangsamoro Transition Commission
Bugti, Brahumdagn, 181, 185
Bugti, Nawab Akbar Khan, 98, 175, 176, 181, 185
Burki, Shahid Javed, 158
Burma. *See* Myanmar
Bush, George W., 2, 3, 60, 113, 128

CAA. *See* India, Citizen Amendment Act
CAATSA. *See* Countering America's Adversaries Through Sanctions Act
CAB. *See* Philippines, Comprehensive Agreement on the Bangsamoro
Canada, 178
CBMs. *See* confidence-building measures
CCP. *See* People's Republic of China, Chinese Communist Party
Charter 08 Manifesto, 70
Chile, 178
China. *See* People's Republic of China
China Overseas Port Holding Company, 178
China-Pakistan Economic Corridor (CPEC), 40, 53, 178–181, 184, 185
Chinese Communist Party (CCP). *See* People's Republic of China
Chinese Metallurgical Construction Company, 178
Christians for Peace, 206, 208
Citizen Amendment Act. *See* India
Civic Culture: Political Attitudes and Democracy in Five Nations (Almond and Verba), 150
Clinton, Bill, 2, 112
Cohen, Stephen, 87, 139, 164
Coll, Steve, 96
Comprehensive Nuclear Test Ban Treaty, 2, 34, 129
confidence-building measures (CBMs), 93–94
Conrad, Joseph, 67
Constable, Pamela, 160
Countering America's Adversaries Through Sanctions Act (CAATSA)
COVID-19, 30, 66, 78, 208
CPEC. *See* China-Pakistan Economic Corridor
Cyclone Diane, 33
Cyclone Idai, 33

democracy: defining legitimacy and citizenship, 68–74; internal security threats, 190–211; liberal democratic legitimacy, 67–68; Pakistan's political culture and implications for, 15, 148–171; in South Asia, 7–11. *See also specific countries*
Democracy Index score, 11
Deng Xiaoping, 69–70, 71, 72, 73

Destro, Robert, 9
Dhungana, Dhaman Nath, 192
Doklam incident, 52, 126
Dung, Nguyen Tan, 101
Durrani, Asad, 172
Durrani, Mahmuc, 96–97
Duterte, Rodrigo, 205–206

Economy, Elizabeth, 71
Egypt, 68: Sharm el-Sheikh, 98
European Union, 200, 207

Facility for Advisor Support for Transition Capacities (FASTRAC), 205, 206, 208
Fair, Christine, 167
FBL Group. *See* Philippines, Faith-Based Leaders Group
Falklands War, 139
FASTRAC. *See* Facility for Advisor Support for Transition Capacities
FATA. *See* Pakistan, Federally Administered Tribal Areas
FATF. *See* Financial Action Task Force
Federalist Papers, 67
Financial Action Task Force (FATF), 43
Fragile States Index, 10–11
France, 30
Freedom House political freedom score, 11
Friends of Peace, 205–206, 208

Galwan Valley, 51, 126, 144
Gandhi, Indira, 138
Gandhi, Mahatma, 75
Gayoom, Maumoon, 202
Germany, 6, 138
Gilani, Yousaf Raza, 98
global governance, 66–67
Gupta, Shekhar, 90, 91
Gyanendra, King, 192

Hague Code of Conduct, 127
Hapilon, Isnilon, 207
"Heart of Asia" conference, 100, 101
Hibbard, Scott, 75
Hitler, Adolf, 67
Holey Artisan Bakery and Café (Bangladesh), 200, 201
Hong Kong, 30, 51, 74, 80

Hu Jintao, 71, 72
Human Development Index scores, 10
human rights issues, 7, 8, 9. *See also specific countries*
Hungary, 68
Hussain, Touqir, 169

IAEA. *See* International Atomic Energy Agency
IAF. *See* Indian Air Force
IMF. *See* International Monetary Fund
India: "Act East" approach, 30; Afghanistan relations, 36–37, 38; Agra, 89–93, 98; Arunachal Pradesh, 52; Assam, 27; Australia Group (chemical and biological controls), 42; Ayodhya, 78; Babri Masjid destruction 78–79; Bharatiya Janata Party (BJP), 67–68, 75–79, 80, 97, 116; Bhuj earthquake, 91, 92; bilateral defense interactions, 28–29; border disputes, 49–51, 52, 61; China relations, 12, 34, 43–44, 49–51, 59–61, 126–127; Citizen Amendment Act (CAA), 9, 76, 77–78, 81; "Cold Start" strategy, 115, 136; confidence-building measures (CBMs), 93–94; Comprehensive Dialogue, 100, 102; Comprehensive Nuclear Test Ban Treaty, 2, 129; Constitution, 76, 77; cooperation-defection cyclicality with Pakistan, 86–108; counterbalance to China, 25, 26–30, 43; COVID-19, 78, 80; Dalit community, 9; defense budget, 52; defense coproduction with United States, 31–32, 141; democracy and development, 7–8, 13; Democracy Index score, 11; democratic legitimacy and citizenship, 67–68, 75–79, 79–82; development aid donor, 7; diplomatic talks with Pakistan, 13–14; economic growth, 96, 102; exports/imports, 6, 7, 30; Falklands War, 139; Fragile States Index, 11; Freedom House political freedom score, 11; GDP, 10, 13, 26; governance challenges, 13, 66–85; Gujarat, 78–79, 100, 101; Gurdaspur, 100, 101; "hard balancing" against China, 25, 30;

Himalayan region, 133, 134; Hindi language, 76; Hindu state, 75–79, 80–81; *Hindutva*, 76, 80; Human Development Index score, 10; human rights issues, 9, 78, 81, 185; humanitarian aid to Afghanistan, 36; increased diplomatic profile in Southeast Asia, 30; Indian Ocean security, 9, 11, 12, 26, 28, 33, 43; Indus Waters Treaty, 100; infrastructure investment projects, 5, 6, 7, 36; interests in Balochistan, 184, 185; internal security threats, 17; Iran relations, 26, 35–36, 43; Joint Investigation Team (JIT), 99–102; Kargil, 88, 89–93, 95, 103, 111–112, 136, 167; Ladakh, 51, 77, 126, 134, 144; Lahore Declaration, 90, 93; language, 76; limited war plans, 115–119; "Look East" approach, 30, 55–56; "Make in India" program, 142, 143, 144; Malabar naval exercise, 32; Marut program, 138; media outlets, 80; military arms deals, 7, 12, 25, 26, 30–33, 34, 36, 43, 135, 137, 138–145; military exercises with United States, 31–32; military spending, 26–27; military tensions with China, 15, 28, 40, 49–65, 120–121, 122, 126–127, 128–129, 135–136, 139, 145; military tensions with Pakistan, 2, 14, 15, 27, 43, 88–108, 109–132, 135–136, 139; Missile Technology Control Regime, 42; Most Favored Nation (MFN) status from Pakistan, 99; Mumbai, 97, 98, 100, 144; Muslims, 9, 76, 77–79, 81; National Register of Citizens (NRC), 76, 78–79, 81; national security advisers (NSA) meeting, 99–100; naval fleet, 27–28; Nepal relations, 57–58, 191–192; "Next Steps in Strategic Partnership," 95; no-first-use policy, 110, 117, 127, 129, 137; nuclear arsenal, 2–3, 14, 28, 34, 42, 50, 52–53, 60, 88–89, 90, 95, 109–132, 123t, 137–138, 167; Nuclear Suppliers Group membership, 3, 129; Office of the Registrar of Newspapers, 80; Oil and Natural Gas Corporation (ONGC), 59–60; oil and natural gas imports, 35, 59–60; Pakistan relations, 35, 36, 41, 43, 79, 86–108, 156, 162, 164, 165, 166–167; Parliament attack, 91, 112; Pathankot, 99, 100, 101, 102; political hardening in, 13; Project Cheetah, 144; Quadrilateral Security Dialogue, 13, 29–30, 34, 43, 60–61; Rajasthan state, 115; religious versus secular nation, 75–79; Russian relations, 26, 33–35, 43–44; Sebu La, 50; security interaction with other countries, 6, 25; Sikkim, 50; Simla accord, 93; Sir Creek dispute, 94, 99; "six-plus-two" Composite Dialogue, 89, 94, 100; social complexity of, 80–81; terrorism threats from Pakistan, 86, 88–95, 97, 102–103, 112–115; trade partner with China, 30; trilateral meetings, 29, 35; tsunami relief operations, 33; Turkmenistan-Afghanistan-Pakistan-India (TAPI) energy pipeline agreement, 99; Udhamur, 100; UN peacekeeping contributor, 4, 42; UN Security Council membership, 3, 59, 129; urban population growth, 176; U.S. defense relations, 28–29, 30–33, 43, 95–96; U.S. economic aid, 2, 10; U.S. economic interest in, 11; U.S.-India Civil Nuclear Agreement, 60, 95; U.S. infrastructure investment projects, 5; U.S. strategic interests, 2–3, 11–12, 25–30, 42, 62–63, 101, 103, 145, 166–167; Wassenaar Arrangement, 42; West Bengal, 27, 80; as world power, 2. *See also* Galwan Valley; Indian Air Force; Jammu; Kashmir

Indian Air Force (IAF): China versus IAF, 134–136; conventional deterrence, 133–134; missions in Kashmir, 113; modernization, 14–15; nuclear mission, 137–138; Pakistan versus IAF, 136–137; U.S. partnership, 141–145; weapons acquisition/production policies, 138–141. *See also* India

Indian Coast Guard, 33

Indian Navy, 29, 33, 113, 115, 144

Indian Ocean security, 9, 11, 12, 26, 28, 33, 43
Indonesia, 33, 191, 195, 203: Gerakan Aceh Merdeka, 195
Indus Waters Treaty, 100
Insiders Mediators' Group, 206, 208
Intense Tropical Cyclone Idai, 33
International Atomic Energy Agency, 41
International Contact Group, 208
International Monetary Fund (IMF), 40
International Republican Institute, 155
Iran: Baloch-populated areas, 174; Chabahar Port project, 35, 36, 185; Global Hawk strike, 144; India relations, 35–36; interests in Balochistan, 184–185; oil sanctions against, 12, 26, 35, 43; Saudi Arabia relations, 185; Sistan-Balochistan province, 184; Sunni Muslims, 184, 186; trilateral meetings, 35
Iraq, 35
ISI division. *See* Pakistan, Inter-Services Intelligence division
ISIS, 200, 202, 204, 207
Islam, 17, 149, 154, 165, 202, 203, 207, 210
Israel, 30, 156
Israel Aircraft Industries, 144
Italy, 6

Jaishankar, Subrahmanyam, 51
Jaish-e-Mohammed terrorist group (JeM), 114, 136
Jammu, 51, 52, 53, 76, 77, 78, 99, 112
Japan: bilateral defense interaction with India, 28, 29; Blue Dot Network, 4–5; destroyer and frigate fleet, 28; development aid donor, 7; exports, 6; GDP, 26; infrastructure investment projects, 5, 6; Lowry Institute scale of power, 27; Malabar naval exercise, 32; military spending, 26–27; National Action Plan on PCVE implementation in the Philippines, 207; Quadrilateral Security Dialogue, 13, 29–30, 61; security links, 6; trilateral leader summits, 29

JeM. *See* Jaish-e-Mohammed terrorist group
jihadi networks, 206–207
Jinnah, Muhammad Ali (Quaid-i-Azam), 154, 159, 174, 182
JIT. *See* India; Pakistan
JMB. *See* Bangladesh, Jamattul Mujahidden Bangladesh
Joint Investigation Team (JIT). *See* India; Pakistan

Karim, Abdul, 181
Kashmir: Comprehensive Dialogue, 100, 102; human rights issues, 9, 185; Hurriyat separatists, 99–100; internal security threats, 17, 52; Legislative Assembly attack, 92; Line of Actual Control (LAC), 50, 51; Line of Control (LOC), 90, 94, 100, 111–114; Maldivian fighters, 202; Pakistan's concessions to China, 53; peace agreement, 93–99; settlement issues, 14, 43, 86–108, 162, 164; Siachen region, 91, 94, 97, 99; Skardu Air Base, 40; "six-plus-two" Composite Dialogue, 89, 94, 100; special status, 51, 54, 76, 77, 78; Uri attacks, 99, 100, 101
Kasuri, Khurshid, 95, 96–97, 98
Khalid, Shazia, 181
Khan, Amanullah, 180
Khan, A. Q., 41
Khan, Ayub, 181
Khan, Imran, 38, 156, 157, 160, 163, 166, 168, 169, 178, 179, 184
Khan of Kalat, 181
Kovind, Ram Nath, 56

LAC. *See* Kashmir, Line of Actual Control
Lahore Declaration, 90, 93
Lambah, Satinder, 95, 96
Lashkar-e-Jhangvi (LeJ), 186, 202
LeJ. *See* Lashkar-e-Jhangvi
Lenin, Vladimir, 67, 69, 72–73
Libya, 41
Line of Actual Control. *See* Kashmir
Line of Control. *See* Kashmir
LOC. *See* Kashmir, Line of Control

Lodhi, Maleeha, 158
Lowry Institute scale of power, 27
Lui Xiaobo, 70

Madagascar, 33
Madison, James, 67
Malaysia, 6, 191, 205
Maldives: anti-terror law, 203; centrality of Islam religion, 203; debt distress and vulnerability to Chinese, 5, 58, 59; democracy and development, 8, 9; development aid to, 7; exporter of religious fighters, 202; gang violence, 203; maritime initiative with India, 33; India's security interaction, 6–7; infrastructure investment projects, 7; internal security threats, 17, 18, 190–191, 202–204, 210; Malé, 202; maritime security, 4; National Action Plan on PCVE, 203; National Terrorism Centre, 203; Preventing and Countering Violent Extremism, 190, 203–204; tsunami relief operations, 33; U.S. economic aid, 10
Mao Zedong, 8, 17, 68, 69, 71, 72, 73, 191–192, 193, 195
Maritime Security Initiative, 4
Marri, Hyrbyair, 181
Marri, Nawab Khair Baksh, 176, 181
Marx, Karl, 69, 72–73
Mauritius, 33
MCC. *See* Millennium Challenge Corporation
Mengal, Attaullah, 176, 181
MFN status. *See* Most Favored Nation status
MILF. *See* Philippines, Moro Islamic Liberation Front
Millennium Challenge Corporation (MCC), 5
Missile Technology Control Regime, 42
MNLF. *See* Philippines, Moro National Liberation Front
Modi, Narendra, 35, 50–51, 58, 77–78, 79, 80, 81, 99–103, 185
Most Favored Nation (MFN) status, 99
Mozambique, 33

Mujahideen, Hizbul, 91
Mukherjee, Pranab, 97
Mullen, Michael, 38
Musharraf, Pervez, 89–99, 102–103, 158, 163, 176, 177, 178
Muslim League, 90, 174
Muslims, 9, 30, 76, 77–79, 81, 154, 164, 184, 186, 199, 204
Mussolini, Benito, 67
Myanmar: All Burma Students' Democratic Forum, 195; Arakan Liberation Army, 195; China relations, 55–56, 197; Chin National Front, 195; Democratic Karen Buddhist Army, Brigade 5, 195–196; human rights issues, 55–56; immigrant persecution, 78; internal security threats, 17–18, 190, 195–196, 205, 208, 209; Joint Ceasefire Monitoring Committee, 196, 197; Kachin, 195; Kachin Independence Army, 196; Karen National Union, 196, 198; Kayan, 195; Kayin, 195; KNU/KNLA Peace Council, 196; Kyaukpyu, 56; Lahu Democratic Union, 196; National League for Democracy (NLD), 195, 196–197, 198; National Peace and Reconciliation Office, 196, 197; Nationwide Ceasefire Agreement (NCA), 196; New Mon State Party, 196; ongoing peace process with Afghanistan, 209; "Panglong," 197; Pa-O National Liberation Army, 196; "peace dividends," 196, 198; Rakhine State, 56, 195, 198; Restoration Council of Shan State, 196; Rohingyas, 56; Shan, 195; Shan State Army-North, 196, 198; transition from military to civilian rule, 195–196; Union Peace Commission, 196; United Wa State Army, 196

Naipaul, V. S., 153–154
Narayanan, M. K., 97
National Register of Citizens. *See* India
national security advisers (NSA) meeting, 99–100
NCA. *See* Myanmar, Nationwide Ceasefire Agreement

NCMRP. See Bangladesh, National Committee on Militancy Resistance and Prevention
Nehru, Jawaharlal, 75, 78, 138
Nepal: China relations, 57–58, 192; Communist Party of Nepal, 192; Comprehensive Peace Agreement, 192; debt distress and vulnerability to Chinese, 5; democracy and development, 8, 9; Democracy Index score, 11; earthquake relief, 57–58, 194–195; economic and security links to China, 6, 57–58; exports/imports, 7; Fragile States Index, 11; Freedom House political freedom score, 11; Human Development Index score, 10; Indian Ocean/Pacific tsunami, 194–195; India's security interaction, 6–7, 191–192; infrastructure investment projects, 7; internal security threats, 17–18, 190, 191–195, 208–209; Kathmandu, 192, 193; Madhes/Terai region, 58, 191, 194; Millennium Challenge Corporation aid, 5; Ministry for Peace and Reconstruction, 193, 209; Maoist insurgency, 8, 191–192, 193, 195; National Transition to Peace Program, 193–194; "nation-building" operations, 193; peace process and peace agreement, 192–195, 205; per capita GDP, 10; Sustainable Development Goals (SDGs), 194; UN peacekeeping contributor, 4; urban population growth, 176; U.S. economic aid, 10
Netherlands Clingendael Institute, 206
New Zealand, 30
"Next Steps in Strategic Partnership," 95
NFC. See Pakistan, National Finance Commission
Nigeria, 60
NLD. See Myanmar, National League for Democracy
Non-Aligned Movement, Summit of the, 45
North Korea, 27, 41
NPT. See Nuclear Nonproliferation Treaty
NRC. See India, National Register of Citizens
NSA meeting. See national security advisers (NSA) meeting
NSG. See Nuclear Suppliers Group
Nonproliferation Treaty (NPT), 3, 60
Nuclear Suppliers Group (NSG), 3, 129
nuclear weapons: civilian nuclear agreement, 3, 129; expansion and deterrence stability, 119–126; nonproliferation efforts, 60; proliferation of, 1–3; risk of use in India-Pakistan crises, 111–119; stability in South Asia, 14, 88–89, 109–132; tactical nuclear systems, 110, 117, 124. See also specific countries

Obama, Barack, 3, 128
O'Donnell, Frank, 135
ONCG. See India, Oil and Natural Gas Corporation
OPAPP. See Philippines, Office of the Presidential Adviser to the Peace Process
Overholt, William, 70

PAF. See Pakistan Air Force
Pakistan: Afghanistan relations, 18, 36–37, 165; Afghanistan war, 25, 37–39, 42; Ahmadiyya Muslim community, 9, 78; anti-India terrorist groups, 42; Awaran, 180, 182; Balakot, 136, 142; Bangladesh independence, 78; Bengalis, 78; Bhuj earthquake, 91, 92; blasphemy law, 159; border disputes, 52; "Brahmanism" rule, 161; bureaucratic subculture, 161–163; Chagai, 178; China-Pakistan Economic Corridor (CPEC), 40, 53, 178–181, 184, 185; China relations, 12, 18, 25, 26, 39–41, 43, 167; civilian nuclear agreement, 3, 129; Civil Service Academy, 161; civil service bureaucracy, 161–163; Commission of Enquiry on Enforced Disappearances, 180; Comprehensive Dialogue, 100, 102; Comprehensive Nuclear Test Ban Treaty, 2, 129; confi-

dence-building measures (CBMs), 93–94; conservatism and protection of privilege, 161–163; conspiratorial behavior, 155–156, 166; Constitution, 183, 186; cooperation-defection cyclicality with India, 86–108; cross-border terrorism, 14; culture and democracy, 148–171; debt distress and vulnerability to Chinese, 5, 40, 177, 178–179; democratic advances/backsliding, 8; Democracy Index score, 11; Dera Bugti, 177, 179, 180, 182, 186; diplomatic talks with India, 13–14; domestic terrorism, 156–157; economic and security links to China, 6, 26, 39–41, 58; economic growth, 96–97, 102, 156, 160, 187; educational system, 149; elections, 153; ethno-nationalist movements, 173–175, 176–177; federal bureaucracy, 151; Federally Administered Tribal Areas (FATA), 16, 98; Federal Ministry of Petroleum and Natural Resources, 178; Financial Action Task Force, 43; Fragile States Index, 11; Freedom House political freedom score, 11; governance and security connections, 150; government corruption, 149–150, 152–155, 162–163; Gwadar, 40, 53–54, 177, 178–181, 182, 184, 185; "Heart of Asia" conference, 100, 101; Hub, 185; Human Development Index score, 10; Human Rights Commission, 180; human rights issues, 9, 180; immigrant persecution, 77–78; Indian Air Force versus Pakistan, 136–137; India relations, 35, 36, 41, 43, 79, 86–108, 156, 162, 164, 165, 166–167; India's limited war plans, 115–119; Indus Waters Treaty, 100; infrastructure investments, 40, 58, 178–179, 184; interests in Balochistan, 184; internal security challenges, 16, 17; Inter-Services Intelligence (ISI) division, 165, 172; Islamic state, 154, 169, 173; Islamization program, 159; JeM (Jaish-e-Mohammed terrorist group), 114; Joint Investigation Team (JIT), 99–102; Kalat state, 174, 181; Karachi, 16, 38, 40, 179, 185; Kargil War, 88, 89–93, 95, 103, 111–112, 136, 167; Kharan state, 174; Khyber province, 16, 114, 176; Kohlu, 179, 182, 186; Lahore, 89–93; Lahore Declaration, 90, 93; Lal Masjid takeover, 98; Lasbella, 174; lawyers' movement, 159; as "Major Non-NATO Ally," 95–96; Makran state, 174; *masjid*, 98; media influences, 149, 166; Minar-e-Pakistan, 90; military arms procurement, 39, 125, 142; military subculture, 149, 159–160, 163, 164–168; military tensions with India, 2, 14, 15, 27, 43, 88–108, 109–132, 167; military ties with China, 26, 39, 53–59; Most Favored Nation (MFN) status to India, 99; Muhajir "ethnic" identity, 173; National Action Plan, 42–43; National Finance Commission (NFC), 183, 186; National School of Public Policy, 161; national security advisers (NSA) meeting, 99–100; no-first-use policy, 117; nuclear arsenal, 12, 14, 25, 26, 41–42, 43, 53, 88–89, 90, 95, 102, 109–132, 125t, 167; nuclear nonproliferation pact with China, 60; "One China and Two Systems" policy with Hong Kong, 74, 80; Pakistan Tehreek-e-Insaaf (PTI) government, 183; Pashtun nationalist movement, 9, 166, 173, 185; patronage-based political system, 161–163; per capita GDP, 10; Peshawar, 38; political culture and implications for democracy, 15, 148–171; political paranoia, 155–157; popular culture, 152–157; Punjab province, 16, 173, 174, 176–177; Qasim, 40; Quetta, 38, 176, 182, 185; Rekodiq, 178; safe haven for terrorists, 38, 95, 185, 202; Saindak Copper Gold Project, 178; Shias, 78; Simla accord, 93; Sindhi province, 9, 16, 173, 174, 177; Sir Creek dispute,

Pakistan (*cont.*)
94, 99; "six-plus-two" Composite Dialogue, 89, 94, 100; Supreme Court, 166; Taliban (*see* Taliban); tax collection/distribution, 153, 183; terrorism threats toward India, 86, 88–95, 97, 102–103, 112–115 (*see also* Kashmir); Turbat, 176, 182; Turkmenistan-Afghanistan-Pakistan-India (TAPI) energy pipeline agreement, 99; UN peacekeeping contributor, 3–4; UN terrorist list, 54; urban middle-class subculture, 151, 157–161; urban population growth, 176; U.S. economic aid, 2, 10, 12, 18; U.S. infrastructure investment projects, 5; U.S. security aid, 39; U.S. state-building efforts in Afghanistan, 36, 166–167; U.S. strategic interests, 11–12, 18, 25–26, 37–42, 95, 101, 103, 112, 156, 160; U.S. talks with Taliban, 38–39, 42. *See also* Balochistan province; Jammu; Kashmir

Pakistan Army, 167, 174
Pakistan Air Force (PAF), 133, 136–137
Pakistan Navy, 39, 115
Pakistan Stock Exchange (PSE), 182
Pakistan Tehreek-e-Insaaf (PTI) government, 183
Pangong Tso, 51
Paris Climate Change Conference, 100
Pashtun Tahafuz Movement (PTM), 166
Patil, Shivraj, 97
PCVE. *See* Preventing and Countering Violent Extremism
People's Liberation Army (PLA), 50–51, 52, 68, 71, 134: Air Force (PLAAF), 133, 134–136; Army Navy (PLAN), 61
People's Republic of China (PRC): America's main "strategic competitor," 25; authoritarian rule, 73, 79–82; Bangladesh relations, 54–55; Belt and Road Initiative, 4, 6–7, 30, 53–54, 55, 58, 71, 178; border disputes, 49–51, 52, 61; CCTV, 73; Charter 08 Manifesto, 70; China-Pakistan Economic Corridor (CPEC), 40, 53, 178–181, 184, 185; Chinese Communist Party (CCP), 67–74, 79–82; Chinese Constitution, 73; Chinese workers in Balochistan, 177; civil war, 71; Consulate, 182; COVID-19 outbreak mishandling, 30; Cultural Revolution, 69; debts owed to, 5–6, 40, 58, 59, 177, 178–179; defense budget, 52; democratic legitimacy and citizenship, 67–74; Democracy Index score, 11; Doklam incident, 52, 126; economic liberation, 69–74; epicenter of global supply chain, 70; exports, 6; Fragile States Index, 11; Freedom House political freedom score, 11; GDP, 10, 13, 26; *Global Times*, 73; governance challenges, 66–85; "Great Firewall," 73, 80; "Great Leap Forward," 69; Himalayan region, 133, 134; Human Development Index score, 10; India as counterbalance to, 25, 26–30, 43; Indian Air Force versus PRC, 134–136; India relations, 12, 34, 43–44, 49–51, 59–61; India's "hard balancing" against, 25, 30; infrastructure investment projects, 4–7, 40, 53–54, 55, 57, 58, 59, 178–179, 184; Lop Nor, 50; Lowry Institute scale of power, 27; Maldives relations, 58; "Maritime Silk Road" development, 58, 71; media control, 73; military arms sales, 6, 7, 26, 39, 56–57, 125, 142; military spending, 27; military tensions with India, 15, 28, 40, 49–65, 120–121, 122, 124, 126–127, 128–129, 145; Myanmar relations, 55–56, 197; National People's Congress, 72; naval forces, 28; Nepal relations, 57–58, 192; no-first-use policy, 127; nuclear arsenal, 14, 28, 50, 52–53, 111, 126–127; nuclear nonproliferation pact with Pakistan, 60; Pakistan as military hub, 40–41, 53–59; Pakistan relations, 12, 18, 25, 26, 39–41, 167, 178–179; Pakistan's actions in Kargil, 92; *People's Daily*, 73; political hardening in, 13; rise as global power, 70–71; role in South Asia security and economics, 4–7;

Scientific Outlook on Development, 73; Social Credit System, 73; Sri Lanka relations, 56–57; surveillance of citizens, 73, 80; technological development, 70, 71, 74; Theory of Three Represents, 73; Tiananmen Square uprising, 70, 79; totalitarian rule, 73, 79–80; trade partners, 30, 54; Uighur Muslims, 30, 81; United States as principal nuclear adversary, 53; U.S.-China fissile material initiative, 129; whistleblowing, 72; World Trade Organization membership, 70; Xinhua (news agency), 73; Xinjiang region, 178–181; Yunnan region, 197; *See also* Galwan Valley; Kashmir; People's Liberation Army

Pew poll, 156

Philippines, 68: Abu Sayyaf Group (ASG), 204, 207; Ahmadiyyas, 208; Anti-Terrorism Council, 207; Armed Forces, 208; Autonomous Region in Muslim Mindanao (ARMM), 204; Bangsamoro Autonomous Region in Muslim Mindanao (BARMM), 204, 206, 208, 210; Bangsamoro Basic Law (BBL), 205; Bangsamoro Islamic Freedom Fighters (BIFF), 207; Bangsamoro Organic Law (BOL), 206; Bangsamoro Transitional Authority, 206, 208; Bangsamoro Transition Commission (BTC), 205; Communists, 204;Comprehensive Agreement on the Bangsamoro (CAB), 204–206; Cordilleran separatists, 204; Davo City, 207; Faith-Based Leaders (FBL) Group, 208; Government-MILF Bangsamoro Transition Commission, 205; Human Security Act, 210; "insider mediation," 209; internal security threats, 191, 197, 204–208, 209; Lanao del Sur, 208; Marawi City, 207; Maute Group, 207; Mindanao peace process, 204–208; Misuari wing of MNLF, 205, 206; Moro Islamic Liberation Front (MILF), 204, 205, 206, 207; Moro National Liberation Front (MNLF), 204, 205, 206; Moros, 24, 204–206, 207; National Action Plan (NAP) on PCVE, 191, 203, 207–208, 210; National Security Council, 207; Office of the Presidential Adviser to the Peace Process (OPAPP), 191, 204–205; Preventing and Countering Violent Extremism, 204, 209; Shias, 208; Sufis, 208;Sunnis, 208; violent extremism, 206–207

piracy, anti– efforts, 4, 33

PLA. *See* People's Liberation Army

PLAAF. *See* People's Liberation Army, Air Force

PLAN. *See* People's Liberation Army, Army Navy

Poland, 68

Powell, Colin, 112–113

PRC. *See* People's Republic of China

Preventing and Countering Violent Extremism (PCVE), 190, 201

PSE. *See* Pakistan Stock Exchange

PTI government. *See* Pakistan Tehreek-e-Insaaf government

PTM. *See* Pashtun Tahafuz Movement

Putin, Vladimir, 101

Qatar, 39

Quadrilateral Security Dialogue (Quad), 13, 29–30, 34, 43, 60–61

Quad. *See* Quadrilateral Security Dialogue

Quaid-i-Azam. *See* Jinnah, Muhammad Ali

Quevedo, Orlando, 206

radicalization/violent extremism, 18, 202–204. *See also* Preventing and Countering Violent Extremism

Raghavan, Pallavi, 87–88

Raghavan, T. C. A., 88

Rajapaksa, Mahinda, 56, 57

Rawat, Bipin, 140

Regional Comprehensive Economic Partnership trade pact, 30

Ren Zhiqiang, 73

"resource crisis," 16

Rouhani, Hassan, 35

Russia: infrastructure investment projects, 6; military arms deals, 6, 12, 26, 34, 43, 135, 137; nuclear deterrence and stabilization, 88–89;

Russia (*cont.*)
nuclear reactor deals, 34; populist illiberal democracy, 68; relations with India, 33–35, 43–44; Ufa, 99–100. *See also* Soviet Union

SAARC. *See* South Asian Association for Regional Cooperation
Saran, Shyam, 87, 97
Saudi Arabia, 35, 185, 202
SCO. *See* Shanghai Cooperation Organization
SDGs. *See* Nepal, Sustainable Development Goals
"Secret Sharer," (Conrad), 67
security issues, 1–4, 17–18
Seychelles, 33
Shah, Amit, 76
Shah, Aqil, 164
Shah of Iran, 184
Shanghai Cooperation Organization (SCO), 44, 51, 98, 99–100
Sharia law, 154
Sharif, Nawaz, 89–93, 97, 99–103, 112, 163, 165–166, 176
Sharif, Raheel, 101
Simla accord, 93
Singapore: bilateral defense interaction with India, 28–29; exports, 6; per capita GDP, 10
Singh, Jaswant, 92
Singh, J. J., 97
Singh, Manmohan, 35, 93–99, 102–103
SIPRI. *See* Stockholm International Peace Research Institute
Sir Creek dispute, 94, 99
Solih, Ibrahim Mohamed, 9, 203–204
South Africa, 44
South Asia: China's role in, 4–7; democracy and development in, 7–11; Democracy Index scores, 11; Fragile States Index, 11; Freedom House political freedom scores, 11; Human Development Index scores, 10; India's security interaction, 6–7; internal security threats, 17–18; international economic aid, 10; maritime security, 4; nuclear stability, 14, 88–89, 109–132; per capita GDP, 10; policy lessons for dealing with insurgencies/violent extremism, 190–211; trade with India, 30; UN peacekeeping efforts, 3–4; U.S. economic aid, 10; U.S. economic interest in, 11. *See also specific South Asian countries*

South Asian Association for Regional Cooperation (SAARC), 100
South China Sea, 30
Southeast Asia: Democracy Index scores, 11; Fragile States Index, 11; Freedom House political freedom scores, 11; Human Development Index scores, 10; per capita GDP, 10. *See also specific Southeast Asian countries*
South Korea, 26, 27, 28, 30
Soviet Union, 199. *See also* Russia
Sri Lanka: China relations, 56–57; Christian community, 9; debt distress and vulnerability to Chinese, 5; democracy and development, 8; Democracy Index score, 11; development aid donors, 7; economic and security links to China, 6, 58; Fragile States Index, 11; Freedom House political freedom score, 11; Hambantota, 57, 59; Human Development Index score, 10; human rights record, 8, 9; immigrant persecution, 78; imports/exports, 6; infrastructure investments, 6–7, 57, 59; internal security threats, 17, 191; Liberation Tigers of Tamil Eelam (LTTE) insurgency, 8, 190; maritime security, 4, 33; military arms procurement, 6, 56–57; Millennium Challenge Corporation aid, 5; Muslim community, 9; per capita GDP, 10; Tamil Nadu, 56; tsunami relief operations, 33, 194; urban population growth, 176; U.S. economic aid, 10; U.S. infrastructure investment projects, 5
Stephens, Bret, 67
Stockholm International Peace Research Institute (SIPRI), 26
Subramaniam, Arjun, 134–135
Sumatra: Gerakan Aceh Merdeka, 194, 195

Sunni Muslims, 184, 186, 208
Swaraj, Sushma, 100–101, 102
Sweden, 39
Syria, 202

Taliban: Afghanistan, 37–38, 185–186; interests in Balochistan, 184; Pakistan, 12, 16, 26, 37–38, 43; "Quetta Shura," 185; U.S. talks with, 12, 26, 38–39, 42
Tamil Tigers. *See* Sri Lanka, Liberation Tigers of Tamil Eelam insurgency
Tan, Tony, 101
TAPI energy pipeline agreement. *See* Turkmenistan-Afghanistan-Pakistan-India energy pipeline agreement
Taseer, Salman, 159
Tellis, Ashley, 87, 142, 143
Thailand, 29, 191, 194
Thein Sein, 195
Tibet, 49
Trump, Donald, 3, 26, 35, 39, 78, 81
Tuladhar, Padma Ratna, 192
Turkey, 39, 68, 99, 128
Turkmenistan-Afghanistan-Pakistan-India (TAPI) energy pipeline agreement, 99

UNDP. *See* United Nations, Development Programme
United Kingdom, 6
United Nations: Bangladesh's National Action Plan-PCVE, 201; Development Programme (UNDP), 193, 203, 205, 206, 207, 208; India-Pakistan dialogue, 89; Musharraf's speech to General Assembly, 93; Nepal's peace process and peace agreement, 192, 193; peacekeeping efforts, 3–4, 209; Security Council (UNSC), 3, 54, 59, 129; Senior Facilitators' Group, 193; Steering Committee on Collaborative Leadership, 193; terrorist list, 54
United States: Afghanistan war, 18, 25, 37–39, 42, 185–186;"Af-Pak" strategy, 2; China as main "strategic competitor," 25; as China's principal nuclear adversary, 53, 129; China's role in South Asia, 4–7; defense coproduction with India, 31–32, 43; democracy and development in South Asia, 7–11; Department of Energy, 41; economic aid to foreign countries, 2, 10, 12; economic interests, 11; India defense relations, 30–33, 127–128, 141–145; infrastructure investment projects, 5; interests in Balochistan, 184; Malabar naval exercise, 32; military arms sales, 7, 25, 30–33, 39, 141–145; military exercises with India, 31–32; National Action Plan on PCVE implementation in the Philippines, 207; Nepal relations, 193–194; "Next Steps in Strategic Partnership," 95; 9/11 attacks, 95, 156; nuclear deterrence and stabilization, 88–89; oil sanctions against Iran, 12, 26, 35; policy implications of India-Pakistan crises episodes, 111, 112–114, 127–129; Quadrilateral Security Dialogue, 13, 34, 43, 61; role in Kargil War, 103; on Russian arms sales to India, 34; security issues, 1–4; separation of state and religion, 75–76; state-building in Afghanistan, 36; strategic interests in India, 11–12, 25–37, 42–44, 62–63, 101, 103, 145, 166–167; strategic interests in Pakistan, 11–12, 25–26, 37–44, 101, 103, 156, 160, 166–167; talks with Taliban, 12, 26, 38–39, 42; trilateral leader summit with Japan and India, 29; U.S.-China fissile material initiative, 129; U.S.-India Civil Nuclear Agreement, 60, 95; war on terror, 95
UNSC. *See* United Nations, Security Council
U.S.-India Civil Nuclear Agreement, 60, 95

Vajpayee, Atal Behari, 89–93, 97, 102, 112
Venezuela, 68
Verba, Sidney, 150
Vietnam, 28, 29, 30, 60
Voice of Baloch Missing Persons, 180

Wahhabi ideology, 202
Wassenaar Arrangement, 42
Weber, Max, 161
Wells, Alice, 9
World Bank, 7: Facility for Advisor Support for Transition Capacities (FASTRAC)
World Trade Organization, 70
World Values survey, 153
Worldwide Threat Assessment, 109

Xi Jinping, 13, 50, 71–72, 74, 81
Xu Zhiyong, 73, 74

Yameen, Abdulla, 203

Zardari, Asif Ali, 98–99, 165
Zaver Pearl Continental Hotel (Gwadar), 179
Zehra, Nasim, 165
Zhou Yongkang, 72
Zia-ul-Haq, Muhammad, 159, 162–163, 173

www.ingramcontent.com/pod-product-compliance
Lightning Source LLC
Chambersburg PA
CBHW021704230426
43668CB00008B/719